THE ECONOMICS
OF PENSIONS AND
VARIABLE RETIREMENT
SCHEMES

SERIES IN
FINANCIAL ECONOMICS
AND QUANTITATIVE ANALYSIS

Further titles in preparation
Proposals will be welcomed by the Series Editor

THE ECONOMICS OF PENSIONS AND VARIABLE RETIREMENT SCHEMES

Oliver Fabel
University of Bielefeld, Germany

JOHN WILEY & SONS

Chichester • New York • Brisbane • Toronto • Singapore

331. 252
File

Published 1994 by John Wiley & Sons Ltd,
        Baffins Lane, Chichester,
        West Sussex PO19 IUD, England

Telephone (+44) 243 779777

Other Wiley Editorial Offices

John Wiley & Sons, Inc., 605 Third Avenue,
New York, NY 10158-0012, USA

Jacaranda Wiley Ltd, 33 Park Road, Milton,
Queensland 4064, Australia

John Wiley & Sons (Canada) Ltd, 22 Worcester Road,
Rexdale, Ontario M9W 1L1, Canada

John Wiley & Sons (SEA) Pte Ltd, 37 Jalan Pemimpin #05-04,
Block B, Union Industrial Building, Singapore 2057

Library of Congress Cataloging-in-Publication Data

Fabel, Oliver.
    The economics of pensions and variable retirement schemes / Oliver Fabel
    p. cm. — (Series in financial economics and quantitative analysis)
    Includes bibliographical references and index.
    ISBN 0-471-94359-2 (cased)
    1. Pensions.   2. Old age pensions.   3. Retirement income.
    I. Title   II. Series.
    HD7105.F24   1994
    331.25'2 — dc20   93–42346
                                                         CIP

British Library Cataloguing in Publication Data

A catalogue record for this book is available from the British Library

ISBN 0-471-94359-2

Typeset in 10/12pt Times from author's disks by Laser Words, Madras
Printed and bound in Great Britain by Biddles Ltd, Guildford, Surrey

Contents

Series Preface

This series aims to publish books which give authoritative accounts of major new topics in financial economics and general quantitative analysis. The coverage of the series includes both macro and micro economics and its aim is to be of interest to practitioners and policy-makers as well as the wider academic community.

The development of new techniques and ideas in econometrics has been rapid in recent years and these developments are now being applied to a wide range of areas and markets. Our hope is that this series will provide a rapid and effective means of communicating these ideas to a wide international audience and that in turn this will contribute to the growth of knowledge, the exchange of scientific information and techniques and the development of cooperation in the field of economics.

Stephen Hall
London Business School, UK

Acknowledgements

Thanks are due to many colleagues who have discussed the issues presented in this book over the past years. My teacher Prof. Wenig, now at the Martin Luther University, Halle-Wittenberg, has provided never ending encouragement and support during the time we worked together at the Universities of Bielefeld and Hagen. Professors Flaschel and Trockel of the University of Bielefeld also contributed many helpful comments on an earlier version presented to them as members of my habilitation board. Parts of this book have entered my lectures and student workshops at the University of Bielefeld and were presented in faculty seminars at the Universities of Bielefeld, Dortmund, Hagen, and Leiden, as well as during the 1992 European Meeting of the Econometric Society in Brussels. Finally, I owe thanks to Prof. Holler, editor of the European Journal of Political Economy, for allowing me to draw on some results published in an article.

Acknowledgements

CHAPTER 1

Introduction

1.1 THE SCOPE OF THE STUDY

The average retirement age has significantly decreased in all industrial countries over the post-war period — in particular, during the 1960s and 1970s. Hence, part of the financial problems of social old-age insurance systems are associated with this change in retirement behavior, rather than merely reflecting unfavorable demographic developments. The growth of social security systems — more precisely, the increase in pensions available at younger ages — is frequently claimed to be responsible for this development. Moreover, the increased 'generosity' of public pension systems in general — hence, the extent of the inter-generational transfers implemented — is usually referred to when focusing on the observed deviations from actuarial fairness in the adjustment rules relating benefit claims to alternative choices of the retirement age. At the same time, the failure to maintain marginal fairness is noted as distorting lifetime labor supply decisions. Thus, removing such inefficiencies may give rise to inter-generational Pareto-efficient transition paths. Yet, the benefit schedules of private, occupational pension plans also lack actuarial fairness. Again, this is often seen to provide additional incentives for early retirement. Furthermore, it generates an interest in examining common explanatory approaches which account for this phenomenon.

From a theoretical point of view these observations provide sufficient motivation to study lifetime labor supply decisions in more detail. However, actual policies recently enacted further highlight the significance of this analysis: In the United States, France, and Germany social security reforms aiming to overcome part of the future financial problems by raising the average retirement age have already been enacted. Similar proposals are on the agenda of many other governments. In this respect, the development has led to an important institutional change. Today, most industrial countries have established flexible retirement age allowances. Hence, influencing the average retirement age can only be carried out by specifying the benefit rules appropriately. In doing so, policy-makers have obviously accepted that (a) the individual choice of the retirement age is induced by pension provisions, and (b) deviations from actuarial fairness have favored excessive early retirement. Interestingly, the regulatory policy concerned with private pension plans has introduced a necessity to utilize actuarial methods in calculating benefits, thus restricting the possibility of redistribution between worker cohorts. Again, the observed lack of actuarial fairness of the benefit schedules, associated with flexible retirement age allowances in such plans, clearly motivates the search for approaches which possess a more general capability of explaining these stylized facts.

Thus, the study presented here contributes to understanding the determinants of individual lifetime labor supply decisions and the design of benefit rules. Since the analysis is based on insurance-theoretic arguments, it applies to both public and private pension arrangements. Thus, it constitutes a prerequisite for the ongoing debate on social security reforms, as well as proposing a more general view of intra-generational efficient variable retirement allowances. Consequently, the results obtained are twofold: Taking a normative perspective, it will be discussed whether introducing, or maintaining, actuarially fair adjustment rules is Pareto-efficient. At the same time, the analysis derives positive implications characterizing the lifetime labor supply decisions of individuals facing such schemes. In doing so, a model of 'induced retirement' constitutes the starting point to formulate an approach towards an institutional theory of flexible retirement age policies.

1.2   OUTLINE OF THE BOOK

The study has been divided into three parts — a literature survey, the introduction of a basic 'induced retirement' model, and the analysis of intra-generational efficient policies assuming heterogeneous populations. Part I highlights some stylized facts in Chapter 2 associated with the development and current structure of the old-age insurance system in developed countries. Particular emphasis is paid to the development of social security claims, including the introduction of flexible retirement programs, and regulatory policies concerned with occupational pension plans. Chapter 3 identifies two explanatory approaches pursued in the economic literature: Insurance-theoretic arguments and analyses of the inter-generational redistributive effects of social security programs. The aim is to provide a motivation for the analysis to follow by isolating the critical issues.

Part II commences by presenting a survey of economic theories of retirement behavior and the respective empirical evidence. Chapter 5 then introduces the basic analytical framework utilized throughout the remaining parts of this study. This model incorporates some 'apparently realistic' features noted in the literature. Due to these assumptions, however, a complete description of the inter-generational welfare effects is precluded. Hence, Chapter 6 resorts to a more restricted view of Pareto efficiency, based on the requirement to maintain fiscal neutrality in analyzing policy alternatives. It is seen that for homogeneous consumer groups efficient lifetime labor supply decisions, given an arbitrary contribution rate, are ensured by specifying an actuarially fair benefit schedule. However, due to the risk-shifting properties of the induced replacement ratio, efficient lifetime allocations more generally require a particular contribution rate as well.

Following this, Part III focuses on intra-generational efficient policies designed for heterogeneous consumer groups. Introducing this analysis, Chapter 7 first derives standard comparative static results. Further, it presents a more detailed account of the observed deviations from actuarial fairness in the benefit schedules of public and private old-age insurances. In Chapter 8 the focus lies on the impact of imposing an identical contribution rate on all participants in the insurance scheme. This reflects an institutional constraint on the design of efficient variable retirement policies. In contrast, the informational constraint, associated with the consumers' private information concerning their survival risk, is the center of interest in Chapter 9. Both approaches are capable of generating deviations from actuarial fairness in the benefit rules applied. Moreover, the particular way of untangling institutional and informational constraints — thus, isolating the impacts of efficient intra-generational redistribution and moral hazard — provides alternative interpretations of the pension provisions and the efficiency of labor supply decisions in flexible retirement schemes. The study concludes by summarizing the line of arguments pursued.

PART I

Social security reform: a survey

CHAPTER 2

Social security policy: an international perspective

2.1 THE DEMOGRAPHICS OF FINANCING PUBLIC PENSIONS

All industrial countries currently face demographic developments which will lead to drastic changes in the age structure of the population[1]. As can be verified from Table 2.1, the average life expectancy is still increasing[2], while the fertility rates are decreasing. Obviously, this 'aging' of the population will induce a variety of social and economic effects. Following Börsch-Supan (1991), for example, it is clear that four areas will be directly influenced:

- The change in the age structure of the working population will affect the average productivity. The exact impact, however, remains rather unpredictable[3].

- Due to the increased fraction of older people with low savings rates, savings may decrease for the economy as a whole[4].

- The demand for housing will increase and induce frictions in the housing markets which show various degrees of regulation in the developed countries[5].

- Very directly, the financial basis of the public old-age insurance will be severely affected.

---

[1] Rosa (1982), OECD (1988a,b). Throughout this study it will be emphasized that the issues discussed possess a rather broad international perspective. For expositional clarity, however, policy discussions will increasingly focus on comparisons between the situations in the United States and Germany.

[2] Kohli (1988) provides evidence for Germany which shows that the life-expectancies have been increasing since the turn of the century. The respective development in the US is discussed in Uhlenberg (1988), for instance.

[3] See Lam (1989) who provides a theoretic analysis, Kotlikoff (1988a) and Schmähl (1986) for some empirical evidence.

[4] This effect is discussed in Auerbach et al. (1989), for instance.

[5] Regulation is particularly strong in Germany, for instance. Here, Wagner and Huinink (1991) stress that the tendency towards smaller family units offsets the relief effect associated with lower fertility rates.

Table 2.1 Life-expectancies and fertility rates for eight OECD countries

Country	Life-expectancy [a]		Fertility-rate [b]	
	1950	1980	1950	1980
Canada	68.4	75.0	3.4	1.8
France	66.8	74.3	2.9	1.9
Germany	66.4	73.3	2.1	1.4
Italy	66.1	74.4	2.6	1.7
Japan	59.2	76.4	2.4	1.8
Netherlands	71.6	75.0	3.1	1.6
United Kingdom	68.9	73.8	3.0	1.8
USA	68.4	73.5	2.2	1.8

Source: Reproduced by permission from OECD (1988a).
[a] Average life-expectancy at birth in years; calculated as the weighted sum of male and female life expectancies.
[b] Age-specific fertility rates summed over all ages in child-bearing period.

Table 2.2 Elderly population and dependency ratios for eight OECD countries

Country	Elderly population [a]				Old-age dependency ratios [b]	
	1950	1980	1990	2030	1980	2030
Canada	7.7	9.5	11.4	22.4	14.1	37.3
France	11.4	14.0	13.8	21.8	21.9	35.8
Germany	9.4	15.5	15.5	25.8	23.4	43.6
Italy	8.0	13.5	13.8	21.9	20.8	35.3
Japan	5.2	9.1	11.4	20.0	13.5	31.9
Netherlands	7.7	11.5	12.7	23.0	17.4	37.8
United Kingdom	10.7	14.9	15.1	19.2	23.2	31.1
USA	8.1	11.3	12.2	19.5	17.1	31.7

Source: Reproduced by permission from OECD (1988a).
[a] Persons 65 and over as % of total population.
[b] Number of persons of age 65 and over per 100 persons aged 15–64.

Focusing on the last of these points, it is clear that, since all public old-age insurance schemes in the industrial countries operate as pay-as-you-go systems[6], the projected changes in the age-structure must be associated with rather drastic adjustments of the contributions and/or the benefit structure, if this financing method is to be maintained. Schmähl (1990) notes that the development of the 'old-age dependency' ratios is usually taken as a point of reference to describe the increase of the 'financial burden' within systems. Holding net migration constant, Table 2.2 reports such ratios for 1980 and the respective projected figures for 2030 — again

---

[6] The only exception can be found in Denmark. Here the 'Additional Pension' ('Arbejdsmarkedets Tillægspension') for non-self-employed workers operates capital-funded. See VDR (1988).

calculated for the OECD countries selected above. From the definition of these figures it is clear, however, that they merely summarize the information about the change in the age-structure as introduced in Table 2.1.

An alternative way of describing these demographic effects constitutes the calculation of contribution rates which are to be expected, if the benefit structure in the public old-age insurance remains unchanged: Schmähl (1990), Breyer (1990, p. 12), and Börsch-Supan (1991) report estimates for Germany which project that the contribution rate must increase from 18.7% in 1989 to 34.8% of gross labor income, given more favorable demographic scenarios, or even above 40% in less favorable scenarios, by 2030. Similarly, Auerbach and Kotlikoff (1984) estimate for the US that the contribution rate must double to about 25% by 2040. Obviously, however, such projections serve to provide arguments for the current debate concerning the necessary adjustments in the systems rather than describing the actual development of the contribution rates. Nevertheless, some participants in this debate have adopted a position which disputes that these estimates possess any informational value at all by pointing at possible developments which may offset the described demographic problems[7].

On the one hand, it is argued that the fertility behavior may change again and, in fact, there is some evidence for Germany that it has. However, as Schmähl (1990) and Breyer (1990, p. 11) point out very convincingly, this will not yield relief since the potential parent generations are already too small[8]. Schmähl (1988, 1990) also dismisses the argument that higher labor force participation rates of women may contribute to a solution. In fact, this will only defer the problem. Moreover, the corresponding increased demand for child-caring services directly counteracts the argument that smaller future generations must be associated with less resources devoted to such activities. Finally, Dinkel (1988) and Uhlenberg (1988) stress that the increased fraction of elderly persons in the population requires additional resources tied to health and senior citizens care programs. However, it must be conceived that changes in net migration flows may in fact alter the demographic scenario considerably[9]. At the time being, only very few economic studies have focused on this issue: Richter (1991) and Homburg and Richter (1991) formulate first approaches which directly associate the migration flows with the state of the national debt (pay-as-you-go financed old-age insurance). Further, Crane (1992) demonstrates that the effect of the immigration of 'poor' individuals on transfers provided voluntarily by the 'rich' in the host country is

---

[7] The characterization of positions as 'disputing', 'reforming', and 'radical' which will be taken up in the following stems from Breyer (1990, p. 12) and Müller and Roppel (1990).

[8] Also, the unification of Germany will not alter these estimates significantly, because the age-structure of the former GDR resembles that of the old Federal Republic rather closely. See the discussion following the study by Börsch-Supan (1991) and Schmähl (1990). A first detailed empirical analysis of this aspect of German unification can be found in Adden (1991).

[9] This point is addressed in Black's discussion of Börsch-Supan's (1991) study, for instance. Also, Dinkel (1990) shows that due to migration the German population has grown again in 1989.

generally ambiguous. Moreover, it remains questionable whether an immigration policy particularly designed to solve the financial problems of the social security systems could be implemented.

Thus, abstracting from such considerations, the problem remains, how to realign the current social security systems given the basic fact that the fraction of elderly persons will significantly increase in the future[10]. Within this long-running debate two further positions can therefore be identified: One group of discussants calls for 'reforms' of the public old-age insurance while maintaining its basic pay-as-you-go character. The other group proposes radical changes in the financing method towards introducing capital funding. Frequently, the latter proposals also involve modifying the benefit structure so as to establish a common benefit level independent of the individual contributions. The individuals should then turn to private insurers to purchase additional old-age insurance according to their preferences.

2.2   THE EVOLUTION OF PUBLIC OLD-AGE INSURANCE

2.2.1   THE STRUCTURE OF OLD-AGE INSURANCE

In order to analyze the effects of changes in the system of old-age insurance it is necessary to develop ideas concerning the question why public pensions have emerged in all industrial countries. Although the different systems show a variety of particular rules and regulations and their significance in providing income for the aged may differ as well, it is clear that this institutional form of supporting the elderly is of prime importance in these countries. Quite generally, however, one may distinguish the following basic instruments available for this purpose:

- Informal (non-traded) agreements between single individuals
- Private savings
- Private pensions and insurance
- The public old-age insurance
- The public welfare system

In the industrialized countries all of these instruments can be seen to be sufficiently developed, while this is typically not the case in developing countries. Breyer (1990, p. 1), Casmir (1989, p. 36–38), and Verbon (1988a, p. 8–15) agree that here — as well as in the pre-industrialized European countries — informal agreements between family members and within the village society dominate[11]. Further, Verbon (1988a, p. 10–12) notes that such informal arrangements imply

---

[10]This constitutes the conclusion in Schwarz (1991) who discusses in more detail the different, possibly offsetting, behavioral changes and their implications for the German case.

[11]Also, the lack of availability of other means to provide for old-age income security has been noted to influence fertility behavior in developing countries. On the 'old-age-security' hypothesis see, for instance, Neher (1971) and Bental (1989a,b).

a pay-as-you-go method of financing. In the absence of legal restraints these agreements can be seen to be enforceable only if (a) the group of participants is sufficiently small, and (b) the group remains intact over a long period of time extending into the future. Both conditions ensure that the 'moral hazard' problem is limited and support the emergence of traditions. At the same time, however, they severely limit the scope of insurable risks. Insufficient harvests due to climatic disturbances or wars not only lead to the failure of the insurance agreement, but may also induce the break-down of the village society itself.

The beginning of the 'industrial revolution' marks a significant disturbance of this security system. Due to the migration of primarily young family members into the cities, the rural traditions of income support fail, which in turn induces additional flows of migrants. Since the early phase of the industrialization is characterized by frequent job changes and extreme regional mobility, the traditional support system cannot be re-established. First, the already existing public welfare programs step in, but very soon employment-related schemes gain importance. It should be noted, however, that 'old-age' security does not constitute a prime concern, since life-expectancies are rather low.

2.2.2   ON THE DEVELOPMENT OF PENSION SYSTEMS

Although Germany is usually referred to as the 'birth-place' of the modern public old-age insurance system, here — as in all other industrial nations — employment-related private schemes were founded first[12]. Moreover, the legislation concerned with old-age insurance begins with attempts to regulate these private arrangements: Since 1849 Prussian law enabled communities to force workers to join an employment-related security scheme, if it existed. The communities' right to force firms to establish such schemes was added in 1854. Consequently, approximately 35% of the laborers in firms employing five or more workers were covered by 1874.

. Yet, between 1881 and 1889 the German government decided to establish an additional public security scheme for workers. Casmir (1989, p. 462) and Verbon (1988a, p. 16–17) agree that the main concern of the government was to undermine the development of the labor movement. The first of these laws to be enacted was the 'Old-Age and Disability Insurance Act'[13] which today is usually referred to as marking the introduction of public old-age insurance in Germany. However, the structure of the scheme proposed can easily be verified to resemble a clearcut disability insurance. Moreover, its application was restricted to blue-collar workers with rather low incomes. The first major reform occurred in 1911[14]: In addition to

---

[12]For obvious reasons this study cannot provide a complete history of the evolution of public old-age insurance. See Casmir (1989) and Uhle (1987) for more details.

[13]'Alters- und Invaliditätsversicherungsgesetz', 1891.

[14]Spelled out in the 'Reichsversicherungsordnung'.

reformulating the benefit rules so as to establish a true old-age insurance, it added the 'survivors' insurance, and most importantly, established a second scheme for white-collar workers. In both schemes capital-funding was required. At first, the reserves exceeded the annual payments by 700% — still being insufficient, however, since the life-expectancies had already begun to increase significantly. During the hyper-inflation of the 1920s the benefits were extended further in order to compensate the losses in private savings and insurances. Practically, this meant the introduction of a pay-as-you-go system, since the government subsidized the scheme. Until the arrival of the Great Depression and during war-time new funds were not accumulated.

The post-war period is then characterized by a number of decisions which extend the benefit claims considerably: In 1957, the two existing schemes were practically, though not formally, merged by imposing a budget balancing requirement between them. Also, the growth of benefits was tied to the rate of growth of gross labor earnings. Beginning in 1984, this was specified to require an automatic adjustment of the benefits according to the rate of growth of the average gross wages. In addition, the 1970s are characterized by several amendments creating benefit claims for periods in which no contributions were paid. In general, the policy can be described as favoring extensions of benefit claims and adjusting contribution rates. The 'Pension Adjustment Act'[15] of 1957 practically already implied the final establishment of the pay-as-you-go method. However, it was not until 1969 that this was legally enacted.

Since 1957 early retirement at age 60 is allowed in cases of unemployment. However, the introduction of the 'flexible retirement age' in 1973 marks an additional significant institutional change: Jacobs and Schmähl (1989) claim that this can be viewed as the first step in a series of legislative acts which led to a drastic decrease in the average retirement age. The normal retirement age for men was set at age 65 (women: 63) with the possibility of early retirement beginning with age 63 (women: 60). This was followed in 1979 (1980) by lowering the early retirement age for persons with health deficits to age 61 (60). Further, by supreme court decision in 1976 partial disability was ruled to be associated with an entitlement to retire unless the possibility of obtaining adequate part-time employment is proven. Finally, on a number of occasions additional early retirement possibilities have been offered when unemployment was particularly high.

From this brief account it should be clear that the development until the mid-1980s is generally characterized by extensions of public old-age insurance. At the same time, however, private savings and employment-related private pension schemes have grown considerably as well. Hornung-Draus (1989), for instance, notes that private household savings have increased from 26% to 83% of total savings over the last 30 years. Also, 'Bundesbank' estimates show that the per-capita net wealth in liquid assets has risen from DM 22 000 in 1970 to DM 67 000 in

---

[15] 'Rentenanpassungsgesetz'.

1985. Further, Uhle (1987, p. 111–118) points out that private pension agreements show a considerable growth at least until the mid-1980s. The 'Private Pension Act'[16] of 1974 here also reflects the lasting desire to regulate such contractual agreements: The 'Pension Insurance Agency'[17] was established in order to provide reinsurance. More importantly, however, the regulation aimed at standardizing the calculation and the vesting of benefits. This has led to an increased use of actuarial methods in the calculation of the benefits. Finally, Schmähl (1974, p. 19–22) draws attention to the fact that the general public welfare system[18] provides additional old-age security for a significant fraction of the population.

Although the social security system in the United States was not introduced until the 1930s, a number of striking similarities can be noted. Munnel (1982, Ch. 2) and Jackson (1977), for instance, stress the importance of employment-related and union-organized pension arrangements prior to the enactment of these laws. By 1929, approximately 10% of the work-force was covered under employment-related schemes, and 40% held additional claims in union schemes. In 1930, some 25% of railway workers approached retirement, while at the same time their companies faced economic problems. The first public old-age insurance was then practically established by the 'Railway Retirement Act' of 1935 in which the government guaranteed the benefit claims of these employment-related schemes. The general social security scheme was discussed and enacted shortly after (1934–1935). Brown (1977) notes that the motive behind this legislative effort was to compensate for the obvious failure of the private arrangements to provide for income security. The scheme established reflects its orientation towards the German system[19].

The level of the benefit is generally related to contributions paid. Moreover, the laws require capital-funding of the system. However, as described in Brown (1977), for instance, immediately after their enactment the social security laws were amended several times: The inclusion of the 'survivors' insurance, certain intra-generational redistributive rules, but mainly the fact that the beginning of the benefit payments was pre-dated considerably, then practically established the pay-as-you-go character of the US OASDI-system ('Old-Age, Survivors, and Disability Insurance'). The post-war period is characterized by further significant extensions of the benefit rules — including the automatic cost-of-living adjustment of benefits set out in the 'Social Security Amendments' of 1972, and the introduction of a variable retirement scheme. The normal age of retirement today is 65, with an early retirement option beginning at age 62. In contrast to the German public old-age insurance, however, the capital-funding requirement has never been removed legally.

---

[16]'Betriebsrentengesetz'.

[17]'Pensionssicherungsverein' — PSVaG.

[18]'Sozialhilfe'.

[19]Compare Verbon (1988a, p. 26). The fact that contributions are formally divided into an employer's and an employee's share can generally be identified to reflect the influence of the German system on other social security schemes. This arrangement is derived from Prussian law postulating an employer's duty to care for needy employees. See Uhle (1987).

However, employment-related private pension arrangements have retained a larger significance in the United States. Börsch-Supan (1991) reports that here 15% of the average retiree's income is derived from private pensions while this figure amounts to only 3% in Germany. At the same time the average social security income provided in the German system exceeds the respective US figure by 33%. Munnel (1982) adds that the average payment from private pension schemes equals approximately 30% of the last yearly income. For 1980, the total wealth accumulated in such plans is estimated at $407.9 billions, with total annual contributions of $68 970 millions and total annual benefit payments of $35 177 millions. At the same time, total annual payments within the OASDI-system amounted to $105 074 millions, for instance. Again, the ERISA legislation ('Employment Retirement Income Security Act') of 1974 reflects new regulative effort: It established the 'Pension Benefit Guarantee Corporation' (PBGC) to control and ensure the liquidity of the private pension plans. Although less standardized than in Germany, most US pension schemes are now 'integrated' — the calculation of the benefits takes account of the respective claims in the OASDI-system[20]. Following Jackson (1977), however, the main consequence of the ERISA-legislation was to introduce full actuarial funding of the plans.

In contrast to these developments the evolution of public old-age insurance has taken a quite different route in the United Kingdom[21]. Here the 'Poor Laws' known from the middle-ages and the development of the so-called 'Friendly Societies' as self-organized and administrated, professional or employment-related income security schemes constitute the starting point. Interestingly, capital-funding was employed very early in the latter[22]. The 'Old Age Pension Bill' of 1908 separates public old-age insurance from the general public welfare system by establishing a tax-financed fixed-benefit scheme. The so-called 'Beveridge Plan' published in 1942 then led to the enactment of the 'National Insurance Act' 1946: At first, it established a fixed-contribution, fixed-benefit plan. Since 1959 it requires a fixed contribution rate while maintaining the basic fixed-benefit structure. However, there exists an additional income-related part of the public pension as well. Pay-as-you-go financing is applied to both the basic fixed-benefit and the additional income-related pension.

Yet, private pension insurances are generally recognized as a means to achieve the individualization of the benefits. Moreover, firms and employees can agree to replace the additional income-related public pension by a private scheme. The 'Graduated Scheme' of 1961 formulated qualifications for private insurance which must be fulfilled in order to be able to 'contract-out'. Following this, 'partial contracting-out' has become dominant. Until 1975 approximately 50% of privately

---

[20]Kotlikoff and Wise (1987), Dyer (1977), and Jackson (1977) stress that the integration of the private pension plans signals a complementarity of private and social old-age insurance.

[21]For more detailed accounts see Benjamin et al. (1987, Ch. 1–3) and Atkinson (1991), for instance.

[22]Palgrave's Dictionary of Political Economy (1910).

employed and a majority of government employees made use of this possibility. 'Contracting-out' was then abolished, only to be reinstated in 1978. Munnel (1982) reports that the difference between 'contracted-out' (basic insurance only) and 'contracted-in' (basic and earnings-related insurance) contribution rates was 7% on average in 1978. However, as can be verified in OECD (1988b, p. 135), the differentiation of contributions and benefits according to labor income yields no obvious actuarial relationship between contracted-out and contracted-in contributions. The British system does not entail a general possibility for early retirement. To some extent this has been introduced by the so-called 'job release allowance'. Conditional on the employer's agreement to replace the released worker by a currently unemployed person, retirement can take place up to three years prior to the normal age of retirement (65 years for men). Moreover, private pension plans usually entail flexible retirement age allowances here.

The possibility of 'contracting-out' clearly reflects the general assumption that public old-age insurance constitutes a necessity for a limited period of economic distress only. Verbon (1988a, p. 24) notes that such considerations prevailed in the Netherlands as well when — following the British 'Beveridge Plan' — it was decided to introduce a fixed-benefit plan between 1946 and 1952. The system lacks the additional income-related public pension, however. Consequently, the Dutch scheme never allowed for 'contracting-out' and its further development led to significant increases in the benefit level. In fact, according to OECD (1992) this system presently provides for the highest replacement rate among all member states. Thus, private pensions completely ceased to be of importance for lower income groups. The remaining private plans are legally required to involve perfect 'integration': any scheme which promises benefits related to income earned must include the social security claim in this guarantee. Despite the fixed-benefit structure of the system there also practically exists a variable retirement scheme: the requirements which allow one to benefit from early retirement rules associated with proven health deficits are very easily fulfilled by persons within a considerable age-bracket prior to the normal age of retirement (65 years). One year of sickness pay received, or a 15% loss of earnings capacity generate an entitlement to retire. Moreover, until 1987 the definition of 'earnings capacity' explicitly accounted for the employment opportunities of the individual[23]. The Dutch system further allows for early retirement (beginning with age 57.5) in cases of unemployment. The benefits are then provided by the unemployment insurance until the normal age of retirement is reached. Finally, there have been voluntary retirement programs (VUT) negotiated by collective bargaining at firm or sectoral level. Within these schemes the retirement age is typically 60–61 years now.

Today, fixed-benefit schemes also exist in Denmark, Sweden, Switzerland, and Japan. Only Japanese laws allow for contracting-out, however. Dyer (1977) points out that, due to the regulation of private pensions in order to qualify for

---

[23]Compare Casmir (1989), VDR (1988), and OECD (1992).

a 'contracting-out' agreement, this possibility is only rarely exercised here. As noted above already, public old-age insurances generally operate as pay-as-you-go systems. Also, private pension schemes are always regulated to some degree[24]. Their importance in providing for old-age income, as well as the respective use of private savings, seems to vary with the extent to which this is achieved by public insurance. Early retirement schemes also constitute a common feature in both public and private old-age insurance programs. Three basic types of such plans can be distinguished: General variable retirement schedules ('flexible retirement age' programs), disability/invalidity schemes, and programs particularly designed to cope with labor market problems. The latter may allow for early retirement of unemployed persons, and/or entail rules conditional on individual or collective bargaining agreements to replace released workers by currently unemployed individuals. The different types of plans frequently co-exist and the respective age intervals of eligibility overlap[25]. Finally, it should be noted that a significant fraction of old-age security is still to be associated with informal arrangements. Here Kotlikoff and Spivak (1981), Kotlikoff, Shoven and Spivak (1987), and Ben-Zion and Gradstein (1988) demonstrate that relatively small groups of individuals may in fact be able to implement considerable risk-shifting.

---

[24]For more details, see Schmähl (1991) and D'Herbais (1991).

[25]Compare OECD (1992), for instance.

CHAPTER 3

Public pensions: economic approaches

3.1 INTRODUCTORY COMMENTS

The previous chapter — despite the necessary brevity — has shown that public insurances evolved as an additional, and currently dominating, form of providing old-age income security within a broader institutional framework. This gives rise to questions concerning the theoretical underpinning of the evolution of such systems. Clearly, this analysis is necessary in order to evaluate the success of both 'reforming' and 'radical' proposals within the current social security debate. Hence, the account presented in the subsequent sections intends to highlight the controversial issues raised in the respective economic approaches.

Following the work of Diamond (1977), Verbon (1988a), Lundholm (1991a), and Berthold (1991), for instance, two separate lines of arguments can generally be identified:

- Private pension contracts and market transactions yield inefficient risk-shifting which can be improved by supplementary public insurance.

- Abstracting from risk-shifting considerations, the implementation of public pay-as-you-go financed insurance implies additional consumption possibilities for all consumers, or particular consumer groups.

Thus, the first type of argument emphasizes the lifetime portfolio decisions of representative consumer groups. In contrast, the latter approaches focus on the inter-generational transfers induced by old-age insurance. It is immediately obvious that the availability, benefits, and shortcomings of the alternative means to generate old-age income must be analyzed thoroughly. In particular, assumptions concerning the substitutability of the different support instruments always turn out to be crucial.

3.2   INSURANCE-THEORETIC ARGUMENTS

Private arrangements to insure old-age risk require that the individuals plan their old-age consumption relatively long periods of time ahead. This basic assumption has been criticized by Cagan (1965), who suggests that the social security system induces an 'educational effect'. Forced to participate, the individual learns about the necessity to provide for old-age income. Katona's (1964) psychological study is based on the fact that individuals devote increased attention to events as the realization dates approach. Both authors conclude that, without social insurance, the consumers would fail to provide for an adequate old-age income. On first sight, the empirical studies by Hammermesh (1984) and Bernheim (1989) seem to support Katona's findings. It is shown that the individuals' projections concerning their retirement date become more accurate as they approach the date eventually realized. However, this may reflect 'uncertainty' rather than 'myopic behavior'. Thus, Hammermesh (1984, 1985), Bernheim (1988, 1989), and Kotlikoff (1979b) clearly demonstrate that even drastic changes in the social security system have been anticipated by the consumers. Moreover, the individuals appear to be able to extrapolate their remaining life-expectancies rather precisely from information about the general development of the life-expectancies in society and their family background.

Still, Lundholm (1991a,b) proposes that the development of public pension systems reflects the attempt of the 'paternalistic' state to correct for the myopic behavior of its citizens. The respective theoretical analysis therefore focuses on models in which the consumers *ex-ante* incorrectly anticipate their loss probabilities (which can be interpreted as survival probabilities). Lundholm demonstrates that a public insurance enforcing a minimum quantity of insurance purchased cannot induce efficient risk-shifting. On the other hand, a tax-subsidy system influencing the individuals' purchasing decisions so as to induce an *ex-post* efficient allocation requires that the policy-maker knows all 'erroneous' loss probabilities. In Feldstein (1985) myopic behavior is associated with 'incorrect' weights attached to the instantaneous old-age utility in the consumer's *ex-ante* lifetime utility function. However, here the introduction of a pay-as-you-go financed public insurance always induces a corresponding decrease in the individuals' private savings as long as the weight attached to the old-age utility does not equal zero. Thus, it turns out that — irrespective of this weight — such an insurance is beneficial only when the pay-as-you-go system is Pareto-superior to capital-funding *per se*[1].

Turning to approaches which are based on market failure without assuming 'myopia' on the part of the consumers, the argument that private insurance arrangements induce 'transaction costs' — such as search and negotiation costs — which can be evaded by enforcing a public insurance is always as compelling as is the reverse. Here Berthold (1991), for instance, stresses the private interests of

---

[1]Following the distinction of arguments outlined above, the discussion of Pareto-comparisons between the financing methods is deferred to the next section.

the administrators in maintaining a large social security bureaucracy. However, Eckstein, Eichenbaum, and Peled (1985a), Eichenbaum and Peled (1987), and Townley and Boadway (1988) introduce models which are based on an 'adverse selection' model[2]: Following Rothschild and Stiglitz (1976) and Wilson (1977) they analyze possible separating and pooling equilibria in private annuity markets when the consumers possess private informatiön concerning their survival probabilities. In the separating equilibrium the risk-groups self-select over a menu of type-specific actuarially fair insurance offers. In contrast, risk-pooling arrangements entail a subsidization of 'high'-risk consumers. As demonstrated by Wilson (1977), however, such equilibria are generally not unique. Specifically, although efficient risk-pooling equilibria still induce a self-selection of individual-types[3], it cannot be ensured that market forces will establish efficient outcomes. Eckstein, Eichenbaum, and Peled (1985a) and Eichenbaum and Peled (1987) thus proceed by demonstrating that the introduction of a public old-age insurance, with mandatory participation and a single insurance offer applied to all consumer-types, gives rise to Pareto-improvements, if additional demand for annuity insurance can be covered in a competitive market. The respective equilibrium in the private insurance market again separates the risk-types.

In addition, this approach can also motivate the necessity to establish a public insurance. Assuming a risk-pooling equilibrium has been established, the insurance firms face a threat of 'cream skimming' by competitors. This refers to the fact that there always exist alternative insurance offers which are (a) only preferred by 'low' risk-types over their pooling-equilibrium offer, and (b) generate positive expected profits, if chosen exclusively by these consumers. Yet, risk pooling may Pareto-dominate the separating solution under certain circumstances. In this spirit, 'adverse selection' is then also noted to motivate the absence of private annuity markets by Eckstein, Eichenbaum, and Peled (1985b), Hubbard (1987), Hubbard and Judd (1987), and Schwödiauer and Wenig (1989, 1990). Here Friedman and Warshawsky (1988, 1990) provide some empirical evidence: investigating realized annuity purchases, it is shown that the respective consumers exhibit life-expectancies which are significantly higher than average. This explains why annuity prices may appear to be unfair and the market is thin. The only offers remaining in the market are those calculated actuarially fair for 'high' risk consumers.

Hoy (1988, 1989) assumes that the consumers' risk-types are *ex-ante* unknown to both the firms and the consumers. Before the event to be insured is realized, however, the agents receive publicly observable signals which allow for imperfect risk categorization. If the *ex-ante* insurance with respect to the realizations

---

[2]The basic argument has been introduced by Akerlof (1970), Pauly (1974), and Leland (1978).

[3]This contrasts with Townley and Boadway (1988), for instance, who — in accordance with many other related studies — only consider risk-pooling equilibria in which all consumer-types purchase an identical insurance offer.

of the signals is incomplete[4], the *ex-post* heterogeneity of the agents must be associated with existing premium risk. Again, it is shown that there exists a signal-contingent Pareto-improving tax-transfer system ('social insurance') which complements the *ex-ante* market transactions. Similarly, Brugiavini (1993) analyzes annuity purchases when the uncertainty concerning the risk-class is resolved as the consumer ages. The *ex-ante* annuity purchases involve insurance against both the longevity and the risk to belong to a particular risk-class. In consequence, annuity coverage is incomplete and the consumers save privately as well. If the income path is additionally subject to uncertainty and income-contingent insurance cannot be obtained, a competitive equilibrium in the insurance market may not exist. Hence, occupational pension plans are interpreted as a means to implement income-contingent insurance.

The non-existence of equilibria, due to dominating pooling and the threat of 'cream skimming', is also noted in Rothschild and Stiglitz (1976) and Wilson (1977) already. The so-called 'E2'-equilibrium concept therefore assumes that an insurance firm anticipates that all competitors would withdraw their offers, if it announces a deviating offer which would induce losses for the other firms by attracting 'good' risks only. Given this assumption pooling equilibria can be supported. However, Jaynes (1978) further shows that all efficient insurance policies can only be implemented if the individual insurance purchases can be monitored by the insurance firms. Consequently, the existence of such equilibria generally implies some 'communication' between firms[5]. If this cannot be taken for granted, private insurances must 'pool' all consumers under a common offer — specifying a single price per annuity claim purchased. Abel (1986) then demonstrates that, due to demand reactions by the heterogeneous consumer-group, the equilibrium price will fall short of the economy-wide actuarially fair rate calculated utilizing the average mortality. This rate can be implemented by a compulsory social security, however. Hence, introducing social security induces welfare effects because private annuities and social insurance are not perfect substitutes, despite the fact that both systems may be capital-funded.

While these approaches stress the impact of asymmetric information structures in private markets, other studies point at the general non-insurability of certain risks. Here the inflation-risk is frequently referred to as being uninsurable in private insurance arrangements[6]. However, Feldstein (1983) and Summers (1983) point out that at least partial inflation protection can be achieved by accumulating human capital and housing property. Moreover, Merton (1983a) and Bodie (1990) show that private firms are able to supply inflation insurance. Yet, Doherty and Garven

---

[4]Due to risk-aversion on the side of the insurance firms, or a co-existing moral hazard problem.

[5]This is specified by Hellwig (1988) who shows that 'communication' must be associated with similar strategic considerations by firms as utilized in Wilson's 'E2'-equilibrium concept. However, Hellwig (1987) and Gale (1992) also point out that there does not exist an equilibrium concept which 'naturally' applies to situations with asymmetric information structures.

[6]Breyer (1990, p. 65).

(1986) and Doherty and Schlesinger (1990) demonstrate that the possibility of bankruptcy of an investment firm induces an additional pay-off risk for the firm's investment offers. Following Mayers and Smith (1983) and Turnbull (1983)[7] who show that the demand for insurance can be derived from an optimal portfolio decision, Schlesinger and von der Schulenburg (1987) therefore propose that the possibility of default in a private insurance influences the respective demand. The model of Feldstein (1983) focuses on deriving the demand for public old-age insurance as an optimal portfolio decision of consumers facing a more risky private old-age insurance which yields a higher expected return than the less risky public insurance.

However, Feldstein puts less emphasis on the possibility of bankruptcy. Rather, the demographic risks of a pay-as-you-go financed public insurance generally differ from the risk associated with the capital returns of funded private insurances. Similarly, Merton (1983b) stresses the different influences of technological uncertainty on the returns of capital-funded and pay-as-you-go financed insurance schemes. Hence, Merton, Bodie, and Marcus (1987) conclude that the integration of social security and private pensions can be viewed as a means to realize an optimal portfolio. Following the classic study by Ehrlich and Becker (1972), however, it must also be conceived that the possibility of 'self-protection' influences the demand for insurance. As far as old-age insurances are concerned, the choice of the retirement age obviously constitutes a means for 'self-protection' as it determines the size of the old-age risk which must be insured. Thus, endogenizing the retirement decision yields the following three options to provide for old-age income: (1) private savings, (2) insurance, and (3) extending the working-life. Following the arguments above, the respective lifetime portfolio decision hinges on the substitutability of the different instruments[8].

3.3   THE PARETO-EFFICIENCY OF FINANCING METHODS

The models discussed above share the feature that pay-as-you-go financing is associated with the necessity to establish a public system while the reverse is generally not true. Thus, in the absence of uncertainty, or given the possibility of achieving efficient risk-shifting via private insurance, the question remains whether this financing method involves further benefits when compared to capital-funding[9]. Aaron (1966) has shown that, if the so-called 'biological' rate of

---

[7] See also the classic studies by Mossin (1968a,b) here.

[8] In a related context Barro and Friedman (1977) emphasize that human capital investments can also be analyzed in terms of lifetime portfolio decisions.

[9] The basic structure of such overlapping-generations models is intensively discussed in Balasko and Shell (1980, 1981), for instance. Breyer (1990, Ch. 2,4), Homburg (1988, Ch. 3–6), and Verbon (1988a, Ch. 4,5) provide more detailed analyses of the issues covered below. Further, Peters (1988; 1989, Parts I,II) and Elbers and Weddepohl (1986) contribute by generalizing the basic two-period overlapping-generations model to allow for continuous time.

return[10], calculated as the sum of population and real wage growth rates, exceeds the market rate of interest, pay-as-you-go financing yields an inter-generational Pareto-dominant allocation: Capital-funded systems induce inter-temporal allocation in which all future generations enjoy lower lifetime utilities. As shown by Famula and Spreemann (1980) and Spreemann (1984), however, it is generally impossible to achieve Pareto-improvements by capital-funding as long as the time horizon is infinite — irrespective of whether the 'Aaron-condition' holds. There simply never exists an obligation to accumulate wealth to cover future benefit claims. Yet, even without reference to such 'Ponzi'-considerations, it can be shown that pay-as-you-go financing is always inter-generational Pareto-efficient, if the time-horizon is infinite. On the other hand, capital-funding is Pareto-efficient in this case, if, and only if, there exists a future period after which the 'Aaron-condition' is violated for all subsequent periods. For finite time-horizons, both financing methods are always inter-generational Pareto-efficient.

The fact that pay-as-you-go systems never accumulate in order to cover future benefit payments has led Samuelson (1958) to conclude that such inter-generational transfers require a mandatory public old-age insurance. However, Gale (1973) shows that the government can achieve any inter-generational redistribution by employing an adequate debt policy. Further, it can be easily shown[11] that the pay-as-you-go financed public old-age insurance is equivalent to a debt-financed public transfer system. The consequences of this result are twofold: First, since the government bonds are tradeable, it contradicts the idea that mandatory participation in a public old-age insurance system is necessary to capture the advantages associated with this scheme[12]. Second, as shown by Diamond (1965), utilizing a neo-classical growth model in the tradition of Solow (1956) and Phelps (1961), the debt policy can be used to achieve 'Golden-Rule'-growth. Samuelson (1975) and van Praag and Poeth (1975) then show in turn that this can be guaranteed by adequately specifying the public old-age insurance as well. Assuming that the benefit claims in the social insurance crowd out private savings, two cases can be identified. If private savings accumulated to provide for old-age income in the absence of a public insurance yield over-accumulation, a pay-as-you-go financed scheme can be formulated so as to achieve 'Golden-Rule'-growth. Similarly, if in the steady-state equilibrium the economy would be under-capitalized, the public old-age insurance must accumulate an adequate capital stock, the returns of which exceed the total benefit payments. In terms of the 'Aaron'-condition over-(under-)capitalization is associated with a steady-state market rate of interest falling short of (exceeding) the population growth rate which equals the rate of growth of the capital stock.

---

[10] Samuelson (1958).

[11] Börsch (1987, Part BIII) and Verbon (1990).

[12] Berthold (1991).

Given the demographic development described above, the second case has obviously gained importance. Breyer (1989; 1990, Ch. 4) and Verbon (1988a, p. 63–71) demonstrate, however, that it is impossible to generate a Pareto-efficient transition to a capital-funded system, even if the application of pay-as-you-go financing fails to achieve 'Golden-Rule'-growth[13]. Although in long-run equilibrium everyone can be made better off, the pay-as-you-go scheme remains inter-generational Pareto-efficient. The loss which would be incurred by the first generation of retirees affected by the transition policy cannot be compensated. Extending the framework of the model, however, the possible existence of a Pareto-efficient transition policy may be confirmed. Pogue and Sgontz (1977) already point out that the pay-as-you-go nature of the social insurance induces incentives to invest in the accumulation of human capital which are usually neglected. More recently, Naquib (1985) notes the equivalence of social security contributions and the general taxation of labor income. Hence, Homburg (1990) and Breyer and Straub (1993) demonstrate that the particular way of collecting contributions and calculating the respective benefits gives rise to inefficient labor supply decisions. The latter in fact prove that a policy with constant per-capita contributions abolishes the labor supply inefficiencies and generates the possibility to achieve a Pareto-efficient transition.

While these studies analyze the standard two-period overlapping-generations model with endogenous labor supply decisions during the working period, Peters (1988; 1989, Parts I,II) focuses on the lifetime labor supply (retirement) decisions within a continuous-time overlapping generations model. The studies reveal that the basic results concerning the Pareto-efficiency of the particular financing methods can be generalized to the case of endogenous retirement. However, efficient labor supply decisions always require that the adjustment of benefits to different choices of the retirement age must satisfy actuarial fairness. In this context, adjustments of benefits to alternative choices of the retirement age are called actuarially or marginally fair when the expected discounted value of prolonged benefit receipts associated with an earlier withdrawal, for example, is reduced by an amount exactly equal to the expected discounted value of foregone contribution payments. Clearly, it is possible to define such an adjustment rule irrespective of the actual financing implemented in the insurance system.

Hence, the argument applies regardless of whether 'Golden-Rule'-growth implies some pay-as-you-go financing to depress savings, or the accumulation of an excessive fund. Since Peters analyzes generations of identical consumers, there is no need to distinguish between individuals with respect to the induced retirement decisions. In contrast, Genosko (1985) emphasizes the deviations from individual marginal fairness of social security arrangements which affect the retirement decisions in heterogeneous consumer-groups. The failure to maintain actuarially fair adjustment

---

[13]Thus contradicting the respective finding in Homburg (1988). Felder (1992) utilizes the same argument to show that switching from a pay-roll to a consumption tax in financing the pensions cannot be Pareto-dominant.

rules is attributed to the inter-generational transfers implemented via pay-as-you-go financing of the pensions. A thorough examination of this claim can be found in Wildasin (1991). This research particularly highlights that, if a growing number of retirees actually translates into increased political power, the benefit rules implemented must be associated with labor supply distortions. Raising benefits available at younger ages — hence, deviating from actuarially fair adjustments — allows the capture of additional welfare gains by avoiding incurring the disutility of labor.

However, such conclusions generally hinge on institutional constraints restricting the possibilities of implementing inter-generational transfers. Hence, Breyer (1991) demonstrates that the anticipation of future adverse labor supply reactions by the generation introducing/maintaining the pay-as-you-go system imposes an upper cap on the contribution rate chosen. This clearly highlights the necessity to focus on the political process of establishing such a scheme in more detail[14]. Here Browning (1975), Townley (1981), Boadway and Wildasin (1989), and Verbon and van Winden (1986), for instance, stress that (a) political majorities may induce the introduction of the pay-as-you-go system, even if funding is efficient, and (b) the contribution rate chosen then always exceeds the rate which would be optimal for all members of each generation at the beginning of their working-life. In addition, Breyer and von der Schulenburg (1987) point out that the distribution of children over the parent generation influences the political majorities[15]. Van Immhoff (1987) stresses that rules inducing intra-generational redistribution affect the political majorities as well[16]. Similarly, Berthold (1991) highlights that in representative democracies voting never applies to a single policy, such as a social security plan. Rather, the citizens decide about policy packages including a variety of intra-generational redistributive rules[17]. More generally, Drissen and van Winden (1991) and Wildasin (1991) note that changes in majorities do not necessarily imply corresponding changes in the political influence of the different groups of the population in representative democracies. Thus, the impact of population aging on the social security legislation is generally ambiguous. Finally, Breton (1974), Niskanen (1971), and Weaver (1982) underline the dependency of the politicians on the bureaucracy, and vice versa. The political incentive to introduce and maintain the pay-as-you-go scheme may reflect interest in supporting a large bureaucracy. Here Browning (1979) and Romer and Rosenthal (1982) add that the bureaucracy can induce public approval for its plans by providing false information about the

---

[14]See also Bernholz and Breyer (1984, Ch. 8,9), Breyer (1990, Ch. 7,8), and Verbon (1988a, Ch. 5–9).

[15]Turner (1984) provides an empirical analysis which shows that a corresponding median-voter model may in fact explain the evolution of the US OASDI-system.

[16]Compare also Verbon (1985, 1987b) on this issue.

[17]This does not imply, however, that the mere existence of such rules can be taken as evidence for a lack of efficiency of the social security policy. As discussed below, approaches based on politically induced intra-generational redistribution again contrast with insurance arguments. See, also Pfeiffer (1989, p. 10–29) and Wagner (1986, p. 20–24).

state of the system, or offering only irrelevant alternatives to its proposals. Moreover, Lindbeck (1985) points out that the bureaucracy can capture the support of interest groups by employing intra-generational redistributive policies.

While these approaches emphasize the role of the political process in introducing, maintaining, and structuring a public old-age insurance, Veall (1986) and Verbon (1986, 1988b) show that this may reflect either political power of the elderly, or altruism on the part of the young. In Verbon (1987a) the young generation's belief in the maintenance of the system can create an 'altruism by habit'. However, Hammond (1975) and Sjoblom (1985) point out that this does not suffice to ensure the stability of the system. Since it is always possible to abolish a system again, only coercion among egoistic generations of agents can generate the complex 'social contract' needed to stabilize such an agreement. In particular, the contract not only requires current generations to maintain the system. In addition, contract breaches by preceding generations must be punished. The latter appears to be rather problematic, if contract breaches are not easily distinguished from necessary adjustments of the system. Due to the threat of being punished, such adjustments may then be avoided. In this context, Sjoblom (1985) specifically refers to unanticipated demographic changes.

This corresponds to Smith (1982) and Green (1977, 1988) who focus on the ability to insure against uncertainty concerning the future wage-interest relation within a 'social contract'. Green emphasizes that pay-as-you-go financing must be second-best since it reduces individuals' ability to react to low realizations of fertility by increasing private savings[18]. Hence, this turns out to be intergenerational Pareto-improving only if the consumers are very risk-averse, the demographic risk is rather significant, and/or labor and capital are poor substitutes. Whereas Green assumes that the system should maximize the expected utility of the members of a specific generation, Brandts and De Bartolome (1992) extend this notion. Here an optimal scheme maximizes the expected utility of a representative consumer who is also uncertain as to which generation he or she will be born into. Thus, pay-as-you-go financing is Pareto-improving, since an unborn individual's risks of becoming a member of a small generation of workers supporting a large generation of retirees and of becoming a member of a large generation of retirees being supported by a small generation of workers, exactly offset.

3.4   THE 'CROWDING-OUT' HYPOTHESIS

3.4.1   THEORETIC CONSIDERATIONS

The individuals' propensity to save, or purchase insurance, and the corresponding reactions to policy changes are of key importance for all of the approaches

---

[18]Also, Gordon and Varian (1988) focus on the optimal structure of an established social insurance given demographic risk.

discussed above. Barro (1974) develops a model of consumer dynasties in which the lifetime utility of a representative member of a generation depends on his or her own consumption possibilities as well as on the attainable utility levels of all predecessors and offspring. Given this assumption, the maximization of this individual's lifetime utility is equivalent to maximizing the lifetime utility of a hypothetical, infinitely long-lived consumer. Hence, individual utility maximization always yields an inter-generational efficient allocation. If the individuals' ability to pass on income transfers received to predecessors and offspring by making gifts and leaving bequests is unconstrained, public debt and social insurance arrangements are perfectly neutral. Since the original allocation is already inter-generational efficient, an additional inter-generational transfer system is exactly offset by respective adjustments in the desired gifts and bequests. The following discussion between Buchanan (1976), Feldstein (1976a), and Barro (1976) highlights the two contrasting points of view with respect to the effects of implementing or extending social insurance: if private savings are accumulated in order to provide for desired inter-generational income transfers — implying a 'bequest-motive' — social insurance is neutral in Barro's sense. On the other hand, if private savings merely constitute a vehicle to transfer income from early periods to later periods of a consumer's life — indicating the 'consumption-motive' — social security claims crowd out private savings[19].

In a series of studies, Laitner (1979a,b,c), however, shows that accounting for uncertain lifetime income opportunities gives rise to binding constraints on the ability to accumulate desired bequests. Hence, Barro's neutrality hypothesis does not carry over here. Whereas this approach emphasizes the lack of risk-shifting arrangements, more recent work focuses on the additional implicit insurance provisions incorporated in public old-age support systems. Thus, Diamond, Helms, and Mirrlees (1980) and Brunner (1990) interpret the intra-generational redistributive aspects of social insurance as implementing risk-shifting between consumers facing random productivity shocks. Peters (1992) highlights that sharing the costs of child-bearing produces additional incentives for parents to invest in the human capital accumulation of their children. Further, Laitner (1988) underlines the insurance effect of intra-generational redistribution, when private capital investments are risky. Here the emphasis lies on increasing the parent generation's incentive to invest in high-yield, but more risky projects. Finally, Gordon and Varian (1988) again focus on the demographic risks affecting the consumers' lifetime income opportunities.

---

[19] In correspondence to the work of Ando and Modigliani (1957) and Modigliani and Brumberg (1954) only this latter motive is frequently associated with the term 'life-cycle savings'. However, this contrasts with the classic studies by Fischer (1973), Hakansson (1969, 1970), Levhari and Srinivasan (1969), Merton (1969), Mossin (1968a, 1968b), Samuelson (1969), and Yaari (1964, 1965) who demonstrate that both savings hypotheses can be derived from the same dynamic model of lifetime consumption and portfolio decisions. It is only important to distinguish whether or not the consumer's utility depends on the utility levels obtained by offspring.

Explicitly accounting for the survival risk also very generally renders the neutrality hypothesis subject to doubts. In Sheshinski and Weiss (1981) the pay-as-you-go social security still provides a perfect insurance of the old-age risk. Hence, the individuals only accumulate in order to leave intended bequests. In contrast, Hu (1986) stresses the incomplete annuity character of public pensions. Since the consumers' risk-aversion then co-determines the accumulation path, the steady-state welfare effects of changing the benefit provisions are ambiguous. Moreover, this ambiguous result does not hinge on the particular financing method employed. This conclusion can be obtained by contrasting Hu (1986) with Abel (1986) — the latter assuming capital-funding. Finally, abstracting from an effective bequest-motive, Abel (1985) and Eckstein, Eichenbaum, and Peled (1985b) also report ambiguous steady-state welfare results of extending the social security system. The decisive element in all of these studies constitutes the fact that, under uncertain lifetimes, private savings and pensions are no perfect substitutes. This research — but also the related work of Davies (1981), Hubbard (1985, 1987), Hubbard and Judd (1987), and Testafion (1984) — therefore highlights that the existence and size of a crowding-out effect hinges on the degree of pension coverage provided and the individuals' risk-taking behavior.

Finally, Feldstein (1974) focuses on the retirement effect of social security in determining a possible crowding-out of private savings: if the public system increases old-age income, the consumers will not only demand more consumption goods, but also more leisure. The study concludes that the retirement age must decrease. This, however, should yield an incentive to increase private savings again in order to provide for additional income over the extended retirement period. Hence, whether or not increasing the public pensions depresses private savings depends on which of the effects dominates. Hu (1978) criticizes Feldstein's partial equilibrium approach. Analyzing long-run effects in a general equilibrium framework, it can be shown that, despite endogenous labor supply decisions, social security can be utilized in order to induce convergence towards 'Golden-Rule'-growth. Again, Hu notes, however, that this requires the absence of labor supply distortions induced by the rules relating contributions and benefits to labor supply decisions.

3.4.2 EMPIRICAL RESEARCH AND INTERPRETATIONS

There exist numerous direct and indirect empirical tests of the 'crowding-out'-hypothesis[20]. First, Ermish (1989) shows very fundamentally that, accounting for the whole set of redistributive rules, redistribution actually favors the elderly in the industrial countries. One type of research then focuses on the hypothesis that in absence of a bequest-motive the elderly should decumulate. However, Mirer (1979),

---

[20] Again, more extensive surveys can be found in von Furstenberg and Malkiel (1977), Clark, Kreps and Spengler (1978), Bernheim (1987a), Kotlikoff (1988b), Modigliani (1988), and Hurd (1990). Kuné (1983) stresses the comparability of country-specific studies.

Kotlikoff and Summers (1981), Danziger *et al.* (1982), King and Dicks-Mireaux (1982), Hall and Mishkin (1982), Menchik and David (1983), David and Menchik (1985), and, with particular reference to housing property, Feinstein and McFadden (1989) and Venti and Wise (1989) report that older persons hold considerable wealth and even accumulate further. On the other hand, Dowell and McLaren (1986), Ng (1992), and, including an empirical analysis again, Börsch-Supan and Stahl (1991) point out that this behavior may also be due to a lack of divisibility of certain consumption goods, or reflect precautionary savings with respect to health risks.

Moreover, Shorrocks (1975) and Hurd (1989) cannot confirm these results when differences in life-expectancies are taken into account. Further, Mirer (1980), Diamond and Hausman (1984a), and Bernheim (1987b), focusing on private wealth excluding housing property, find that older persons in fact decumulate. This again contrasts with Bernheim, Shleifer and Summers (1985), Bernheim (1991) and Fitzgerald (1987) which put particular emphasis on life-insurance purchases. Here the empirical results support the existence of a strong bequest-motive. The first of these studies also highlights that only 2% of the retirees investigated hold private annuity claims. Yet, following Friedman and Warshawsky (1988, 1990) again, this may be attributed to the fact that annuity prices are actuarially unfair for the average individual. However, the latter also maintain that the savings behavior of the very old cannot be explained without reference to a bequest-motive. On the other hand, comparing families with and without children, Hurd (1987) finds no significant differences in the savings behavior. Similarly, adjusting household income for family size, Gehrels (1991) cannot confirm an additional bequest-motive for Germany, either.

Although these studies directly focus on the savings motive, Bernheim, Shleifer and Summers (1985), Bernheim (1991) and (implicitly) Gehrels (1991) stress that, even if savings are accumulated in order to leave bequests, this does not necessarily imply the presence of altruistic considerations. Rather, bequests can also reflect a strategic behavior in the sense of Kotlikoff and Spivak (1981), Kotlikoff, Shoven and Spivak (1987), and Ben-Zion and Gradstein (1988). Such inter-generational transfers constitute a reward part of informal security arrangements among non-altruistic family members. In particular, life-insurance purchases can here be seen to reduce a possible moral hazard problem which arises when the savings of the elderly cannot be perfectly verified by the young. A second type of study therefore examines whether changes in social security transfers influence aggregate lifetime consumption. If this can be confirmed, the system is concluded not to be perfectly neutral.

Again the empirical evidence is split: The work of Kochin (1974), Tanner (1979), Plosser (1982), and Kormedi (1983) generally supports the neutrality hypothesis. Feldstein (1982b), however, criticizes the specification of such empirical models and provides alternative estimates which do not confirm these findings. Thus, Aschauer (1985) stresses that due to a lack of adequate data neither the neutrality hypothesis nor its converse can be supported. For Germany, Franz (1976), with particular reference to the social security system, and Flaig (1987), for instance, show that lifetime consumption is influenced by fiscal decisions. However, the latter also states again that the neutrality hypothesis cannot be contradicted. Again, the possibility of involuntary bequests, when survival is uncertain and private annuities cannot be obtained, constitutes a very general problem in assessing the impact of social security wealth on lifetime consumption behavior. Thus, Leimer and Richardson (1992) estimate two different subjective discount rates for social security and private wealth accounting for the different risk-spreading properties. The respective estimate of lifetime consumption as a function of the two wealth components reveals that social security induces a substantial crowding-out of private savings.

Finally, a third type of empirical work concentrates on the effect of social security on individual savings. However, there is little reference as to the nature of this accumulation. Here Feldstein (1974, 1976b, 1980, 1982a) and Munnell (1974), for instance, confirm the 'crowding-out'-hypothesis. However, Leimer and Lesnoy (1982), utilizing the same set of data as Feldstein (1974), stress the lack of robustness of these findings with respect to alternative measures of the wealth equivalent of social security claims. In effect, their results contradict the earlier studies. Further, Todo-Rivera and Pérez-Amaral (1988), analyzing survey data associated with the 1976 decision of the University of California employees to join the social security system, point out that Feldstein's assumption concerning the expected rise in future benefits overestimates the true expectations. The impact of different assumptions concerning the calculation of the actuarial value of future social security benefits is also reflected in the variety of results obtained in other studies: For the US, Kotlikoff, Spivak and Summers (1982), for instance, find that a one dollar increase in social security crowds out substantially less than one dollar of private savings. On the other hand, Kotlikoff (1979a) and Thornborrow (1985) confirm the existence of a strong crowding-out effect. Dicks-Mireaux and King (1984), analyzing Canadian data covering roughly the same period of time, conduct tests of robustness and report that crowding-out is weak, but statistically significant. For Germany, Pfaff, Hurler and Dennerlein (1979), for instance, find no evidence that social security replaces private savings. Quite generally, Kuné (1983) shows that the results of respective empirical studies for other developed countries do not allow for clearcut conclusions either.

Further, Leimer and Lesnoy (1982) and Burkhauser and Turner (1982) demonstrate that, if the retirement effect of the public pensions is ignored, a possible crowding-out effect will be overestimated. This argument is picked up by Diamond and Hausman (1984a) and Fields and Mitchell (1984). Both studies conclude that the incentive to increase private savings induced by earlier retirement is not sufficiently strong to offset the replacement effect of public pensions on private savings. Thus, a considerably weaker, but significant, crowding-out effect of social security is confirmed. The more recent study by Börsch-Supan (1991) shows that this result carries over to the situation in Germany as well.

3.5   IMPLICATIONS FOR REFORM PROPOSALS

Given the current demographic development it is unlikely that the pay-as-you-go scheme has been implemented in order to induce an inter-generational Pareto-dominant allocation. In particular, the transition to a capital-funded insurance system appears to be necessary in order to generate convergence to a 'Golden-Rule'-growth path. On first sight, this clearly favors the 'radical' position to (re-)introduce capital-funding into the system and, possibly, to reduce its size in order to allow for more private savings/insurance[21]. Basically two qualifications must be added, however:

(1)   The historical development and a number of theoretical studies highlight the fact that public insurance may correct deficits of private risk-shifting arrangements. This can be seen to limit the possibility of privatizing the old-age insurance, and/or require additional regulation of private insurances. It has been noted also that pay-as-you-go financing can be viewed as an instrument to insure inter-temporal risk.

(2)   If the pay-as-you-go system is inter-generational Pareto-efficient, the political implementability of such proposals is still in question. A similar conclusion can be drawn from the political theories of social security schemes[22].

The first point is taken up by Schmähl (1988, 1990) and Holler (1986), for instance, who note that the complexity of the institutional framework of old-age insurance has been neglected in most studies. Verbon (1988a, p. 241–242) addresses the second issue when stating that questions concerning the future of the pay-as-you-go schemes can be answered only by asking the currently young whether they believe that this system will survive. More importantly yet, the underlying conclusion that the economy's growth path is characterized by under-capitalization, rests on the assumption that the social security system is non-neutral with respect to inter-temporal allocation. Although the empirical findings support this assumption to some extent, there is also evidence to the contrary. Obviously, the 'reforming' position is based on the assumption that the social security system is neutral[23]. However, even if the neutrality of the system is taken for granted, two questions cannot be avoided:

---

[21]See, for instance, Neumann (1986), Jäger (1990), and Longman (1990). The benefits of privatization are particularly stressed in von Wartenberg (1987), Neumann (1987), and Feldstein (1978).

[22]Due to these qualifications, participants in the reform debate may call for 'reforms', rather than radical changes, without necessarily accepting the 'reforming'-position as defined in Section 2.1.

[23]In the relevant German literature this position is usually defended by reference to the so-called 'Mackenroth'-hypothesis: Mackenroth (1952) claims that, due to the fact that in every society the working population must provide the consumption possibilities for all other members of the society as well, it does not matter whether the necessary distribution of income is implemented openly in the form of a pay-as-you-go social security system, or the individual members of the society choose different means to achieve this goal. Obviously, this hypothesis assumes the strict neutrality of the social security system.

(3)   Very generally, it is critical to ask why there is a need for public insurance at all, if the neutrality of the system is accepted. An institutional framework, in which inter-generational income transfers are implemented by issuing trade-able public debt, could serve just as well. In particular, it should be noted that 'myopic behavior' is hardly compatible with the set of assumptions needed to generate the neutrality result.

(4)   Moreover, even if — due to the transaction costs of transforming the system, for instance — it appears to be beneficial to maintain public old-age insurance as a vehicle for inter-generational transfers, it remains unclear whether mere adjustments of the contribution/benefit structure accounting for the demo-graphic changes suffice. In particular, the rules applied in tying benefit claims to contributions have been noted to give rise to further inefficiencies.

Given the fundamental differences in the assumptions on which 'radical' and 'reforming' positions are based and the qualifications noted above, clearcut conclu-sions about the benefits of the respective proposals cannot be drawn from this survey. Yet, this overview very clearly highlights that the attention cannot be confined to the pure demographic developments. In particular, two generally competing approaches towards explaining both the inter-generational and the intra-generational transfers have been isolated: Either the systems are viewed as providing additional welfare enhancing insurance arrangements, or the transfers are associated with group interests.

Moreover, points (2) and (4) can also be seen to introduce some common interest: if, due to the particular way of organizing the system, the public insurance induces labor-supply inefficiencies, both 'radicals' and 'reformers' should be interested in their abolition. On the one hand, removing such distortions has been argued to raise the possibility of achieving a Pareto-efficient transition path. However, the argument possesses a more general virtue as well. Following Hu (1978) and Peters (1988, 1989), efficient lifetime allocations constitute a prerequisite for inter-generational efficiency — irrespective of the financing method employed. Thus, even maintaining the basic pay-as-you-go system, two possible effects appear to be of importance: First, if — ensuring the current flow of contributions and benefits — the welfare of a generation can be improved, there also exist fiscally favorable policy changes which do not yield deteriorations of the consumers' lifetime utility. Second, given that the current structure of the retirement policy in fact induces inefficient early retirement, such policy changes should be associated with delayed retirement decisions.

The pure fiscal effects of raising the average retirement age can again be illus-trated by alternative calculations of old-age dependency ratios — as provided in Table 3.1 for Germany, for instance. Further, assuming such changes were possible, projections of the implied contribution rates summarize this information. Hence, Breyer (1990, p. 12) reports that, if the average retirement age in Germany can be increased by three years, the contribution rate necessary to finance the benefits, holding the benefit structure constant, would only have to be increased to 26%,

Table 3.1   Alternative definitions of the old-age dependency ratio for Germany

Earnings interval	Dependency ratios 1985	2030	%-Increase 1985–2030
20–60	38.5	81.2	110.9
20–65	25.5	51.0	100
15–65	21.3	48.3	126.7

Source: Reproduced by permission of Springer-Verlag and the author from Schmähl (1990).

Table 3.2   Financial effects of an increase in pension age by five years

Year	1980[a]	2000		2025	
Country		No change	Increased age	No change	Increased age
Germany	7.8	9.1	8.2	13.7	10.8
Japan	3.4	6.0	5.6	10.4	9.4
UK	4.4	4.9	4.6	7.2	6.1
US	4.2	4.7	4.4	7.4	5.9

Source: Reproduced by permission from OECD (1988b).
[a]Original pension ages: 63 for Germany, 60 for Japan, 65 for the United States, and 65 for men and 60 for women in the United Kingdom.

instead of 34.8%, by 2030. Focusing on the developments of the old-age pension shares for selected countries — reported in Table 3.2 above — also merely represents an alternative means of investigating the relationship between changes in the average retirement age and the fiscal burdens of social security systems. These estimates assume that the average replacement ratio is held constant and pension age increases by one year every five years beginning in 1995. While such projections thus underline that increases in the retirement ages can significantly contribute to easing the fiscal burden in the social old-age insurances, they clearly do not provide information as to how the assumed change in the retirement behavior is to be brought about. On first sight similarly, Thompson (1983) reports estimates of the US Social Security Administration showing that an increase in the normal age of retirement from 65 to 67 years would reduce the projected deficit in the OASDI-system by 71% over the next 75 years. Here, the underlying estimation explicitly accounts for the change in the retirement behavior to be expected after the 1983 OASDI-reform, however.

Again it is interesting to compare this legislation with the German reform of 1992[24]: Whereas the US system has reintroduced partial capital-funding[25], the German legislation strengthens the pay-as-you-go nature further by reducing the

---

[24]This year marks the date when the respective laws — enacted in 1989 — became effective.

[25]More details can be found in Verbon (1988a, p. 29–39) and Schultze (1990), for instance.

social security agency's reserves. Here indexing the benefits to net real wages, instead of gross wages, and providing more tax-financed subsidies has been chosen as a means to decrease the financial burden in the system. Although this can be viewed as reflecting fundamental differences in the perception of the benefits associated with pay-as-you-go financing, the problem of political implementability of the reform proposals plays an important role as well: For Germany, Dinkel (1988), for example, notes that the contribution rate would have to be doubled in order to ensure that existing unfunded claims can be maintained, while at the same time introducing capital-funding of future claims[26]. It is concluded that such contribution rates are not politically feasible. Similarly, Schwarz-Schilling (1987) and Jäger (1990) therefore suggest only partial capital-funding to be introduced in a first step. On the other hand, Verbon (1988a, p. 30) warns that, since the US system will now build up considerable reserves until 2015, there will exist an incentive for politicians to use these funds for further extensions of the benefits. Further, Cook (1990) provides evidence which shows that a considerable fraction of the members of the US congress favored a 'reform position' in the debate on the 1983-legislation as well.

Quite clearly stressing the conclusions obtained above again, both the US and the German legislation have taken steps to increase the average retirement age. In particular, it has been decided to adjust the flexible retirement age allowances[27]. Larger increases in benefits associated with delayed retirement, and larger deductions associated with earlier retirement, respectively, are expected to provide incentives to retire later. In this context, it is also noted[28] that currently both systems favor (inefficient) early retirement, since the calculation of early benefits is actuarially unfair. Casey (1989) adds that *'plans to cut down on opportunities for publicly financed early retirement and even to increase the age at which full public pensions can be claimed are on the agenda of many governments [...]'*. Thus, France has also recently adopted a policy of adjusting the early retirement scheme. Japan has taken steps towards increasing the age of retirement for women, taking account of the fact that female life-expectancies are significantly higher than male. Also, the lack of actuarial fairness in calculating the early benefits is noted to be an obstacle for achieving a long-term solution to social security financing in Sweden by Kruse and Söderström (1989). Finally, Petersen (1989), considering the Danish case, warns that the development towards an actuarially fair early retirement scheme, which has taken place during the 1970s, has largely been offset again by amendments enacted in 1979.

Moreover, proposals to adjust the benefit schedules are not confined to general flexible retirement age programs only. Schmähl (1988), for instance, emphasizes the

---

[26]See also Müller and Roppel (1990) on calculations concerning the capital-requirement associated with currently existing claims.

[27]In the US the normal (full-benefit) age will be gradually increased to 67 from 2002 to 2027. The 1992 reform in Germany rules that the age-limits of the variable scheme will be raised starting in 2001.

[28]See Börsch-Supan (1991), for instance.

adverse effects of the special early retirement allowances for unemployed persons in Germany. Clearly, if the eligibility rules for early disability benefits are lax, the same objections apply. The fact that retirement due to disability hides long-term unemployment among the elderly has been noted to be particularly important in the Netherlands, for instance[29]. By the same argument it can be guessed that such rules introduce a hidden variable retirement scheme in which actuarial fairness is of minor importance. On the other hand, the very existence of such other early retirement options clearly motivates a more detailed investigation of the determinants of individual lifetime labor supply decisions.

---

[29]OECD (1992).

PART II

Individual retirement decisions

CHAPTER 4

Determinants of the lifetime labor supply

4.1 LABOR SUPPLY AND RETIREMENT

Despite considerable differences in interpretations, the basic phenomenon that the average retirement age has significantly decreased over the post-war period is virtually undisputed among economists[1]. This is usually illustrated by reference to the developments of the participation rates of older workers as reported in Table 4.1. Although the figures also show some variation (in particular for Italy), they can be seen to highlight two fundamental facts. First, the participation rates of the elderly decrease rather drastically over the period from 1966 to 1990 in all of the countries included. Since in some of these countries the respective female participation has actually increased, the male employment ratios reported also stress this conclusion further. Second, this development appears to have been particularly strong between the late 1960s and the early 1980s. The period between 1968 and 1980 is associated with decreases in the participation rates of the following magnitudes: Canada 4.7%, France 10.3%, Germany 16.5%, Italy 4.1%, Japan 6%, United Kingdom 11.3%, and United States 6%. The more recent figures then signal some stabilization — the subsequent reductions of the participation rates are generally smaller. As pointed out in Chapter 2, the 1970s are characterized by significant expansions of the social security system. Hence, it appears to be rather straightforward to associate the observed change in retirement behavior with the changes in the social security legislation which have occurred.

Obviously, the figures reported in Table 4.1 provide a rather crude picture of the basic developments. More detailed investigations — in particular, when attempting to focus on international comparisons — encounter several severe difficulties, however. Whereas the economic theorist is free to define 'retirement' as complete withdrawal from the labor market, empirical studies face problems in

---

[1] This observation constitutes the starting point for Boskin (1977), Diamond and Hausman (1984a,b), Genosko (1985), and Schmähl (1988, 1990), among many others. Börsch-Supan (1991) stresses the similarity of the respective developments in the US and Germany again.

Table 4.1 Labor force participation and male employment ratios of older workers for eight OECD countries

Country	Canada		France		Germany		Italy	
Year	LFPR[a]	MER[b]	LFPR	MER	LFPR	MER	LFPR	MER
1966	36.4	42.6	36.4	—	46.5	—	10.3	17.7
1968	36.0	42.5	34.6	58.4	38.6	52.5	16.1	27.6
1970	35.2	52.2	32.2	54.2	34.5	48.6	14.2	25.3
1972	33.5	49.6	29.1	50.2	29.0	41.9	12.1	21.8
1974	32.5	48.5	26.1	46.0	24.9	36.5	12.1	21.7
1976	31.7	46.2	24.8	43.4	22.8	32.3	11.0	19.8
1978	31.6	45.0	24.3	42.5	22.2	30.3	12.3	20.1
1980	31.3	44.7	24.3	41.7	22.1	29.9	11.5	18.7
1982	30.4	41.9	22.7	38.5	22.0	29.5	10.8	14.8
1984	29.2	39.7	20.4	33.9	21.1	28.2	10.8	18.5
1986	27.9	37.9	19.5	32.0	20.8	28.5	10.7	18.1
1988	27.4	36.7	18.7	30.1	—	—	9.8	16.8
1990	26.5	35.3	17.6	28.4	—	—	9.7	16.9

Country	Japan		Netherlands		UK		US	
1966	52.2	—	—	—	53.8	—	37.7	53.1
1968	50.2	70.4	—	—	53.3	—	37.7	53.5
1970	48.9	68.5	—	—	52.7	55.4	37.4	52.3
1972	47.0	66.7	24.1	37.5	50.5	51.2	36.1	50.0
1974	46.1	65.5	22.3	35.0	48.3	49.1	34.0	47.8
1976	44.8	62.6	20.9	33.4	47.2	46.4	32.8	44.4
1978	44.3	60.8	19.7	32.6	44.3	43.4	32.5	44.5
1980	44.2	61.0	18.1	29.3	42.0	40.3	31.7	43.0
1982	44.2	60.4	15.8	24.9	39.6	34.4	31.9	41.6
1984	43.9	59.4	14.9	21.3	37.9	33.5	29.7	38.9
1986	43.3	58.8	12.9	20.0	35.4	30.8	29.1	37.9
1988	43.4	58.9	—	—	35.5	31.4	29.0	37.6
1990	44.2	60.0	—	—	36.5	33.0	29.1	37.0

Source: Reproduced by permission from OECD (1992).
[a]LFPR: Labor Force Participation Rate; Persons aged 55 and over employed or actively seeking employment per 100 workers in this age group.
[b]MER: Male Employment Ratio; Male employment component of the LFPR.

identifying actual retirement decisions. Following the discussion in Fields and Mitchell (1984, Ch. 1) and Peracchi and Welch (1991), for instance, there basically exist two sources of distortions:

(1)   Since an individual may choose to reduce his/her labor supply at different stages of his/her economic life, it is generally unclear which degree of withdrawal must be associated with 'retirement'.

(2)   The particular institutional framework — including the co-existence of flexible retirement age programs, disability schemes, and unemployment insurance,

the various eligibility rules applied, tax-allowances for post-retirement jobs, and the employment opportunities in the shadow sector — further obscure the possibility of identifying the employment status 'retired' in the available data.

Moreover, the two problems can be guessed to be highly interrelated. A number of countries have introduced 'gradual retirement options' to their public pension system, for instance[2]. Also, partial disability is frequently associated with the necessity to take up part-time work, and, consequently, the possibility for full retirement, if the availability of adequate employment cannot be proven. Thus, it is rather difficult to distinguish 'retirement' from 'unemployment' in these cases. The same problem arises, when there exist specific programs which relate an entitlement for full retirement to the labor market status of the individual. In fact the OECD (1992) study, from which the figures in Table 4.1 are taken, also underlines these potential difficulties. Throughout, there is no reference to actual retirement ages in international perspective. Instead this work proceeds by discussing the relative importance of the various early retirement rules — adding separate passages concerned with the use of disability schemes and the incidence of long-term unemployment among the elderly for selected countries.

This may be contrasted with the information on retirement ages compiled in Table 4.2. These figures, taken from OECD (1988b), define 'retirement' with reference to the age when the payment of social security old-age benefits commences. Hence, the list only selects countries where an explicit flexible retirement age program exists. For comparisons the respective figures for the United Kingdom have been added — exemplifying the development in countries where no such program exists[3]. Although the basic findings are confirmed, the scope appears to be more limited than necessary. As illustrated by Table 4.3, the institutional frameworks

Table 4.2 Average male retirement ages in old-age pension schemes

Country	Canada	Germany		France[a]	US	UK
		Blue Collar	Employees			
1960	—	65.2	65.2	—	66.8	—
1970	66.7	65.2	65.1	—	64.4	—
1975	66.2	64.0	64.2	63.6	64.0	65.6
1980	65.2	62.5	61.9	63.4	63.9	65.4
1983/4	65.1	61.9	62.0	62.4	63.6	65.4

Source: Reproduced by permission from OECD (1988b).
[a] Figures for employees entitled to 'Droits Directes'.

[2] See the international surveys provided by Schmähl (1989) and OECD (1992).

[3] In general, the information presented in Table 4.2 seems to suggest that the development has been less dramatic than that expressed by comparisons of the participation rates. It should be noted, however, that comparably small changes in the average retirement age possess rather significant impacts on the financial status of the pension systems. See Table 3.2 above.

Table 4.3 Legal retirement ages in general public schemes

Legal rule	Standard pension		Reduced pension		Special arrangements	
Country	Male	Female	Male	Female	Male	Female
Canada	65	65	60	60	—	—
France	60	60	—	—	55/50	55/50
Germany	65	65	63	63	58	58
Italy	60	55	50	50	55	50
Japan	65	65	—	—	—	—
Netherlands	65	65	—	—	59	59
UK	65	60	—	—	60	59
US	65	65	62	62	—	—

Source: Reproduced by permission from OECD (1988b).

can be verified to allow for more early retirement options[4]. Moreover, the information suggests that the variable retirement options offered may be quite complex and show considerable variation between countries. This contrasts with the fact that — despite such differences — the respective developments of the participation rates show striking similarities.

4.2 THEORIES OF RETIREMENT BEHAVIOR

4.2.1 INTRODUCTORY REMARKS

The theoretical literature on retirement decisions distinguishes three basic approaches which can be verified to be closely associated with the discussion above. In particular, there exist

- analyses of disability contingent retirement rules,
- models which focus on the role of mandatory retirement agreements in long-term labor contracts, and
- 'induced retirement' approaches relating the retirement decision to the income opportunities provided by public and/or private pension plans.

The brief overview provided in the following will discuss the basic arguments of these different approaches. At the same time, however, it attempts to point out common aspects. With respect to the latter, the discussion intends to highlight two issues. On the one hand, results concerning the calculation of benefits — in particular, the role of actuarial fairness — are emphasized. Second, the focus lies on the determination of the retirement age within these approaches. As will be

---

[4]Casey (1989) provides a very detailed international comparison of the different early retirement options.

seen, the different analyses can again be identified as either stressing the impact of additional implicit insurance arrangements, or focusing on the role of benefit provisions in inducing retirement decisions.

4.2.2   MORAL HAZARD AND DISABILITY BENEFITS

In a series of studies Diamond and Mirrlees (1978, 1985, 1986) have analyzed the impact of moral hazard on the design of disability benefit schedules. The basic framework consists of a three-period model in which the possibility of retiring in the second period is contingent on disability. Disability is a random event. In the third period all workers are retired. The focus is on the optimal provision of disability benefits. Instantaneous utility functions are defined as follows: The marginal utilities of consumption generally differ between retired and non-retired persons. If the person is disabled, the utility when working exceeds that of non-disabled workers, while the marginal utilities of consumption are independent of the health status. Given that 'disability' can be publicly observed, the best policy equates the marginal utilities of consumption between employment states. This implies that the 'disability' pension equals the normal pension — disabled persons retire in the second period, however, while non-disabled consumers must wait until the third period. If the equality of the marginal utilities of consumption between active and non-active individuals implies that retired persons receive an income which is greater than or equal to the net labor income, a moral hazard problem arises when 'disability' constitutes private information.

In this case an incentive-compatible benefit rule must set the disability benefit so as to guarantee the indifference of healthy individuals with respect to the second-period employment status. This explains why disability benefits are lower than normal pension payments. Yet, actuarial fairness does not apply to the calculation of the two benefits. Instead, the indifference condition determines the pension levels — the disability insurance is at its highest possible level, given the incentive problem. Whinston (1983) adds the analysis of the adverse selection problem which arises when consumers are characterized by different disability probabilities and this constitutes private information as well. The study demonstrates that an optimal policy always pools the risk-classes. Hence, disability benefits only depend on the health-status of the consumers. The incentive-compatible benefit rules, which solve the moral hazard problem, also eliminate the necessity to account for adverse selection.

Although Whinston's model is particularly well suited to analyzing the effects of moral hazard and adverse selection in pure health insurance provisions, it is interesting to note the following again: the results, if transferred to pension problems, imply that an actuarial differentiation according to risk-classes encounters an additional moral hazard problem. If 'good' risks would receive generally higher benefits — thus, also higher disability benefits — the incentive to claim to be disabled would increase for all consumer-types. However, following Hoy (1988) this result necessarily requires the possibility of implementing perfect risk-shifting with respect to risk-type uncertainty. If, due to transaction costs, or risk-aversion on the side of the insurance agency, this cannot be attained, the optimal insurance will entail an *ex-post* separation of risk-classes. Consequently, actuarial differences between consumer groups influence the premium/benefit relationship[5].

Diamond and Mirrlees and Peters (1989, Part III) also generalize the basic model to allow for continuous time and introduce a density function relating the probability of becoming disabled to age. In this case, the optimal system under moral hazard can be seen to yield an increasing benefit schedule. However, the model maintains the *assumptions* that (a) there exists an exogenous normal retirement age, and (b) disabled consumers always retire at the date of occurrence of the health shock. Here an additional effect arises, however. Higher benefits provided at later ages serve to increase the incentives, not to cause 'shirking' at younger ages. Again, the slope of the benefit schedule is determined by the trade-off between insurance and incentives, rather than following actuarial considerations. Peters further claims that the model would allow for an endogenous determination of the normal retirement age, given a budget constraint on the actuarial value of the expected pension payments. This is addressed by Nalebuff and Zeckhauser (1985) who demonstrate that, depending on budget requirements, an optimal policy may involve a maximum ('normal') retirement age as well. Yet, the study maintains that disabled consumers always immediately retire when the health shock is realized. Existing moral hazard then implies an increasing benefit profile — again determined by the fact that healthy consumers must be indifferent between withdrawing and remaining in the labor force.

4.2.3 LABOR CONTRACTS AND RETIREMENT CLAUSES

Turning to the second point noted above, the traditional view of the role of private pensions has primarily focused on the 'tax-shelter'-argument. Pensions can be used to evade high payroll taxes on labor income by deferring wage-payments to the retirement period over which personal income taxes are significantly lower. However, Lazear (1979) notes that the private pension arrangements in the United States traditionally also incorporate mandatory retirement rules. Such requirements can hardly be explained by a pure 'tax-shelter' argument[6]. Thus, Lazear proposes to analyze the nature of mandatory retirement rules within the

---

[5]This is denoted 'premium risk', since the risk-averse consumers would always prefer complete insurance. In a related context, Hoy (1989) demonstrates that differences in the *ex-post* information structure also determine whether or not an optimal insurance policy will entail 'premium risk'.

[6]Moreover, the ERISA-legislation of 1974 has also established 'Individual Retirement Accounts' (IRA) which in the 1981 'Economic Recovery Act' has been extended to everyone, regardless of other pension coverage. Since IRA-savings are tax-sheltered as well, they can be viewed as equivalent to occupational pension plans. This conclusion is not necessarily valid, however, if the whole structure of taxation and social security is taken into account. See Mumy (1985) and Sanmartino and Kasten (1985) for more details.

context of long-term firm–labor relationships. The typical increasing age–earnings (tenure–earnings) profile observed in such arrangements is associated with an implicit *ex-ante* contract, in which a termination date must be specified. This date has to be explicit — implying enforceability[7]. Otherwise, the firm would incur losses, if the worker decided *ex-post* to stay with the firm receiving the high final wage, which exceeds the value of the marginal product[8].

As introduced by Becker (1962), increasing age–earnings profiles may reflect an optimal sharing of the costs of and the returns to non-firm-specific human capital. Further, Donaldson and Eaton (1976), for instance, show that the firm as the sole investor can also design increasing age-earnings profiles which achieve the attachment of the workers until the pay-off to a one-off human capital investment is collected. This highlights the role of age-earnings schedules as incentive devices. Thus, Lazear (1979) points out that such schemes provide incentives to preclude 'shirking' on the job. In addition, Lapp (1985) stresses that, if the employment contract entails an implicit insurance against random productivity shocks, the increasing wage-schedule reduces retirements of workers who realize better than average productivities. Moreover, given that productivity also depends on accumulated human capital, the remaining implicit productivity insurance can be verified to induce an increased demand for training by the workers. The adverse effects of retirement threats on the process of human capital accumulation, the workers' acceptance of health and safety standards, and effort supply decisions are also analyzed by Viscusi (1980). Here the increasing earnings-schedule reduces inefficient retirements which arise when workers learn about their productivity over the course of a long-term labor contract.

These arguments are picked up by Lazear (1983, 1985) and Viscusi (1985) who propose that the pension provisions themselves must also be viewed as mobility-reducing incentive devices. This obviously bears significant implications for the calculation of the benefits. Rather than following actuarial rules, the pensions constitute part of the complex package of incentive mechanisms designed to preclude retirements and to induce particular effort supplies. Hence, the pensions are contingent upon individual, or group-specific productivities, reservation wages, risk-taking behavior, and tastes for consumption and on-the-job leisure. Moreover, these studies draw the attention to possible adverse effects which stem from regulatory policies aiming at standardizing and integrating private pensions. As noted above, such regulation has been introduced by the US ERISA-legislation, the German 'Private Pension Act', the British 'Graduated Scheme', and the general integration requirement imposed in the Netherlands, for instance. These policies obviously reduce a firm's ability to utilize pensions as incentive devices.

---

[7]Following Newberry and Stiglitz (1987), for instance, a contract breach may be open (observable for both parties), but not enforceable due to a lack of public verification.

[8]This argument obviously implies the existence of other institutional constraints restricting the possibility of decreasing wages again, or to fire workers.

In contrast, the earlier study by Lazear (1979) focuses on the impact of the 1978 amendments to the US 'Age Discrimination in Employment Act'. This legislation introduces a minimum age (70 years) for mandatory retirement clauses in private pension plans, and bears similar implications for the social security program as well[9]. Again, a similar development has taken place in Europe[10]. In Germany, the 1992 Social Security Reform law[11] explicitly abolishes the employer's right to terminate a labor contract conditional upon the employee reaching the normal age of retirement (65 years). Today, most public schemes not only allow for downward flexibility of the pension age, but also entail the possibility to postpone retirement beyond the normal age. The OECD study (1988b) further stresses the interaction between flexible retirement age allowances contained in most private plans and the social security system. It is concluded that there exists a general tendency to respect individual decisions, rather than imposing mandatory retirement ages. Consequently, the attention shifts towards analyzing the effects of both private and public pension schemes on *inducing* retirement decisions.

4.2.4   INDUCED RETIREMENT

As pointed out before, induced retirement behavior has first been studied by Feldstein (1974). Utilizing a two-period model, the retirement decision is identified with second-period labor supply. In accordance with the standard, static model of consumption/leisure choices, it is shown that the introduction of a public pension system raises lifetime income and therefore increases the demand for leisure. The respective decrease in the labor supply is then associated with a decision to retire earlier. Two-period models of this type, or relating retirement to first-period labor supply, while holding the respective second-period supply constant, constitute a major part of the respective literature. Hu (1979), Breyer (1991), Breyer and Straub (1993), and Wildasin (1991) can be noted to introduce this basic static approach into overlapping-generations models. The efficiency of the labor supply decision is generally associated with the well-known condition that the marginal rate of substitution between consumption and labor must equal the labor income per unit of labor supplied. Whereas Hu concludes that, as long as the efficiency of the labor supply decision is maintained, the basic intertemporal efficiency analysis with respect to financing methods carries over, the latter studies particularly stress labor-supply inefficiencies which arise due to the structure of contributions and benefits. In all of these studies the benefits are income-related and, thus, the labor supply decision codetermines the benefit level. Watson (1982) adds the analysis of uncertainty with respect to the future price of consumption, the wage-rate, and the level of

---

[9]Further, in 1986 mandatory retirement clauses have been ruled illegal in most private pension plans. See, also, Burkhauser and Quinn (1989).

[10]OECD (1988b, p. 81–82).

[11]'Rentenreformgesetz'.

benefits. Here the impact of an exogenous increase in second-period income on the respective labor supply is generally ambiguous.

Interestingly, Watson associates the benefit uncertainty with existing survival uncertainty. This, however, stresses that retirement decisions may be qualitatively quite different from static labor supply reactions. Weiss (1972) can be verified to highlight this difference: Analyzing a life-cycle model with endogenous instantaneous labor supplies, it is demonstrated that, if savings are unconstrained, the labor supplies always increase when the instantaneous wage-rate rises. Only if the consumers are liquidity constrained may this result be reversed. Yet, given that a public pension system exists, in which payments are tied to a withdrawal decision, the optimal choice of the retirement age again induces a division of the total life-span into two distinct subintervals. Hence, comparing Weiss (1972) and Feldstein (1974), the very existence of such programs induces retirement — defined as complete withdrawal from the labor market. Therefore, the question to be addressed is not whether the programs decrease the lifetime labor supply in contrast to models with unconstrained instantaneous labor supply decisions[12]. Rather, what must be analyzed is whether the particular structure of the retirement program induces inefficiencies within a theoretical framework incorporating complete withdrawal decisions[13].

Although the structure of the social security program and the differential taxation of post- and pre-retirement income can thus be assumed to influence the degree of withdrawal[14], analyses of the retirement behavior therefore usually assume an exogenously fixed labor supply during the working-life and determine the optimal length of this age interval. Hemming (1977) shows that, ignoring the disutility of labor, this choice maximizes lifetime income. In contrast, Hu (1978) stresses that, if the move into retirement induces changes in the instantaneous preferences, the optimal retirement age is also contingent on this preference structure. In particular, optimal retirement is characterized by achieving an equality between the marginal utilities of consumption for dates within working-life and old-age. Peters (1989, Part I) then draws the connection between these marginal utilities and the normality, neutrality, and inferiority of labor in the instantaneous utility function. Sheshinski (1978) stresses the annuity character of the public pensions as opposed to private savings. Assuming additively separable utility and the equality of the subjective discount rate and the market rate of interest, it can be shown that the optimal consumption path equalizes income over the course of the consumer's lifetime. Given these assumptions, the introduction of an exogenous annuity significantly decreases the optimal retirement age, since it reduces the necessity to accumulate

---

[12]As Lupu (1984) states: 'Retirement programs by definition undercut work effort'.

[13]See Chang (1991), for instance, who presents a model with endogenous instantaneous labor supply and the possibility of complete withdrawal induced by the development of the 'reservation wage'.

[14]This aspect is particularly stressed in the research of Blinder, Gordon, and Wise (1980), Dye (1985), Quinn and Burkhauser (1983), and Lupu (1984), for instance.

privately in order to achieve equalization of income. If, however, benefits increase marginally fairly with the retirement age chosen, this effect is diminished.

The latter requires that the consumers anticipate the adjustment of the benefits when making the retirement decision. Similarly, Blinder, Gordon, and Wise (1980) demonstrate that, if the public pension system entails a benefit schedule in which the present value of benefits exceeds the respective present value of contributions, this system actually induces a delay of the retirement date compared to the pure private savings solution. Finally, Peters (1989, p. 71–73) and Kahn (1988) demonstrate that anticipated, marginally fair adjustments of the benefits are 'neutral' with respect to the induced retirement decision. 'Neutrality' here implies that the timing of the inter-generational transfers over the consumer's lifetime bears no consequences for the individual retirement decision. Rather, only the expected present values of the income flows — associated with particular choices of the retirement age — matter[15]. At the same time, Kahn draws an important distinction, however. It is demonstrated that this neutrality result requires that the consumers are unconstrained in accumulating — respectively, decumulating — private savings. This implies that social security claims are freely marketable. If, however, the consumers are liquidity constrained, the structure of contributions and benefits, as well as their effect on the discounted lifetime income, determine the optimal retirement date. Additional lifetime income which can only be captured by increasing the retirement age, also raises the replacement ratio. Hence, given that the possibility to achieve consumption-smoothing by borrowing against this future social security income cannot be taken for granted, choosing a later retirement age in order to increase lifetime income can yield a sub-optimal consumption path. Thus, there exists an additional trade-off. Crawford and Lilien (1981) further show that, if survival is uncertain, the annuity character of the pension also contributes a welfare effect. Since private savings accumulated during the working-life give rise to accidental bequests, a higher annuity coverage increases welfare by diminishing the necessity to save for old age. Again, this effect is determined by the induced replacement ratio which is associated with a particular retirement decision.

Crawford and Lilien[16] illustrate this point further by explicitly comparing a version of their model under certain lifetimes and without liquidity-constrained consumers with a second variant incorporating these assumptions. In the first version a marginally fair benefit schedule in fact turns out to be neutral with respect to the retirement decision. Here only deviations from this adjustment rule — possibly induced by inter-generational redistribution — affect the retirement

---

[15]Thus, this concept of 'neutrality' relates to Barro's (1974) notion in two ways. Technically, whereas Barro refers to the fact that the inter-temporal timing of the transfers bears no impact on the inter-generational allocation, the focus here is on lifetime allocations. Since lifetime allocational decisions are relevant for the inter-temporal allocation as well, however, 'neutrality' as defined in Kahn (1988) also constitutes a prerequisite for inter-generational neutrality.

[16]See also Breyer (1990, Ch. 5).

choice compared to the case in which old-age income is derived exclusively from private savings. However, the second version shows that, even with marginally fair adjustments, the retirement effect of expanding the social security system is generally ambiguous. The authors conclude that '[t]hree strong assumptions — perfect capital markets, actuarial fairness, and certain lifetimes' can be shown to '[..] imply that social insurance has no effect on the individuals' incentives to retire'. Hence, Crawford and Lilien (1981) and Kahn (1988) highlight that models of individually optimal retirement decisions can yield qualitatively quite different results[17] given the following assumptions:

(1) Survival is uncertain and there does not exist a private annuity market.

(2) The consumers are liquidity constrained.

Moreover, Crawford and Lilien (1981) conclude that the results derived under conditions (1) and (2) above 'isolate a number of apparently realistic influences that Social Security and some private pension plans might have on workers' retirement decisions'. This statement can also be contrasted with the discussion in Feldstein (1978) on the economic effects of private pensions. Here, only 'unanticipated' pension payments are seen to induce deviations of the savings and retirement plans of the individuals compared to the pure private savings solution. The argument thus obviously assumes again that private savings and 'anticipated' private pensions are perfect substitutes, since the latter are necessarily capital-funded. However, as shown by Crawford and Lilien (1981) and Kahn (1988), even 'anticipated', marginally fair adjustments can be shown to be associated with additional retirement incentives. Thus, analyzing retirement behavior, given the conditions (1) and (2), can now be verified to be of much broader interest. It also provides insights into the possibilities of inducing retirement via private pension plans. As noted above, this is particularly important, if mandatory retirement rules cannot be implemented due to institutional restrictions.

4.3   EMPIRICAL TESTS OF THE HYPOTHESES

Focusing directly on the role of retirement rules in long-term labor contracts, Lazear (1979) finds that, adjusting for several socio-economic variables, job tenure exhibits a negative impact on the mandatory retirement date specified for a particular worker. Since job-tenure is associated with the worker's entrance date, this is seen to support that expected wage-payments and expected productivity are

---

[17]This is in contrast to Blinder, Gordon, and Wise (1980), Chang (1991), Hemming (1977), Hu (1978), Sheshinski (1978), and Peters (1989). Moreover, Chang (1991) can be verified to implicitly underline that the qualitative differences also arise in comparisons to two-period models. The study shows that, only if survival probabilities are constant, the maximum life-span is infinite, and the consumers are not liquidity constrained, there exists a two-period, certain lifetime model which is equivalent to the continuous-time formulation.

equalized in long-term contracts[18]. Similarly, Kotlikoff (1988a), comparing workers with different entrance dates, concludes that age-earnings profiles are steeper than age–productivity profiles. Further, Lapp (1985) demonstrates that workers subject to mandatory retirement clauses face steeper age–earnings schedules than others. Morrison (1988) proceeds by presenting evidence which underlines the importance of existing mandatory retirement rules for realized retirement decisions. In fact, the study concludes that raising the minimum mandatory retirement age from 65 to 70 years yields a 5% increase in the average retirement age.

This, however, contrasts sharply with Burkhauser and Quinn (1983, 1989). If the financial incentives which stem from the social security system are taken into account, the impact of additional mandatory retirement clauses on the realized retirement behavior is considerably less important. Interestingly, Burkhauser and Quinn (1989) also show that the legal restrictions on the use of such clauses introduced in 1978 and 1986 have not induced changes in the actual retirement pattern in the US. Rather extensive calculations provided by Lazear (1985) illustrate that the present value of private pension benefits exceed the respective actuarial value of the contributions. This is concluded to support the hypothesis that pensions are used as incentive devices. Moreover, the study notes large increases in the private pension coverage which have taken place prior to the enactment of the age-discrimination laws. Thus, these changes may have been anticipated. Consequently, the firms have turned to 'induced retirement' strategies, well before the legal restrictions were enacted. This again corresponds to the evidence presented in Burkhauser and Quinn (1989).

The empirical research on the impact of disability pensions on retirement decisions has been motivated by Boskin (1977). The study notes two basically contradictory developments. On the one hand, the observed increase in life-expectancies can be associated with improvements in the overall health status of the population. Yet, early retirement due to claimed health deficits has been a prime factor in determining the decrease in the participation rates over the post-war period, in particular the 1970s. Thus, Boskin concludes that this phenomenon can only be explained by the increased 'generosity' of the disability benefits which has induced more disability-contingent early retirement. This conclusion is not undisputed, however. Crimmins and Pramaggiore (1988), for instance, claim that the health status of male workers has actually deteriorated despite the observed increase in life-expectancies. Second, the subjective perception of 'disability' may have changed. Disability benefits are increasingly claimed in situations which would not have been associated with a necessity to receive such transfers some years ago. On the other hand, Kohli (1988) and Uhlenberg (1988) can be seen to support Boskin's basic finding. The authors note that the standard retirement age (65 in most countries) does not constitute a natural productivity barrier any more.

---

[18]Bellmann (1989), however, reports split evidence as far as tenure-earnings profiles are concerned. This study also compares the situations in the US and Germany.

Haveman and Wolfe (1984) provide an empirical test of the induced retirement argument with respect to disability pensions. The research shows that an increased generosity in these transfers in fact yields significant decreases in the retirement age of persons claiming such benefits. In this context, it is interesting to note that there exists a considerable discrepancy between self-reported 'poor health' and the actual claiming of disability benefits[19]. As noted by Boskin (1977) this may correspond to the fact that 'poor health' is a 'socially acceptable' reason to retire early. Yet, the hazard rate analyses of Diamond and Hausman (1984a,b) demonstrate that the probability of retirement is significantly influenced by 'poor health'-proxies and age. These impacts are distinct from the social security income rules and have gained importance over time. Moreover, Diamond and Hausman (1984b) note considerable time-lags between the date when 'poor health' is first reported and the actual beginning of the respective disability benefit claims. This is seen to warrant caution in interpreting the increased significance of disability claims as merely reflecting an 'increased generosity' effect.

As pointed out before, the differences between the original work by Feldstein (1974) and Leimer and Lesnoy's (1982) and Burkhauser and Turner's (1982) re-examinations are partially due to the fact that the expansion of the social security system proves to have significantly decreased the average retirement age. This can be seen to contrast with Gordon and Blinder (1980) who focus on individual retirement data. Here, the realized retirement decisions are explained by the 'normal' effects of aging and private pensions on 'market wages' (productivity) and 'reservation wages'. The 'normal' effects of aging are associated with declining health, depressed human capital accumulation, and shifts in preferences towards favoring leisure. The study attempts to capture these effects by introducing dummy variables for the individual's health status and age. It turns out that the health status, the autonomous age effect, and private pension income possess a considerably stronger impact on the retirement pattern than social security variables introduced as well.

Following this, a number of subsequent studies have focused on discriminating between the determinants of retirement behavior[20]. Kotlikoff (1979b) reports that individual retirement decisions respond to changes in the expected social security wealth. Hanoch and Honig (1983) confirm the existence of an autonomous age effect, but also strong negative impacts of pension coverage and, additionally, of currently available social security benefits on the retirement age. Mitchell and Fields (1984) utilize a linear regression model with the retirement age as the dependent variable, and a Logit-estimation focusing on the probability of retiring at a certain

---

[19]Packard and Reno (1988).

[20]The method used in these empirical studies has changed over time. While earlier research utilizes standard linear regression, more recent studies generally turn to hazard rate models. Also, the studies usually ignore certain effects which then appear in other research. Rust (1989) can be seen to design a structural model of retirement decisions which is theoretically suited to capture all of the possible effects. At the same time, however, this demonstrates the extreme complexity of such an approach. Hence, some simplification will always be required in empirical studies.

age. Both analyses confirm strong negative impacts of both private pensions and social security income on the retirement age. This result is confirmed by Burtless and Moffitt (1984, 1985), also demonstrating that 'poor health' possesses a significant, separate effect. The very detailed research by Fields and Mitchell (1984) and Diamond and Hausman (1984a,b) further adds that the individual's experience of unemployment induces earlier retirement. Diamond and Hausman (1984b) again note that unemployment, poor health, low permanent income, and age are highly correlated. Further, a significant fraction of workers experience considerable delays between the reported dates of disability or retirement and the beginning of pension payments. Thus, the induced retirement argument may fail for these workers and the authors conclude that policies aimed at modifying the incentives to retire must be associated with further welfare losses for this group. Hurd and Boskin (1984) confirm an additional significant impact of mandatory retirement rules. Thus, these studies suggest that all of the theoretical approaches described above can partially explain the retirement pattern. More general in focus, Hammermesh (1984) and Bernheim (1988, 1989) demonstrate that individuals anticipate changes in the institutional framework when planning their retirement.

Also, the very fact that the studies reviewed show that the *structure* of contributions and benefits, and other determinants of the *instantaneous* incomes, prove to have statistically significant impacts on the retirement decision, can be seen to emphasize the importance of existing liquidity constraints. This is further stressed by Kahn (1988). In contrast to Blinder, Gordon, and Wise (1980) who utilize the market rate of interest to discount all future income flows, Kahn first estimates the labor earnings potential of retired workers based on several socio-economic variables, including education and health status. Given these estimates, the study calculates the potential change in social security wealth associated with delaying the retirement decision. The probability to retire is then seen to depend on a choice between receiving these potential earnings or social security benefit payments as of the time when this decision is actually made. The results strongly support the hypothesis that the structure of the social security system matters. In particular, early retirement options are important factors in explaining the observed pattern of retirement.

Turning to the problem of retirement vs. variations of the instantaneous labor supply, Gustman and Steinmeier (1986) conclude that the observed pattern of retirement and part-time work can be associated with existing non-linearities in the income structure. However, Peracchi and Welch (1991) cast doubts on the induced retirement hypothesis in this context[21]. They point out that there exist rather significant exit rates well before the legal early retirement ages are reached. Yet, a number of studies — including Burkhauser and Turner (1982), Burtless and Moffitt (1984, 1985), Burkhauser and Quinn (1989), Gustman and Steinmeier (1986), and Hanoch

---

[21] See also Diamond and Hausman (1984b) again.

Table 4.4   Male participation rates and retirement in the US and Germany

Age	United States			Germany		
	Full-time[a]	Part-time[b]	Retired[c]	Full-time	Part-time	Retired
50–54	76.6	11.0	12.4	91.5	0.6	7.8
55–59	65.9	17.4	16.7	79.1	1.5	19.4
60–64	38.8	16.9	44.3	37.7	1.6	60.8
65–69	12.2	22.3	65.4	4.1	7.5	88.4
70–74	7.4	13.7	79.1	1.7	3.2	95.3
75–79	2.5	12.7	84.8	2.5	1.7	95.7
80+	1.6	4.8	93.5	1.2	0.0	98.8

Source: Reproduced by permission of Economic Policy from Börsch-Supan (1991).
[a] More than 35 hours per week.
[b] 15–35 hours per week.
[c] Less than 15 hours per week.

and Honig (1983), for instance — support the conclusion that social security induces moves from full-time employment into full-time retirement.

This variety of empirical research available for the United States can be seen to be best suited to highlight the different aspects of retirement behavior. Although the empirical research on the determinants of retirement is much less developed for other countries, the following studies can be verified to present some evidence on the basic fact that retirement programs induce complete withdrawal. For the United Kingdom, Zabalza, Pissarides, and Barton (1980) analyze the joint choice between full-time employment, part-time employment, and retirement. The latter is shown to depend on age, the health status, and the statutory pension age. Given the discussion above, the absence of a general flexible retirement age program may be also assumed to induce the use of disability programs for early retirement here. For Germany, Genosko (1983) and Börsch-Supan (1991) can be verified to highlight the influence of the eligibility rules for the different social security retirement programs for induced complete withdrawal. As illustrated by the figures compiled in Table 4.4, this effect can be concluded to be even stronger than in the United States.

4.4   SUMMARY AND OUTLOOK

Although this review of theoretical approaches and empirical studies reveals that there does not exist a sole explanatory approach, it also highlights some stylized facts.

(1)   The 'induced retirement' argument can be seen to provide an explanation for the observed retirement pattern. However, it cannot be ignored that other influences — such as poor health, employment opportunities, and productivity effects of aging — are also important, distinct factors. Hence, 'induced

retirement' models may only explain the retirement behavior of a subgroup of the population.

(2)   However, 'induced retirement' effects may also be of importance in analyzing the economic effects of special retirement programs. As far as disability schemes are concerned, this can be assumed to depend on the institutional framework under consideration — in particular, whether there exists a flexible retirement age option in the old-age pension system. Moreover, inducing retirement can be seen to provide an instrument to achieve separation in long-term labor contracts.

(3)   A considerable fraction of the population moves from full-time employment into full-time retirement. There is evidence that this decision may be influenced by other factors — such as unemployment, part-time employment opportunities, and tax laws — in addition to the incentives provided by the social security system itself.

(4)   The retirement decision is not only contingent on the present value of the lifetime income flow. The income structure implied by the system matters as well. This lends support to the hypothesis that consumers are liquidity-constrained as far as their possibility to borrow against future social security income is concerned.

The first two points motivate interest in analyzing 'induced retirement' models. At the same time, they can be verified to limit the scope of such an analysis. In particular, this applies to policy proposals which intend to remove retirement incentives in disability and other special programs. However, given the necessary caution in making such proposals, the interest in analyzing the implications of 'induced retirement' arguments for the design of these programs is also quite obvious. In particular, given the discussion in Section 3.5, this approach clearly constitutes a natural starting point for the present investigation into the nature of variable retirement schemes. Points (3) and (4) then isolate some basic requirements for modeling individual retirement decisions adequately. They will be picked up in the following again. The basic model introduced — and carried through the remaining parts — is particularly aimed at incorporating these features. This will necessarily imply a loss of generality with respect to possible other determinants of retirement behavior, however.

CHAPTER 5

A basic analytical framework

5.1 BASIC ASSUMPTIONS AND DEFINITIONS

This chapter will introduce the basic setting for the analysis of the induced retirement behavior which will be pursued in the following[1]. Although the chapter adds new results and interpretations, the basic model outlined follows the framework proposed by Crawford and Lilien (1981) rather closely. In fact, as far as the assumptions used are concerned, the generalization is only very slight. This approach will be seen to serve well to isolate effects which stem from particular assumptions introduced at later stages. As noted before, the model particularly allows for uncertain survival and liquidity constraints. (Conditions (1) and (2) in Section 4.2.4 above.) These two properties have been argued to be of prime importance if individual retirement decisions are to be analyzed. This section will now briefly sketch out and discuss the additional characteristic assumptions.

To begin with, the consumers are assumed to possess identical, instantaneous preferences over consumption $c \in C = [0, \infty)$ and labor l which can be expressed by a utility function v. In particular, utility is additively separable in the two arguments. Hence, the utility of a survivor aged t years equals

$$v(t) = U(c(t)) - g(l(t)). \tag{5.1}$$

The function $U(\cdot)$ exhibits the usual properties: $U'(c) > 0$, $U''(c) < 0 \; \forall \, c \in C$, and $\lim_{c \to 0} U'(c) = \infty$. Obviously, (5.1) already implies the absence of an altruistic bequest motive. In contrast to Kahn (1988) the instantaneous preference structure does not entail an autonomous age effect. Specifically, the model abstracts from possible age-related changes in the disutility of labor. Further, it is assumed that the instantaneous labor supply equals unity when working, and zero otherwise. For simplicity, $g(0) = 0$ and $g(1) = G$.

---

[1] In part, the exposition in this chapter is based on Fabel (1992).

Assuming that the utility of a non-surviving consumer attains the value 0, the instantaneous expected utility associated with age t — hence, to be calculated immediately prior to reaching this age — is obtained according to

$$\mathcal{V}(t) = F(t)v(t) + (1 - F(t))0$$
$$= F(t)v(t). \tag{5.2}$$

Here $F(t)$ is the survival probability at age t — assumed to be known *ex-ante*. Throughout, we will ignore problems associated with new information revealing possible changes in the survival risk which may arrive as the individual ages. Thus, the *ex-ante* probabilities in fact correctly characterize the *ex-post* survival risk.

Let date 0 denote entrance to the labor-force, R the retirement age, and T the maximum life-span of an individual. Retirement is perceived as a one-time decision to withdraw from the labor market completely. The possibility of re-entrance is excluded. Then, assuming that the consumer *utilizes* the market rate of interest r for subjective discounting, the expected discounted lifetime utility can be written as[2]:

$$V = \int_0^T \mathcal{V}(t)e^{-rt}dt$$
$$= \int_0^T U(c(t))F(t)e^{-rt}dt - G\int_0^R F(t)e^{-rt}dt. \tag{5.3}$$

It is obviously plausible that the survival probabilities decrease with age. This is illustrated by the typical, empirical survival frequency functions provided by Dinkel (1988) and Ng (1992), for instance. Hence,

$$\dot{F}(t) < 0. \tag{5.4}$$

For convenience, it is assumed that $F(0) = 1$ and, by definition, $F(T) = 0$.

Working individuals receive a constant wage-income w and must pay contributions. The contribution rate p is assumed to be constant as well. Thus, income equals $w(1 - p)$ at each date during the working-life. When retired the consumer's income consists of a constant stream of benefits x. The assumptions concerning the constancy of income flows simplify the analysis considerably, but also induce some loss of generality. Thus, it should be noted that introducing an increasing age–earnings relationship does not yield qualitatively different results here. Moreover, the assumptions can be seen to reflect the stylized fact that pension systems

---

[2]More precisely, the expression derived below should be denoted 'discounted lifetime value of expected utilities'. Yet, the term 'expected discounted lifetime utility' appears to be more commonly used throughout the literature and is, thus, applied here as well. Nevertheless, it should be noted that — since integration is carried out over ages, rather than probabilities — the respective unit of measure must be 'utility × years'. However, integration is introduced merely as a matter of convenience — avoiding summations. None of the results obtained in the following needs to be re-interpreted as a consequence of the slightly differing notion of expected utility appearing in this study.

generally do not allow for *age-dependent* contributions and benefits. Private wealth $\omega(t)$ is accumulated according to:

$$\dot{\omega}(t) = \omega(t)r + [w(1 - p) - c(t)]; \quad t \in [0, R) \tag{5.5}$$

$$\dot{\omega}(t) = \omega(t)r + [x - c(t)]; \quad t \in [R, T]. \tag{5.6}$$

This specification implies that there does not exist a private market for annuity insurance, nor the possibility to bequeath wealth to creditors. Thus, private savings and insurance are only imperfect substitutes, since they are associated with a positive probability to leave involuntary bequests. In terms of Ehrlich and Becker (1972), private savings can be identified with 'self-insurance'. Hence, self-insurance constitutes an inferior instrument to provide for old-age income, compared with the possibility of accumulating pension claims. As pointed out in Chapter 3, the absence of private annuity markets is a rather common feature of models which focus on the role of pensions under uncertain lifetimes. While Crawford and Lilien (1981) and Abel (1985) do not seek to provide an explicit motivation, Eckstein, Eichenbaum, and Peled (1985b), Hu (1986), Hubbard (1987), Hubbard and Judd (1987), Schwödiauer and Wenig (1989, 1990), and Leimer and Richardson (1992), among others, stress the importance of market failure due to adverse selection. Further, it will be assumed that private wealth holdings are restricted to be non-negative:

$$\omega(t) \geq 0 \quad ; \quad t \in [0, T]. \tag{5.7}$$

This liquidity constraint is often 'naturally' associated with the very fact that survival is uncertain. Yaari (1965), for instance, seems to suggest that it reflects the usual assumption that lifetime consumption must be financed out of lifetime income known from models with certain lifetimes. Obviously, (5.7) implies that *realized* lifetime consumption may never exceed *realized* lifetime income. Yet, Kotlikoff, Shoven, and Spivak (1987) and Chang (1991), for instance, can be verified to analyze uncertain lifetime models without introducing a non-negativity constraint on private wealth. Here, the survival probabilities only affect the individuals' discounting of the utility derived from consumption at later ages. Thus, the optimal consumption path is exclusively determined by the preference structure and the annuity character of the public pension. However, (5.7) can be further motivated, if there exist institutional constraints limiting the consumers' possibility to borrow against future income. Thus, the constraint can either reflect general capital-market imperfections, or legal restrictions of the ability to borrow against old-age benefits. Obviously, the liquidity constraint (5.7) affects the trade-off between self-insurance, via private savings, and insurance, by means of accumulating social security claims. As will be seen, the constraint will be responsible for the effect of alternative replacement ratios on the optimal consumption path. Merely for convenience again, it will also be assumed that

$$\omega(0) = 0. \tag{5.8}$$

For the time being, the particular retirement policy in focus will be characterized by the following budget equation:

$$\int_0^R F(t)e^{-rt}\,\mathrm{d}t\; pw - \int_R^T F(t)e^{-rt}\,\mathrm{d}t\; x = B. \tag{5.9}$$

Here, B is an exogenous value indicating that the financing method actually implemented may be either capital-funding, or pay-as-you-go. Clearly[3], fully funded pensions require $B = 0$. Obviously, (5.9) can be taken to define benefits x as an implicit function of several policy variables and other parameters of the model. Assuming that the consumers are actually free to choose retirement ages conditional only on ensuring that (5.9) remains satisfied, gives rise to the following marginal rate of transforming changes in the retirement age into respective benefit realignments:

$$MRT^{x,R}(p, R, x) \equiv \left.\frac{\mathrm{d}x}{\mathrm{d}R}\right|_{\substack{dB=0\\dp=0}} = \frac{F(R)e^{-rR}[pw + x]}{\displaystyle\int_R^T F(t)e^{-rt}\,\mathrm{d}t}. \tag{5.10}$$

Obviously, (5.10) characterizes an actuarially, or marginally fair adjustment rule. In the following, let $x = \xi^M(R; p, B)$ denote a marginally fair benefit schedule with slope given by (5.10). Throughout the subsequent analysis it will be assumed that

$$\frac{\partial^2 \xi^M(R; p, B)}{\partial R \partial R} = \frac{\partial MRT^{x,R}}{\partial R} \geq 0. \tag{5.11}$$

An explicit derivation and an example, considering a specific type of survival probability functions, is provided in the Appendix.

Similarly, the marginal rate of transformation

$$MRT^{x,p}(p, R, x) \equiv \left.\frac{\mathrm{d}x}{\mathrm{d}p}\right|_{\substack{dB=0\\dR=0}} = \frac{\displaystyle\int_0^R F(t)e^{-rt}\,\mathrm{d}t\; w}{\displaystyle\int_R^T F(t)e^{-rt}\,\mathrm{d}t} \tag{5.12}$$

defines the benchmark case of marginally fair adjustments of the benefit to changes in the contribution rate — given a retirement date. Once again, it should be noted that (5.10) and (5.12) refer to possible adjustment rules. Only if full capital-funding were required, would these equations also describe necessary adjustments. Given pay-as-you-go and the possible existence of additional tax-financing, there is no such obvious reason to require actuarially fair adjustments of the benefits.

---

[3]Chapter 6 below will address the relationship between this 'budget surplus parameter' and the financing method employed in more detail.

5.2 THE OPTIMAL CONSUMPTION PATH

In a first step the consumers maximize their expected lifetime utility (5.3) by choosing an optimal consumption path. This decision is made subject to the income flows generated — given a contribution rate p, a retirement age R, and the corresponding benefit x. Let $\{z(t)\} = \{z(t; p, x, R)\}$ denote the optimal consumption path. For the following analysis it is very convenient to note that this path can be characterized as follows[4]:

Lemma 1 (Yaari (1965)). *(i) If $w(1 - p) > z(t_1)$, for some $t_1 \in [0, R)$, then $w(1 - p) > z(t), \forall\, t \in [t_1, R)$.*

(ii) If $x > z(t_3)$, for some $t_3 \in [R, T]$, then $x > z(t), \forall\, t \in [t_3, T]$.

Sketch of proof. Consider case (i) and suppose there exist $t_1 < t_2 < R$ such that $w(1 - p) > z(t), \forall\, t \in [t_1, t_2)$, and $w(1 - p) \leq z(t_2)$. This implies $U'(z(t_2 - \eta)) F(t_2 - \eta) > U'(z(t_2))F(t_2)$, where $\eta \in (0, t_2 - t_1]$. Note that if the consumer increased consumption at date $t = t_2 - \eta$ by an amount ε and decreased consumption at date $t = t_2$ by the amount $\varepsilon e^{r(t_2 - (t_2 - \eta))} = \varepsilon e^{r\eta}$, private wealth $\omega(t_2)$ would remain unchanged. However, differentiating with respect to ε — evaluated at $\varepsilon = 0$ — shows that the expected utility changes according to

$$[U'(z(t_2 - \eta)) F(t_2 - \eta) - U'(z(t_2))F(t_2)]e^{-r[t_2 - \eta]} . \tag{5.13}$$

This ensures that the consumer's expected utility could be increased by redistributing consumption in a (small) vicinity around t_2 as proposed above. Thus, $\{z(t)\}$ cannot be an optimal consumption path in this case. The same argument can be utilized to prove part (ii) of the lemma. Q.E.D.

Thus, given Lemma 1, (5.7), and (5.8), it follows that the search for the optimal consumption plan can be restricted to such paths, where

$$c(t) \leq (1 - p)w, \quad \forall\, t \in [0, R); \tag{5.14}$$

$$c(t) \geq x, \quad \forall\, t \in [R, T]. \tag{5.15}$$

Here, (5.15) has been derived utilizing the additional 'natural' boundary condition

$$\omega(T) = 0. \tag{5.16}$$

Obviously, since there does not exist an altruistic bequest motive, it can never be optimal not to consume all wealth until date T. Hence, (5.8) and (5.16) imply

---

[4]The lemma presented here relies on the assumption that the consumers utilize the market rate of interest for subjective discounting. Yaari (1965) — among others — actually provides a more general discussion of optimal consumption paths under varying subjective discount rates. However, the qualitative results obtained in the following carry over as long as these paths are non-increasing over the consumer's working-life and old-age, respectively.

that total discounted lifetime consumption must equal total discounted lifetime income:

$$\int_0^T c(t)e^{-rt}dt = \int_0^R e^{-rt}dt \, w(1-p) + \int_R^T e^{-rt}dt \, x. \qquad (5.17)$$

These preliminary considerations can now be used to formulate an optimization problem which is more easily handled. Maximizing (5.3) subject to (5.8) and (5.14)—(5.17) with respect to the consumption path $\{c(t)\}$, for given values (p, R, x), gives rise to the following characterization of the optimal path $\{z(t)\}$:

Proposition 1 (Crawford and Lilien (1981)).   *(i) If $(1 - p)w > x$, then there exist $t_L \in [0, R)$ and $t_U \in (R, T]$, such that $U'(z(t))F(t) = \lambda^*, \forall\, t \in [t_L, t_U]$. This implies $z(t) = w(1 - p), \forall\, t \in [0, t_L], z(t) < w(1 - p), \forall\, t \in (t_L, R), z(t) > x, \forall\, t \in [R, t_U)$, and $z(t) = x, \forall\, t \in [t_U, T]$.*
(ii) If $(1-p)w \le x$, then $z(t) = (1-p)w, \forall\, t \in [0, R)$, and $z(t) = x, \forall\, t \in [R, T]$.

Proof.   Define the following Lagrangian:

$$L \equiv \int_0^T U(c(t))F(t)e^{-rt}dt$$

$$-\lambda\left\{\int_0^T c(t)e^{-rt}dt - \int_0^R e^{-rt}dt \, w(1-p) - \int_R^T e^{-rt}dt \, x\right\}$$

$$-\int_0^R \gamma_y(t)\{w(1-p) - c(t)\}dt - \int_R^T \gamma_o(t)\{c(t) - x\}dt. \qquad (5.18)$$

Maximizing L with respect to consumption $\{c(t)\}$ yields the first-order conditions:

$$U'(z(t))F(t) = \lambda^* - \gamma_y^*(t)e^{rt}; \quad t \in [0, R) \qquad (5.19)$$

$$U'(z(t))F(t) = \lambda^* + \gamma_o^*(t)e^{rt}; \quad t \in [R, T], \qquad (5.20)$$

where superscripts '$*$' denote the optimal values of the multipliers.

It is easily obtained that $\lambda \ge 0$, $\gamma_y(t)$, $\gamma_o(t) \le 0$. Let $S(t)$ denote the induced, optimal path of private wealth $\omega(t)$. Now, suppose there exists t_L such that $w(1 - p) > z(t_L)$, $t_L < R$. It follows from Lemma 1 (i) that $w(1 - p) > z(t), \forall\, t \in [t_L, R)$—hence $S(R) > 0$. Moreover, it is easily obtained that (5.16) implies the existence of $t_U \le T$ such that $S(t) = 0, \forall\, t \in [t_U, T]$ (by Lemma 1 (ii)). Thus, if there exists an interval $[R, t_1]$, where $t_1 < t_U$, with $z(t) = x$, for $t \in [R, t_1]$, and $z(t) > x$, for $t \in (t_1, t_U]$, then $\gamma_o(t) \le 0$ would imply that $U'(x)F(\tau) < U'(z(t))F(t)$, where $\tau \in [R, t_1]$ and $t \in (t_1, t_U]$. The concavity of $U(c)$ and (5.4) assure that this cannot be the case. If follows that, if $w(1-p) > z(t)$, for $t \in [t_L, R)$, then $z(t) > x$, for $t \in [R, t_U)$. Hence

$$U'(z(t))F(t) = \lambda^*; \quad t \in [t_L, t_U] \qquad (5.21)$$

in this case. Thus, $S(R) > 0$ implies the existence of a 'free' interval[5] $[t_L, t_U]$ as defined above. Further, (5.14), (5.15), and (5.21) prove that $(1 - p)w > x$ is necessary for $S(R) > 0$. Setting $z(t) = (1 - p)w$, $\forall\ t \in [0, R)$, and $z(t) = x$, $\forall\ t \in [R, T]$, and recalling that $\gamma_y(t)$, $\gamma_o(t) \leq 0$, then reveals that $(1 - p)w > x$ is also sufficient for $S(R) > 0$.
Q.E.D.

Hence, depending on the (net) replacement ratio $x/(1 - p)w$ the proposition defines two 'accumulation-regimes': If the replacement ratio is smaller than unity, the consumers accumulate private wealth in addition to contributing to the pension program. On the other hand, replacement ratios greater than or equal to unity induce no further private accumulation. Moreover, the optimal consumption path, given $x/(1 - p)w < 1$, can additionally be described by:

Corollary 1 (Crawford and Lilien (1981)).   *Let θ_L and θ_U, respectively, denote the optimal values of t_L and t_U defined in Proposition 1(i). Then, $\theta_U < T$, if pension payments x are positive. Further, the optimal consumption path $\{z(t)\}$ is continuous at $t = \theta_L$, for $\theta_L > 0$, and $t = \theta_U$. It follows that*

$$\dot{z}(t) = -\frac{U'(z(t))\dot{F}(t)}{U''(z(t))F(t)} < 0, \ \forall\ t \in [\theta_L, \theta_U].$$

Proof.   Differentiating (5.21) with respect to t directly proves that optimal consumption must decrease with age. Further, (5.20) implies

$$U'(z(t))F(t) \leq U'(x)F(t), \ \forall\ t \in [t_L, t_U].\qquad(5.22)$$

Taking $\lim_{t_U \to T}$ the RHS of this expression equals zero at $t = t_U$. However, the LHS must be equal to $\lambda^* > 0$. This contradicts $\theta_U = T$. Hence, utilizing the information from Proposition 1 (i) (thus, assuming the case $w(1 - p) > x$) the optimization problem can be reformulated as[6]:

$$\max_{t_L, t_U, c(t)} L_S \equiv$$

$$\int_0^{t_L} F(t)e^{-rt}dt\, U((1 - p)w) + \int_{t_L}^{t_U} U(c(t))F(t)e^{-rt}dt + \int_{t_U}^{T} F(t)e^{-rt}dt\, U(x)$$

$$- \lambda \left\{ \int_{t_L}^{t_U} c(t)e^{-rt}dt - \int_{t_L}^{R} e^{-rt}dt\, (1 - p)w - \int_{R}^{t_U} e^{-rt}dt\, x \right\} - \phi t_L.\quad(5.23)$$

---

[5]Yaari (1965) has introduced the notion of 'blocked' versus 'free' intervals according to whether or not the constraints (5.14) and (5.15), respectively, are binding.

[6]Due to the arguments above, $t_U \leq T$ cannot constitute a binding constraint and has, therefore, been omitted.

The respective first-order conditions read

$$F(\theta_L)e^{-r\theta_L}[U((1-p)w) - U(z(\theta_L))] - \lambda^*e^{-r\theta_L}[(1-p)w - z(\theta_L)] = \phi^*$$

(5.24)

$$F(\theta_U)e^{-r\theta_U}[U(z(\theta_U)) - U(x)] - \lambda^*e^{-r\theta_U}[z(\theta_U) - x] = 0 \qquad (5.25)$$

and — restating (5.21) —

$$U'(z(t))F(t) = \lambda^*, \ \forall\, t \in [\theta_L, \theta_U]. \tag{5.26}$$

Note that the concavity of $U(c)$ implies $U(y_1) - U(y_2) \le U'(y_2)[y_1 - y_2]$, with strict equality, if, and only if, $y_1 = y_2$. This confirms the continuity statements contained in Corollary 1.
Q.E.D.

Proposition 1 and Corollary 1 can now be utilized to define the consumers' expected lifetime utility — after optimization with respect to the consumption path — as follows:

$$V^*(p, R, x) \equiv \beta(p, R, x) \cdot L_S^*(p, R, x)$$

$$+[1 - \beta(p, R, x)] \cdot L_{NS}^*(p, R, x) - G \int_0^R F(t)e^{-rt}dt \,, \qquad (5.27)$$

where $L_S^*(p, R, x)$ is derived from (5.23), for $t_L = \theta_L$, $t_U = \theta_U$, and $\{c(t)\} = \{z(t)\}$. Similarly,

$$L_{NS}^*(p, R, x) \equiv \int_0^R F(t)e^{-rt}dt\, U((1-p)w) + \int_R^T F(t)e^{-rt}dt\, U(x) . \quad (5.28)$$

Finally, it must be true that

$$\beta(p, R, x) = \begin{cases} 1, & \text{if } (1-p)w > x \\ 0, & \text{if } (1-p)w \le x. \end{cases} \qquad (5.29)$$

Throughout the following analysis it will be assumed that the consumers always choose an optimal consumption (savings) path given the social security policies offered. Hence, (5.27) constitutes the respective objective function of individuals facing a particular policy. Preparing for the arguments to follow, (5.27) can now be utilized to define the marginal rates of substitution:

$$MRS^{x,R}(p, R, x) \equiv$$

$$\left.\frac{dx}{dR}\right|_{\substack{dV^*=0 \\ dp=0}} = \begin{cases} \dfrac{F(R)e^{-rR}[G - U'(z(R))[w(1-p) - x]]}{\displaystyle\int_R^T U'(z(t))F(t)e^{-rt}dt}, & \text{if } \beta = 1 \\[6mm] \dfrac{F(R)e^{-rR}[G + U(x) - U((1-p)w)]}{\displaystyle\int_R^T F(t)e^{-rt}dt\, U'(x)}, & \text{if } \beta = 0 \end{cases} \qquad (5.30)$$

and

$$MRS^{x,p}(p, R, x) \equiv$$

$$\frac{dx}{dp}\bigg|_{\substack{dV^*=0 \\ dR=0}} = \begin{cases} \dfrac{\displaystyle\int_0^R U'(z(t))F(t)e^{-rt}dt\; w}{\displaystyle\int_R^T U'(z(t))F(t)e^{-rt}dt}, & \text{if } \beta = 1 \\[3em] \dfrac{\displaystyle\int_0^R F(t)e^{-rt}dt\; U'((1-p)w)w}{\displaystyle\int_R^T F(t)e^{-rt}dt\; U'(x)}, & \text{if } \beta = 0. \end{cases} \tag{5.31}$$

In both (5.30) and (5.31) λ^* has been substituted according to (5.26) given the case $\beta(p, R, x) = 1$. For the subsequent analysis it is assumed that

$$\frac{\partial MRS^{x,R}}{\partial R} > 0 . \tag{5.32}$$

Again, an explicit derivation illustrating the necessary qualifications can be found in the Appendix.

Obviously, the choice of the retirement age determines the replacement ratio. Thus, this choice can be identified with the decision to achieve a certain degree of 'self-protection' — in terms of Ehrlich and Becker (1972) again. Broadly speaking, retiring later (earlier) decreases (increases) the size of the old-age risk which needs to be insured. Due to the particular institutional framework, it also determines the degree of income insurance provided, however. Thus, it can be assumed that the choice of the retirement age affects the trade-off between 'insurance' and 'self-insurance'. In fact, the opportunity costs of increasing the self-protection will be seen to determine the accumulation regime — consequently, also the amount of additional self-insurance via private savings.

5.3   OPTIMAL RETIREMENT AND 'ACCUMULATION-REGIMES'

In the next step, the consumers now choose their optimal retirement age R^* and benefit x^*. The notion of 'optimality' here is confined to choices which maximize the expected lifetime utility, as defined in (5.27), subject to the constraint (5.9). For this optimization problem the required contribution rate p and the policy parameter B are taken as exogenously given. Assuming an interior maximum exists, the optimal combination (x^*, R^*) must be characterized by the following first-order conditions:

$$\beta(p, R^*, x^*) \int_{R^*}^T U'(z(t))F(t)e^{-rt}dt$$

$$+ (1 - \beta(p, R^*, x^*)) \int_{R^*}^T F(t)e^{-rt}dt\; U'(x^*) = \psi^* \int_{R^*}^T F(t)e^{-rt}dt \tag{5.33}$$

$$\beta(p, R^*, x^*)F(R^*)e^{-rR^*}[G \ - \ U'(z(R^*))((1-p)w - x^*)]$$
$$+ \ (1 - \beta(p, R^*, x^*))F(R^*)e^{-rR^*}[G \ + \ U(x^*) \ - \ U((1-p)w)] \ =$$
$$\psi^* F(R^*)e^{-rR^*}[pw + x^*]. \qquad (5.34)$$

Here $\psi^* \geq 0$ denotes the optimal value of the multiplier associated with the constraint (5.9). As in (5.30) and (5.31), for $\beta = 1$, all first-order effects associated with variations of the consumption path vanish again, since $\{z(t)\}$ is chosen optimal conditional on (p, R, x). Further, λ^* has been substituted. Obviously, in terms of the definitions above, combining (5.33) and (5.34) yields

$$MRS^{x,R}(p, R^*, x^*) = MRT^{x,R}(p, R^*, x^*). \qquad (5.35)$$

Yet, in order to be able to interpret this condition further, it is necessary to know whether $\beta(p, R^*, x^*)$ equals unity or zero. Note that the induced benefit level x^* —calculated according to (5.9) for $R = R^*$ —may either be associated with the accumulation regime of part (i), or of part (ii) of Proposition 1. Faced with this problem, Crawford and Lilien (1981) *assume* that the induced replacement ratio is smaller than unity. Fortunately however, interior solutions to the optimization problem above entail a separation property which identifies the accumulation regime:

Proposition 2.   *Let $\tilde{p}$ be the contribution rate defined by the equation*

$$U'((1 - \tilde{p})w)w = G$$

and assume that there exists an interior solution (R^*, x^*) to the optimization problem

$$\text{Max}_{x,R} \ (5.27)$$
$$\textit{subject to } (5.9).$$

If the contribution rate p required satisfies:
(a) $p < \tilde{p}$, $w(1 - p) > x^*$. Thus, $\beta(p, R^*, x^*) = 1$. Hence the consumers save privately in addition to accumulating claims in the pension system.
(b) $p = \tilde{p}$, $w(1 - p) = x^*$. Thus, $\beta(p, R^*, x^*) = 0$ and there is no private accumulation.
(c) $p > \tilde{p}$, $w(1 - p) < x^*$. Again, $\beta(p, R^*, x^*) = 0$ and the consumers do not save.

Proof.   The proof follows by contradiction. Thus, suppose the social security agency requires $p < \tilde{p}$, but $w(1 - p) < x^*$. Taking the respective expressions for $\beta(p, R^*, x^*) = 0$ in (5.33) and (5.34) and rearranging yields

$$U((1 - p)w) \ - \ U(x^*) \ + \ U'(x^*)[pw + x^*] = G. \qquad (5.36)$$

By the concavity of $U(c)$ it follows that

$$U((1-p)w) - U(x^*) < U'(x^*)[(1-p)w - x^*] < 0 . \qquad (5.37)$$

Inserting into (5.36) gives rise to

$$U'(x^*)w > U((1-p)w) - U(x^*) + U'(x^*)[pw + x^*] = G. \qquad (5.38)$$

However, note that $x^*>w(1-p)>w(1-\tilde{p})$ implies $U'(x^*)w<U'((1-\tilde{p})w)w = G$, where the equality follows from the definition of $\tilde{p}$. Thus, $p < \tilde{p}$ and (5.38) contradict. Consequently, such contribution rates cannot induce an interior solution with $\beta(p, R^*, x^*) = 0$.

Next, assume that $p \geq \tilde{p}$ and $\beta(p, R^*, x^*) = 1$. From (5.33) and (5.34) it follows that the interior solution is characterized by

$$\frac{\int_{R^*}^{T} U'(z(t))F(t)e^{-rt}\,dt}{\int_{R^*}^{T} F(t)e^{-rt}\,dt}[pw + x^*] + U'(z(R^*))[(1-p)w - x^*] = G. \qquad (5.39)$$

Recall that the first-order conditions (5.24)–(5.26) imply $w(1-p) > z(R^*) > z(t)$, for $t \in (R^*, T]$. Hence

$$\left(\frac{\int_{R^*}^{T} U'(z(t))F(t)e^{-rt}\,dt}{\int_{R^*}^{T} F(t)e^{-rt}\,dt} - U'(z(R^*))\right)[pw + x^*] > 0 . \qquad (5.40)$$

Utilizing this information in (5.39), it must therefore be true that

$$U'(z(R^*))w < G = U'((1-\tilde{p})w)w \leq U'((1-p)w)w , \qquad (5.41)$$

where the last (weak) inequality follows from the assumption $p \geq \tilde{p}$. However, it can be seen that $z(R^*) < (1 - p)w$ contradicts (5.41). Consequently, contribution rates greater than or equal to $\tilde{p}$ cannot yield interior solutions with $\beta(p, R^*, x^*) = 1$.

Finally, it can be easily obtained that $p = \tilde{p}$ necessarily requires $x^* = (1-\tilde{p})w$. This follows from the fact that the second part of this proof has demonstrated that $p = \tilde{p}$ cannot induce additional private savings. However, (5.36) can only be satisfied if $(1 - \tilde{p})w = x^*$ in this case. Since the cases are exclusive, the proof is complete.

Q.E.D.

Thus, if the attention is confined to interior maxima, Proposition 2 demonstrates that the required contribution rate alone determines which accumulation regime prevails. The respective optimal choices of the retirement age contingent on this rate induce replacement ratios which can be identified with a particular savings regime only. Thus, it remains to be shown under which conditions the optimization problem entails an interior solution. It is rather straightforward to see that basically two sets of qualifications must be satisfied in order to guarantee the existence of an interior maximum. The first is associated with the question of whether the tangency condition indeed characterizes a local maximum. This can be taken for granted — given the assumptions made about the slopes of the marginal rates of substitution and transformation. The second issue to be addressed relates to the existence of dominating corner solutions — e.g. $R^* = 0$ and $R^* = T$. In general, such solutions can be precluded, if $|B|$ is sufficiently small. In particular, it must be possible to achieve perfect income insurance — given the contribution rate specified. Again, the Appendix provides a detailed investigation.

In Figure 5.1 the i-curves depict (x, R)-combinations such that the consumers' expected utility remains constant. As for the respective transformation curves, they are derived assuming $p = p_1 < \tilde{p}$, $p = \tilde{p}$, and $p = p_2 > \tilde{p}$, respectively. Hence, the respective utility levels are *not* equal at crossing points of the indifference curves. The superscripts '*' denote the optimal retirement ages and benefits given these contribution rates. For $p = \tilde{p}$, $\tilde{R} = R^*(\tilde{p})$ and $\tilde{x} = x^* = (1 - \tilde{p})w$ as spelled

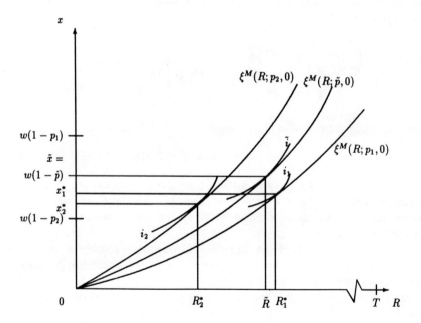

Assumed $p_1 < \tilde{p}$, $p = \tilde{p}$, and $p_2 > \tilde{p}$. Also, $B = 0$.

Figure 5.1 The optimal retirement age

out in Proposition 2. In this figure note that the optimal benefits x_1^* and x_2^* have been indicated to fall short of $\tilde{x}$. In fact, the following can generally be shown to hold:

Corollary 2.   *The contribution rate $\tilde{p}$ maximizes the optimal, induced benefit level.*

Proof.   Since we can now identify the accumulation regime with the contribution rate chosen, the statement follows directly for cases with $p \geq \tilde{p}$ from (5.38). If $p < \tilde{p}$, the interior solution is characterized by (5.39). Subtracting $U'(\tilde{x})[pw + x^*]$ on both sides of the equation, recalling that $G = U'(\tilde{x})w$, and some simple rearrangements yield

$$U'(\tilde{x}) \left(\frac{\displaystyle\int_{R*}^{T} \frac{U'(z(t))}{U'(\tilde{x})} F(t) e^{-rt} dt}{\displaystyle\int_{R*}^{T} F(t) e^{-rt} dt} - 1 \right) [pw + x^*]$$

$$= [U'(\tilde{x}) - U'(z(R^*))][w(1 - p) - x^*]. \tag{5.42}$$

The RHS of (5.42) can easily be verified to be positive by virtue of (5.41). However, $x^* > \tilde{x}$ implies $U'(z(t)) < U'(\tilde{x})$, $\forall\, t \in [R^*, T]$. Hence, the LHS of (5.42) would turn out to be negative. It follows that the optimal benefit level x^* must fall short of $\tilde{x}$ in this savings regime as well. *Q.E.D.*

So far the analysis has shown that there exists a 'benchmark'-contribution rate $\tilde{p}$ which divides the range of possible contribution rates into two subintervals $[0, \tilde{p})$ and $[\tilde{p}, 1)$ such that rates within the lower (upper) interval must be associated with replacement ratios smaller (greater or equal) to unity. The Inada-condition $\lim_{c \to 0} U'(c) = \infty$ obviously guarantees that $\tilde{p} < 1$ exists. Thus, in order to ensure the existence of this benchmark contribution rate, it suffices to assume

$$U'(w)w < G . \tag{5.43}$$

Clearly, if G is sufficiently large (5.43) can always be satisfied for $p > 0$. The next section will show, however, that one can find an additional, rather appealing argument to assume that the benchmark rate $\tilde{p} \in (0, 1)$ exists. Summing up, Proposition 2 demonstrates that the opportunity costs of self-protection and the amount of income insurance required — measured by the fraction of labor income p, which must be paid into the insurance — determine the accumulation regime. Further, Corollary 2 shows that, regardless of whether the contribution rate induces under-insurance ($w(1 - p) > x^*$), or overinsurance ($w(1 - p) < x^*$), the absolute amount of the pension x^* falls short of $\tilde{x}$, which constitutes the realized benefit, given that the contribution rate $p = \tilde{p}$ induces perfect income insurance ($w(1 - \tilde{p}) = \tilde{x}$).

5.4   CONTRIBUTION RATES AND INDIVIDUAL WELFARE

In this section, we shall consider the effects of changing the contribution rate p on the discounted expected utility of the consumers. Obviously, the contribution rate may be determined by considerations which are outside the scope of the present model, if the financing method does not require full-funding. However, it is still interesting to analyze the respective individual welfare effects, assuming the respective adjustments of benefits and retirement age to changes in the contribution rate must be marginally fair. Hence, let W denote the objective function of the optimization problem $\text{Max}_{x,R}$ (5.27), subject to (5.9). Further, $W^*(p, B) \equiv W(R^*(p, B), x^*(p, B); p, B)$. Maintaining that the retirement age and the benefit level are chosen optimally, conditional on the contribution rate p and B, the envelope theorem can be utilized to obtain

$$
\frac{\mathrm{d}W^*(p, B)}{\mathrm{d}p} = -\beta^*(p, R^*, x^*)\int_0^{R^*} U'(z(t))F(t)\mathrm{e}^{-rt}\mathrm{d}t\, w
$$

$$
- (1 - \beta^*(p, R^*, x^*))\int_0^{R^*} F(t)\mathrm{e}^{-rt}\mathrm{d}t\, U'((1-p)w)w
$$

$$
+\psi^*\int_0^{R^*} F(t)\mathrm{e}^{-rt}\mathrm{d}t\, w. \tag{5.44}
$$

Inserting for ψ^* from the first-order conditions therefore yields

$$
-\frac{\mathrm{d}W^*(p, B)}{\mathrm{d}p} = \beta^* w\int_{R^*}^{T} U'(z(t))F(t)\mathrm{e}^{-rt}\mathrm{d}t
$$

$$
\times \left[\frac{\int_0^{R^*} U'(z(t))F(t)\mathrm{e}^{-rt}\mathrm{d}t}{\int_{R^*}^{T} U'(z(t))F(t)\mathrm{e}^{-rt}\mathrm{d}t} - \frac{\int_0^{R^*} F(t)\mathrm{e}^{-rt}\mathrm{d}t}{\int_{R^*}^{T} F(t)\mathrm{e}^{-rt}\mathrm{d}t}\right]
$$

$$
+(1 - \beta^*)wU'(x)\int_{R^*}^{T} F(t)\mathrm{e}^{-rt}\mathrm{d}t
$$

$$
\times \left[\frac{\int_0^{R^*} F(t)\mathrm{e}^{-rt}\mathrm{d}t\, U'((1-p)w)}{\int_{R^*}^{T} F(t)\mathrm{e}^{-rt}\mathrm{d}t\, U'(x)} - \frac{\int_0^{R^*} F(t)\mathrm{e}^{-rt}\mathrm{d}t}{\int_{R^*}^{T} F(t)\mathrm{e}^{-rt}\mathrm{d}t}\right]. \tag{5.45}
$$

Thus, the sign of this expression depends on the difference $MRS^{x,p} - MRT^{x,p}$ as defined above. Given the distinction of cases in Proposition 2, the following can easily be verified to be true now:

Proposition 3.   *The induced change in consumer's expected lifetime utility asso-ciated with increases in the contribution rate p is positive, if $p < \tilde{p}$, equals zero, for $p = \tilde{p}$, and is negative, if $p > \tilde{p}$.*

Proof.   Consider the three cases defined in Proposition 2: If $p < \tilde{p}$, then $\beta^* = 1$, $U'((1-p)w) < U'(x^*)$, and $\dot{z}(t) < 0$, $\forall\ t \in [\theta_L, \theta_U]$ reveal that

$$\frac{\displaystyle\int_0^{R^*} U'(z(t))F(t)e^{-rt}\,dt}{\displaystyle\int_{R^*}^{T} U'(z(t))F(t)e^{-rt}\,dt} < \frac{U'(z(R^*))\displaystyle\int_0^{R^*} F(t)e^{-rt}\,dt}{U'(z(R^*))\displaystyle\int_{R^*}^{T} F(t)e^{-rt}\,dt}, \tag{5.46}$$

due to the concavity of $U(c)$. Also, $p \geq \tilde{p}$ implies $U'((1-p)w) \geq U'(x)$. Q.E.D.

Proposition 3 clearly suggests that $p = \tilde{p}$ maximizes the consumer's welfare. In fact, there exists a rather simple insurance-theoretic interpretation of this result: Consider an individual consumer who maximizes his or her discounted expected utility given a retirement scheme specifying a mandatory retirement date R. Differentiating (5.27) with respect to p and x gives rise to indifference curves in (p, x)-space. The slope of these curves is given by $MRS^{x,p}$ as defined above. Similarly, differentiating (5.9) yields the slope of the budget-constraint $MRT^{x,p}$. Figure 5.2 depicts two of such indifference curves, i and i', and the transformation line. For convenience, the graphical illustration has been transferred into $((1-p)w, x)$-space, thus reflecting the trade-off between two goods from the point of view of the consumers.

Note that our arguments above imply that for $w(1-p) > (=, <) x$ the slope of the indifference curves is steeper (equal to, flatter) than the slope of the budget-line. Clearly, for a given retirement date R, the consumers' expected utility can be increased by increasing (decreasing) premium rates if $(1-p)w > x$ $((1-p)w < x)$. In Figure 5.2 points A and B on the i'-curve represent (p, x)-combinations which are dominated by the combination $((1-p^o)w, x^o)$ depicted by point C on the i-curve. Since all of these combinations lie on the transformation line, the consumers' expected lifetime utility is maximized at point C, given the budget constraint (5.9). Obviously, combination C implies perfect income insurance: $(1-p^o)w = x^o$. Thus, relative to any arbitrarily chosen retirement date, the premium $p^o(R)$ which is selected so as to yield

$$(1-p^o(R))w = \frac{-B + wp^o(R)\displaystyle\int_0^R F(t)e^{-rt}\,dt}{\displaystyle\int_R^T e^{-rt}F(t)\,dt} = x^o(R), \tag{5.47}$$

perfect income insurance, maximizes the consumers' welfare. As this holds for any retirement date, it must also be true if retirement is chosen optimally. Therefore

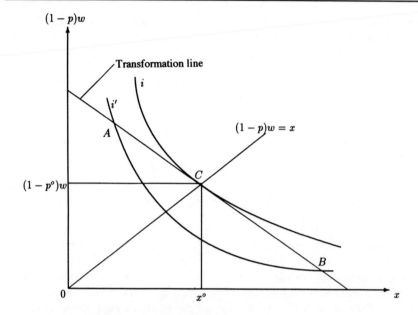

Perfect income insurance as optimal
insurance for a given retirement age *R*.

Figure 5.2   The optimal replacement ratio

restricting our attention to finding the optimal retirement date given $p = p^o(R)$, $x = x^o(R)$ — and assuming that a replacement ratio greater or equal to unity is feasible — the following can be obtained:

Proposition 4.   *Suppose there exists a contribution rate* $\tilde{p} \in (0, 1)$, *as defined in Proposition 2, and*

$$(1 - \tilde{p})w = \tilde{x} = \frac{-B + \int_0^{\tilde{R}} F(t)e^{-rt}\,dt\,\tilde{p}w}{\int_{\tilde{R}}^T F(t)e^{-rt}\,dt}$$

is possible for some $\tilde{R} \in (0, T)$. *Further, consider the set of policies with contribution rates* $p \in (0, 1)$, *which offer free choices of the retirement age R within the age interval* [0, T], *calculating the attainable benefit levels according to*

$$x = \xi^M(R; p, B) = \frac{-B + \int_0^R F(t)e^{-rt}\,dt\,pw}{\int_R^T F(t)e^{-rt}\,dt} \,.$$

Then—given the value for B—the policy with contribution rate $\tilde{p}$ maximizes the consumers' expected, discounted lifetime utility among all policies in this set. By virtue of Proposition 2, the respective induced benefit level $\xi^M(R^*(\tilde{p}, B); \tilde{p}, B) = \tilde{x}$ and $R^*(\tilde{p}, B) = \tilde{R}$.

Proof. The qualifications noted in the proposition again refer to the existence of an interior solution. The equation

$$(1 - p^o(R))w = x^o(R) ,\qquad(5.48)$$

which expresses the fact that perfect income insurance is always optimal given the retirement age R, can be used to calculate

$$p^o(R) = \frac{\displaystyle\int_R^T F(t)e^{-rt}dt}{\displaystyle\int_0^T F(t)e^{-rt}dt} + \frac{B/w}{\displaystyle\int_0^T F(t)e^{-rt}dt}\qquad(5.49)$$

$$x^o(R) = \frac{\displaystyle\int_0^R F(t)e^{-rt}dt\,w}{\displaystyle\int_0^T F(t)e^{-rt}dt} - \frac{B}{\displaystyle\int_0^T F(t)e^{-rt}dt}.\qquad(5.50)$$

Clearly, for $B = 0$, $p^o(R) \in (0, 1)$ and $x^o(R) \in (0, w)$ can be guaranteed. In general, however, $|B|$ must be assumed to be sufficiently small. Taking this for granted, the following optimization problem can be set up:

$$\max_{R\in[0,T]} U(x^o(R)) \int_0^T F(t)e^{-rt}dt - G \int_0^R F(t)e^{-rt}dt.\qquad(5.51)$$

Let R^o denote the solution. The necessary condition for the interior solution can be obtained as

$$U'(x^o(R^o))w = G.\qquad(5.52)$$

From the definition above, this obviously implies $x^o(R^o) = \tilde{x}$. Hence, $p^o(R^o) = \tilde{p}$ and the optimal retirement age equals $R^o = \tilde{R}$. Moreover, the second-order condition can easily be verified to ensure that, if there exists $x^o(R)$ such that (5.52) can be satisfied, this benefit level in fact characterizes a maximum. Also, the concavity of $U(c)$ guarantees that the solution is unique. Hence, it must only be checked whether the corner solutions $R^o = 0$ and $R^o = T$ can be excluded. Again, the explicit derivation of the necessary arguments has been deferred to the Appendix.
Q.E.D.

Hence, assuming the 'benchmark' rate $\tilde{p}$ exists can now be seen to state that — within the imposed institutional framework — *perfect* income insurance remains to be *optimal*, when the opportunity costs of self-protection are taken into account. In fact, the economic intuition underlying Propositions 2–4 can now be seen to hinge on a rather simple mechanism: Assume, for example, the contribution rate p is set such as to exceed (fall short of) $\tilde{p}$. If the consumers chose their retirement age in order to obtain perfect income insurance, the *certain* marginal utility of consumption would consequently be larger (smaller) than the instantaneous disutility of labor G. Clearly, in this case it would be possible to achieve welfare improvements by increasing (reducing) the working-life. However, this adjustment would automatically induce a replacement ratio exceeding (falling short of) unity.

The analysis of the preceding sections can now be fully appreciated: a number of studies before have shown that low contribution rates induce more private savings. However, these conclusions are always based on the *assumption* that the replacement ratio falls short of unity. Introducing the possibility of self-protection by endogenizing the retirement age, this ratio is determined endogenously itself. However, the analysis has shown that, given a utility function as defined above, a similar conclusion carries over: If the contribution rate falls short of (is greater or equal to) $\tilde{p}$, the accumulation regime *given optimal retirement* is characterized by (no) private wealth accumulation. Further, if the survival risk is perfectly insured ($p = \tilde{p}$), the consumer will choose the retirement date such as to maximize the benefit payments. In all other cases the induced benefits will be smaller. This result is particularly interesting for the case $p > \tilde{p}$, hence $(1 - p)w < x^*$, which may be interpreted as 'overinvestment' in social security claims ('overinsurance'). In general, this finding — as well as the fact that 'insurance' only perfectly crowds out the 'self-insurance' if the contribution rate is greater than or equal to the welfare maximizing level — can be attributed to a complementarity of 'insurance' and 'self-protection' characterizing the present model. Increasing or decreasing the degree of insurance coverage can only be purchased at the expense of incurring additional opportunity costs associated with the retirement decision.

5.5   INDUCED CHANGES IN THE RETIREMENT AGE

The preceding sections have shown that the government's choice of the contribution rate p induces retirement at a certain date, determines the 'accumulation regime', and bears welfare implications. Hence, taking a positive point of view, it is also worth while to address the relationship between the contribution rate and the consumers' optimal retirement date in more detail. As will be seen the respective results cannot be obtained as easily as the welfare analysis above may suggest. In particular, the following can be shown to hold, for instance:

Proposition 5.   (a) If $p \geq \tilde{p}$ and, therefore, $w(1-p) \leq x^*$, the optimal retirement age decreases with an increasing contribution rate: $dR^*/dp < 0$.
(b) If $p < \tilde{p}$—hence, $w(1-p) > x^*$—the impact of changes in the contribution rate on the optimal retirement date is generally ambiguous.

Proof.   Suppose $p \geq p^p$. Differentiating (5.36) can easily be verified to yield

$$\frac{dR^*}{dp} = -\frac{U''(x)[pw + x^*]MRT^{x,p} + [U'(x) - U'((1-p)w)]w}{U''(x)[pw + x^*]MRT^{x,R}}. \qquad (5.53)$$

Since $U''(c) < 0$ and $w(1-p) \leq x^*$ in this case, part (i) of the proposition follows.

Turning to the more complicated case where $p < \tilde{p}$, a clear-cut result cannot be obtained. From (5.39) let

$$\Delta W^* \equiv \frac{\lambda^* \displaystyle\int_{R^*}^{\theta_U} e^{-rt}dt + U'(x^*)\displaystyle\int_{\theta_U}^{T} F(t)e^{-rt}dt}{\displaystyle\int_{R^*}^{T} F(t)e^{-rt}dt}[pw + x^*]$$

$$+ \frac{\lambda^*}{F(R^*)}[(1-p)w - x^*] - G. \qquad (5.54)$$

Differentiating (5.54) confirms the result obtained by Crawford Lilien (1981): due to the existence of counteracting income and substitution effects the sign of dR^*/dp remains indeterminate. The fact that within a small vicinity around $\tilde{p}$ (5.53) applies does not generalize. This can be verified as

$$\frac{d\Delta W^*}{dp} = \frac{\displaystyle\int_{R^*}^{\theta_U} e^{-rt}dt \left(\dfrac{d\lambda^*}{dp}[pw + x^*] + \lambda^* MRT^{x,p}\right)}{\displaystyle\int_{R^*}^{T} F(t)e^{-rt}dt}$$

$$+ \frac{\displaystyle\int_{\theta_U}^{T} F(t)e^{-rt}dt \left(U''(x^*)[pw + x^*] + U'(x^*)\right)MRT^{x,p}}{\displaystyle\int_{R^*}^{T} F(t)e^{-rt}dt}$$

$$+ \frac{d\lambda^*}{dp}\frac{w(1-p) - x^*}{F(R^*)} - \frac{\lambda^*}{F(R^*)}MRT^{x,p}. \qquad (5.55)$$

Defining $H(\cdot) \equiv [U'(\cdot)]^{-1}$, the fact that total, discounted consumption must equal the discounted value of the income flow over the age interval $[\theta_L, \theta_U]$, and $U'(z(t))F(t) = \lambda^*$, can be used to formulate

$$\int_{\theta_L}^{\theta_U} H\left(\frac{\lambda^*}{F(t)}\right)e^{-rt}dt = \int_{\theta_L}^{R^*} e^{-rt}dt\, w(1-p) + \int_{R^*}^{\theta_U} e^{-rt}dt\, x^*. \qquad (5.56)$$

However, differentiating with respect to p yields

$$\frac{d\lambda^*}{dp}\frac{1}{\lambda^*} = \frac{-\int_{\theta_L}^{R^*} e^{-rt}\,dt\,w + \int_{R^*}^{\theta_U} e^{-rt}\,dt\,MRT^{x,p}}{\int_{\theta_L}^{\theta_U} H'\left(\frac{\lambda^*}{F(t)}\right)\frac{\lambda^*}{F(t)}e^{-rt}\,dt}. \tag{5.57}$$

Thus, $H'(\cdot) < 0$ does not induce a particular sign for this expression. Moreover, even if (5.57) could be signed, this would not suffice to specify the direction of the reaction

$$\frac{dR^*}{dp} = -\frac{\dfrac{d\Delta W^*}{dp}}{\dfrac{d\Delta W^*}{dR}}. \tag{5.58}$$

The second-order sufficient condition for the maximization of W here only guarantees that the term $d\Delta W^*/dR$ is negative.
Q.E.D.

However, it is worthwhile to focus on a special case[7] which shows that the result $dR^*/dp < 0$ may carry over to the regime with $p < \tilde{p}$ as well. This is stated as:

Corollary 3. *Let the utility of consumption function be of the constant relative risk-aversion (CRRA) type, $U(c) = (1/(1-\alpha))c^{1-\alpha}$, for $\alpha > 0$ and $\alpha \neq 1$, and $U(c) = \ln(c)$, for $\alpha = 1$, and assume $B = 0$. Then*

$$(i) \quad \frac{\int_{\theta_L}^{R^*} e^{-rt}\,dt\,w}{\int_{R^*}^{\theta_U} e^{-rt}\,dt\,x^* + \int_{\theta_L}^{R^*} e^{-rt}\,dt\,(1-p)w} \leq 1$$

and

$$(ii) \quad \alpha\left(1 - \frac{\int_{\theta_L}^{R^*} e^{-rt}\,dt\,w}{\int_{R^*}^{\theta_U} e^{-rt}\,dt\,x^* + \int_{\theta_L}^{R^*} e^{-rt}\,dt\,(1-p)w}\right) \geq 1$$

are sufficient for $dR^*/dp < 0$, given $w(1-p) > x^*$.

---

[7]The CRRA-functions introduced below are frequently utilized in studies focusing on optimal consumption/savings plans under uncertainty. See, for instance, Fischer (1973), Hakansson (1970), Kotlikoff, Shoven, and Spivak (1987), Levhari and Srinivasan (1969), Merton (1969), Mossin (1968a,b), and Samuelson (1969).

Proof.   Given this type of utility function, the property $H'(y)y = -(1/\alpha)H(y)$ can be utilized to derive

$$\frac{d\lambda^*}{dp}\frac{p}{\lambda^*} = -\alpha + \alpha \cdot \frac{\displaystyle\int_{\theta_L}^{R^*} e^{-rt}\,dt\,w}{\displaystyle\int_{R^*}^{\theta_U} e^{-rt}\,dt\,x^* + \int_{\theta_L}^{R^*} e^{-rt}\,dt\,(1-p)w}. \tag{5.59}$$

Also $B = 0$ implies

$$w + MRT^{x,p} = w\left(1 + \frac{\displaystyle\int_0^R F(t)e^{-rt}\,dt}{\displaystyle\int_R^T F(t)e^{-rt}\,dt}\right), \tag{5.60}$$

and

$$pw + x = pw\left(1 + \frac{\displaystyle\int_0^R F(t)e^{-rt}\,dt}{\displaystyle\int_R^T F(t)e^{-rt}\,dt}\right). \tag{5.61}$$

Hence, condition (i) can be seen to ensure that $d\lambda^*/dp \le 0$. Hence, turning to (5.55) $d\lambda^*/dp(p/\lambda^*) \le -1$ guarantees that the first term in this expression is non-positive. This is ensured by condition (ii). Since the latter implies $\alpha > 1$, the second term in (5.55) is negative.
Q.E.D.

Interpreting these results, it can be noted that condition (i) in Corollary 3 implies that aggregate, discounted income over the savings interval $[\theta_L, \theta_U]$ must increase if the contribution rate is increased (holding everything else constant). It corresponds to 'Condition A' in Crawford and Lilien (1981, p. 527) who state that, under this condition, a negative income effect prevails: 'Increasing p increases feasible planned consumption and leisure and, thus [...] tends to encourage earlier retirement'. However, since this also encourages pre-retirement consumption and, therefore, induces an incentive to prolong the working-life, it must be ensured that the 'marginal utility of consumption falls off rapidly enough', such that 'the income effect dominates the substitution effect'. The latter can now be seen to be implied by condition (ii) in Corollary 3. For cases with $p > \tilde{p}$ the 'substitution' effect is absent since the consumer is constrained in shifting income from old-age to working-life. Also, increasing the contribution rate always increases lifetime income and, thus, induces earlier retirement.

This discussion also highlights the possible effects of varying the budget parameter B on the optimal retirement age R^*. Here, the income effect is unambiguous.

Increasing B always reduces lifetime income, since

$$\frac{\partial \xi^M(R^*; p, B)}{\partial B} = -\frac{1}{\displaystyle\int_{R^*}^{T} F(t)e^{-rt}dt} < 0 . \tag{5.62}$$

Again, however, this may induce a counteracting substitution effect for the case $p < \tilde{p}$. Hence follows

Proposition 6. *(a) If $p \geq \tilde{p}$, $dR^*/dB = \left(F(R^*)e^{-rR^*}[pw + x^*]\right)^{-1} > 0$.*
(b) If $p < \tilde{p}$, the sign of dR^*/dB is generally ambiguous.

Proof.   From (5.36) it follows that

$$\frac{dR^*}{dB} = -\frac{\dfrac{\partial \xi^M(R^*; p, B)}{\partial B}}{MRT^{x,R}} . \tag{5.63}$$

On the other hand, differentiating (5.54) with respect to B yields

$$
\begin{aligned}
\frac{d\Delta W^*}{dB} &= \frac{\displaystyle\int_{R^*}^{\theta_U} e^{-rt}dt}{\displaystyle\int_{R^*}^{T} F(t)e^{-rt}dt}\left(\frac{d\lambda^*}{dB}[pw + x^*] + \lambda^*\frac{\partial \xi^M(R^*; p, B)}{\partial B}\right) \\[2em]
&\quad \frac{\displaystyle\int_{\theta_U}^{T} F(t)e^{-rt}dt}{\displaystyle\int_{R^*}^{T} F(t)e^{-rt}dt}\left(U''(x^*)[pw + x^*] + U'(x^*)\right)\frac{\partial \xi^M(R^*; p, B)}{\partial B} \\[2em]
&\quad + \frac{d\lambda^*}{dB}\frac{(1-p)w - x^*}{F(R^*)} - \frac{\lambda^*}{F(R^*)}\frac{\partial \xi^M(R^*; p, B)}{\partial B} .
\end{aligned}\tag{5.64}
$$

Further,

$$\frac{d\lambda^*}{dB}\frac{1}{\lambda^*} = \frac{\displaystyle\int_{R^*}^{\theta_U} e^{-rt}dt}{\displaystyle\int_{\theta_L}^{\theta_U} H'\left(\frac{\lambda^*}{F(t)}\right)\frac{\lambda^*}{F(t)}e^{-rt}dt}\frac{\partial \xi^M(R^*; p, B)}{\partial B} > 0 , \tag{5.65}$$

since $H'(\cdot) < 0$, reveals that the income effect can be signed unambiguously. However, upon inspection of (5.64) this can be seen to be insufficient in order to determine the direction of dR^*/dB in this case.
Q.E.D.

Again, specifying the utility of consumption function a sufficient condition can be derived which guarantees the dominance of the income effect.

Corollary 4.   *Let the function $U(c)$ be of the CRRA-type defined in Corollary 3. Then*

$$\frac{\alpha[pw + x^*]}{x^*} \geq 1 + \frac{\int_{\theta_L}^{R^*} e^{-rt}\, dt}{\int_{R^*}^{\theta_U} e^{-rt}\, dt}\, \frac{w(1-p)}{x^*}$$

is sufficient for $dR^*/dB > 0$, given that $p < \tilde{p}$.

Proof.   Note that

$$\frac{d\lambda^*}{dB}\frac{1}{\lambda^*}[pw + x^*] + \frac{\partial\xi^M(R^*; p, B)}{\partial B} =$$

$$\frac{-\alpha\int_{R^*}^{\theta_U} e^{-rt}\, dt\,[pw + x^*] + \int_{R^*}^{\theta_U} e^{-rt}\, dt\, x^* + \int_{\theta_L}^{R^*} e^{-rt}\, dt\, w(1-p)}{\int_{R^*}^{\theta_U} e^{-rt}\, dt\, x^* + \int_{\theta_L}^{R^*} e^{-rt}\, dt\, w(1-p)}\, \frac{\partial\xi^M(R^*; p, B)}{\partial B}.$$

(5.66)

This can be seen to be non-negative, if the condition noted in the Corollary holds. Moreover, since the condition implies $\alpha > 1$ the second term in (5.64) is positive. Thus, $d\Delta W^*/dB > 0$ and

$$\frac{dR^*}{dB} = -\frac{\dfrac{d\Delta W^*}{dB}}{\dfrac{d\Delta W^*}{dR}} > 0,$$

(5.67)

if the second-order sufficient condition for the maximization problem is satisfied. *Q.E.D.*

The conditions noted above reveal that 'normal' reactions of the optimal retirement age with respect to the parameters p and B are more likely, the larger the degree of relative risk-aversion and the smaller the difference $[w(1-p) - x^*]$. For changes in the contribution rate, one must add the additional qualification that lifetime income is actually increased when p increases. Otherwise, the statement above must obviously be exactly reversed. The very fact that increases in p can be associated with increases in the lifetime income hinges on the imposed complementarity of self-protection and insurance, again. Due to the assumed budget relationship (5.9) any increase in the contribution rate, measuring the relative importance of insurance, *ceteris paribus* increases the benefit level. Hence, decreasing the level of self-protection by choosing lower retirement ages does not necessarily imply a loss of lifetime income. Whether or not the retirement age is actually decreased as a response to higher contribution rates, then depends on the desired substitution of insurance and self-protection by self-insurance (private savings). Here, the overall significance of private savings in providing for old-age income is limited, if $[w(1 - p) - x^*]$ is positive but small, or if the consumers are rather risk-averse and therefore strongly oppose the possibility of leaving involuntary bequests. Moreover, if shifting income from old-age to working-life via negative pre-retirement private savings would be optimal ($[w(1 - p) - x] < 0$), such that the non-negativity constraint on savings is binding, the role of private savings completely ceases to be of importance. In these cases the choice will be to decrease the amount of self-protection/insurance, since higher contribution rates *ceteris paribus* induce an increase in lifetime income.

5.6   SUMMARY

Since the results of the analysis have been extensively discussed in the course of the preceding sections, it is only necessary to briefly summarize the basic findings which will become important in the following:

(1)   There exists a contribution rate $\tilde{p}$ such that the range of possible contribution rates can be divided into a lower interval $[0, \tilde{p})$ and an upper interval $[\tilde{p}, 1)$. The induced optimal retirement age yields net replacement ratios smaller (greater or equal) than unity, if the contribution rate required lies in the lower (upper) subinterval.

(2)   Hence, the insurance agency's choice of the contribution rate determines whether or not there will be private savings in addition to the accumulation of insurance claims.

(3)   The contribution rate $\tilde{p}$, defined by the equation $U'((1 - \tilde{p})w)w = G$, is associated with an induced net replacement ratio equal to unity and maximizes the consumers' expected lifetime utility among all policies, in which the adjustment of benefits to choices of the retirement age is marginally fair.

(4)   While in the regime with contribution rates $p \in (\tilde{p}, 1)$ the optimal retirement age R^* decreases with expansions of the insurance system ($dR^*/dp < 0$) and increases when the value of attainable benefits is further reduced compared to fully funded pensions ($dR^*/dB > 0$), the respective reactions are generally ambiguous for contribution rates $p \in (0, \tilde{p})$.

As pointed out, all of these conclusions require the existence of an interior maximum with respect to choices of the retirement age. In the following this will always be taken for granted. The last result noted above can be verified to be the center of interest in Crawford and Lilien (1981), Kahn (1988), and Breyer (1990, Ch. 5). It illustrates that, if survival is uncertain and the consumers are liquidity constrained, the co-existence of private savings and insurance claims gives rise to income and substitution effects, which obscure the possibility of deriving clearcut reactions of the choice of the retirement age associated with the policy parameter p. This is particularly interesting if compared to models assuming certain lifetimes and the absence of liquidity constraints in which a marginally fair system can be shown to be neutral with respect to the retirement decision. In contrast to these studies, the present analysis does not resort to assuming that the induced net replacement ratio is smaller than unity, however. The division between regimes characterized by under-insurance (over-insurance, respectively) is determined endogenously contingent only on the contribution rate required and the disutility of labor[8].

Once again it should be noted that all of the results obtained crucially depend on the assumed complementarity of self-protection and insurance. Two observations stress this further. First, as shown in Section 5.4, perfect income/consumption smoothing would always be optimal if the replacement ratio could be chosen independently of the retirement decision. Second, assuming that the opportunity costs of self-protection were zero ($G = 0$), (5.33) and (5.34) also imply $1 - p = x^*$, $\forall\ p$, if $R^* \in (0, T)$. It is easily checked that in this case an interior solution with respect to R again requires that the consumer can attain a replacement ratio greater or equal than unity by participating in the insurance scheme. Moreover, so far it has been taken as exogenously given that all adjustments of the benefits to alternative choices of the retirement age, but also considering changes in the contribution rate, are actuarially fair. In particular, the latter are assumed not to be absorbed by simultaneously altering the budget parameter B. If this cannot be taken for granted, the reactions of the consumers to changes in the contribution rate would obviously turn out to be quite different. With respect to the present study, the first three results are of prime importance. In the following, it will be questioned whether marginal fairness constitutes an efficiency requirement. Since this can in fact be shown, the question remains of why variable retirement schemes most often appear to be unfair.

APPENDIX

The slope of the budget line equals

$$
MRT^{x,R} = \frac{F(R)e^{-rR}[pw + x]}{\int_R^T F(t)e^{-rt}\,dt} \,. \tag{A5.1}
$$

---

[8]Considering both possible accumulation regimes constitutes more than a mere theoretical exercise. Börsch-Supan (1991) presents evidence that an over-annuitization of the elderly may in fact characterize the situation in Germany. Similarly, Uhle (1987, p. 117–118) notes that firms frequently claim an already existing overinsurance to be responsible for the fact that they do not expand their private pension plans further. Hence, the 'overinsurance' case cannot be ruled out on empirical grounds.

Differentiating with respect to R yields

$$\frac{\partial MRT^{x,R}}{\partial R} = \frac{(\dot{F}(t)e^{-rR} - rF(t)e^{-rR})[pw + x]}{\int_R^T F(t)e^{-rt}dt}$$

$$+ \frac{(F(R)e^{-rR})^2 [pw + x]}{\left(\int_R^T F(t)e^{-rt}dt\right)^2} + \frac{F(R)e^{-rR}MRT^{x,R}}{\int_R^T F(t)e^{-rt}dt}. \quad (A5.2)$$

For this expression to be positive, it suffices to assume

$$\frac{\dot{F}(t)}{F(t)} + \frac{2F(R)e^{-rR}}{\int_R^T F(t)e^{-rt}dt} - r > 0. \quad (A5.3)$$

Using partial integration this can be shown to equal

$$\frac{\dot{F}(t)}{F(t)} - \frac{\int_R^T \dot{F}(t)e^{-rt}dt - e^{-rR}}{\int_R^T F(t)e^{-rt}dt}. \quad (A5.4)$$

Assume, for example, $F(t) = (1 - (t/T))^\zeta$, with $\zeta \in [0, 1]$. This particular function implies $\ddot{F}(t) < 0$ which proxies actual relative survival frequencies rather well—except for the typical kink during childhood[9]. $\zeta = 0$ can be associated with a certain lifetime, while $\zeta = 1$ implies that the expected lifetime equals $T/2$. Note that (A5.3) is always satisfied in this case, since

$$1 < \frac{\int_R^T \frac{\dot{F}(t)}{F(R)}e^{-rt}dt}{\int_R^T \frac{F(t)}{F(R)}e^{-rt}dt} = \frac{\int_R^T \frac{T-R}{T-t}\frac{F(t)}{F(R)}e^{-rt}dt}{\int_R^T \frac{F(t)}{F(R)}e^{-rt}dt}. \quad (A5.5)$$

For the case $p \geq \tilde{p}$,

$$\frac{\partial MRS^{x,R}}{\partial R} = \frac{F(R)e^{-rR}MRS^{x,R}}{\int_R^T F(t)e^{-rt}dt\, U'(x)} + \mathcal{D}\left(\frac{\dot{F}(R)e^{-rR} - rF(R)e^{-rR}}{\int_R^T F(t)e^{-rt}dt\, U'(x)}\right.$$

---

[9]See Dinkel (1988) and Ng (1992).

$$
+ \frac{F(R)\mathrm{e}^{-rR}U'(x) - \displaystyle\int_R^T F(t)\mathrm{e}^{-rt}\,\mathrm{d}t\, U''(x) MRS^{x,R}}{\left(\displaystyle\int_R^T F(t)\mathrm{e}^{-rt}\,\mathrm{d}t\, U'(x)\right)^2} \Bigg), \tag{A5.6}
$$

with $\mathcal{D} = [G + U(x) - U((1-p)w)]$. It is easily obtained that (A5.6) is positive, if (A5.2) is positive. Moreover, given $MRT^{x,R} = MRS^{x,R}$, it can be verified that the expression above is greater than the respective derivative in (A5.2). This implies an interior maximum as illustrated in Figure 5.1.

If $p < \tilde{p}$, the convexity of the indifference curve requires further assumptions, however. The expression

$$
\frac{1}{MRS^{x,R}}\frac{\partial MRS^{x,R}}{\partial R} =
$$

$$
\frac{G}{\mathcal{D}'}\left(\dot{F}(R)\mathrm{e}^{-rR} - rF(R)\mathrm{e}^{-rR}\right) + \frac{2\lambda^*\mathrm{e}^{-rR}}{\displaystyle\int_R^T U'(z(t))F(t)\mathrm{e}^{-rt}}
$$

$$
- \frac{\left(\dfrac{\partial\lambda^*}{\partial R} + \dfrac{\partial\lambda^*}{x}MRS^{x,R}\right)[w(1-p) - x]}{\mathcal{D}'}
$$

$$
- \frac{\left(\dfrac{\partial\lambda^*}{\partial R} + \dfrac{\partial\lambda^*}{\partial x}MRS^{x,R}\right)\displaystyle\int_R^{\theta U}\mathrm{e}^{-rt}\,\mathrm{d}t}{\mathcal{D}'\displaystyle\int_R^T U'(z(t))F(t)\mathrm{e}^{-rt}\,\mathrm{d}t}, \tag{A5.7}
$$

with $\mathcal{D}' = \left(GF(R)\mathrm{e}^{-rR} - \lambda^*\mathrm{e}^{-rR}[w(1-p) - x]\right)$, cannot be signed unambiguously. Similar to the derivations in Section 5.5 above, it can be obtained that $\partial\lambda^*/\partial R$ and $\partial\lambda^*/\partial x$ are both negative as required. However, the assumptions ensuring that (A5.2) is positive, do not suffice to imply non-negativity for (A5.7) here. Hence, this must be guaranteed by assumption[10].

Focusing on corner solutions, it is clear that $R^* = 0$ can only occur if $B < 0$. Otherwise, $z(t) \leq 0$, $\forall t \in [0, T]$. Hence,

$$
\frac{\mathrm{d}W^*}{\mathrm{d}R}\Big|_{R^*=0} = U'(x^*)[pw + x^*] - G - U(x^*) + U((1-p)w)
$$

$$
= \left(U'(x^*) - U'(\hat{c})\right)[pw + x^*] + \left(U'(\hat{c}) - U'(\tilde{x})\right) \tag{A5.8}
$$

---

[10] $\mathcal{D}'$ can be seen to be necessarily positive at the optimum. Some further rearrangements verify that (A5.7) is more likely to be positive, if $[(1-p)w - x]$ is small, (A5.2) is positive, and the consumers are sufficiently risk-averse.

with

$$
\hat{c} \begin{cases} \in (w(1-p), x^*), & if \quad w(1-p) < x^* \\ = x^* & , \quad if \quad w(1-p) = x^* \\ \in (x^*, (1-p)w), & if \quad w(1-p) > x^* \end{cases} \tag{A5.9}
$$

defined by the mean value theorem. It can be verified that $|B|$ sufficiently small implies a positive sign for the expression (A5.8). Similarly, $B > 0$ can only induce a corner solution $R^* = T$, which must be associated with non-participation as the consumers pay the contribution p without ever receiving benefits. The solution $R^* = T$ can be excluded for $B < 0$, since $F(T) = 0$ implies that it is always optimal to withdraw at some date smaller than T, if there exists a positive annuity which can be obtained. For $B > 0$ it must again be assumed that $|B|$ is sufficiently small to allow for retirement age $\bar{R} < T$, such that

$$
\bar{x} = \frac{\displaystyle\int_0^{\bar{R}} F(t)e^{-rt}dt\ pw\ -\ B}{\displaystyle\int_{\bar{R}}^T F(t)e^{-rt}dt} = (1-p)w\ . \tag{A5.10}
$$

If this is the case, then

$$
W^*|_{R^*=T}\ -\ W(\bar{x}, \bar{R}) = \int_0^T F(t)e^{-rt}dt\ U((1-p)w)\ -\ G\int_0^T F(t)e^{-rt}dt
$$

$$
-\ \int_0^{\bar{R}} F(t)e^{-rt}dt\ U((1-p)w) - \int_{\bar{R}}^T F(t)e^{-rt}dt\ U(\bar{x}) + G\int_0^{\bar{R}} F(t)e^{-rt}dt
$$

$$
= -G\int_{\bar{R}}^T F(t)e^{-rt}dt\ < 0\ . \tag{A5.11}
$$

Thus, it will always be optimal to retire at some age before T.

CHAPTER 6

Marginal fairness and Pareto-efficiency

6.1 INTRODUCTORY COMMENTS

The model outlined in Chapter 5 above highlights the induced retirement behavior of expected utility maximizing agents facing a marginally fair retirement scheme. Clearly, the positive implications of this approach are interesting as such — in particular, when contrasted with models assuming certain lifetimes and unconstrained personal accumulation[1]. Yet, the question remains whether this particular adjustment rule possesses a more general virtue as well. As far as private pension plans and capital-funded public systems are concerned, the financing method employed is often seen to imply that the adjustments of benefits to alternative choices of the retirement age must necessarily be actuarially fair[2]. However, the link between requiring marginal fairness of the benefit schedule and inter-generational Pareto-efficiency is generally less obvious in pay-as-you-go financed public pension systems.

Assuming an exogenous lifetime labor supply, this financing method can be shown to be always inter-generationally efficient[3]. Moreover, since pay-as-you-go is in fact implemented in the public pension systems of all industrial countries, the scope of the preceding analysis — as far as both its positive and normative implications are concerned — therefore appears to be severely limited. On the other hand, Homburg (1990), Hu (1978), Breyer (1991), Breyer and Straub (1993), and Peters (1988; 1989, Parts I,II) have been noted to provide analyses which show that, if the individual lifetime labor supply decisions are endogenous, this conclusion does not carry over. Here, the pension system bears two effects: first, it generates inter-generational transfers; second, it induces individual labor supply decisions contingent on these transfers. If, given the rule which relates

---

[1] Crawford and Lilien (1981), Kahn (1988), and Breyer (1990, Ch. 5).

[2] See, for instance, Feldstein (1978) and Breyer (1990, p. 117–118), respectively.

[3] Breyer (1989; 1990, Ch. 4) and Verbon (1988a, p. 63–71).

attainable benefits to alternative labor supply decisions, the individually optimal labor supplies are inefficient, the pension system as such is inter-generationally inefficient as well[4]. The labor supply decision is denoted inefficient, if — holding the inter-generational transfers constant — there exist alternative lifetime allocations which are preferred by the consumers. Hence, reducing these inefficiencies generates Pareto-improvements and thus possibly also an inter-generationally efficient transition path.

Among these studies only Peters (1988; 1989, Parts I,II) utilizes a continuous-time overlapping generations model with endogenous retirement decisions. However, this study restricts the attention to the case of certain lifetimes and non-liquidity-constrained consumers. The analysis then proceeds in two steps. First, it is shown that, if the adjustment of the benefit level to alternative choices of the individual retirement age is marginally fair, the individually optimal retirement age is contingent only on the discounted value of the lifetime income flow. This result reflects the neutrality of the labor supply decision with respect to the timing of the transfers again. The discounted value of the lifetime income flow, however, depends on the realized inter-generational transfers. Thus, the analysis turns to comparing steady-state growth equilibria. Since such equilibria are characterized by constant inter-generational transfers, it is clear that they are compatible with sequences of identical consumer generations, all of which would choose the same individually optimal retirement age, if offered a marginally fair retirement scheme and holding these transfers constant. Steady-state growth paths can then be compared with respect to the inter-generational welfare effects of different financing methods[5]. This separation into two distinct problems — the individual labor supply analysis and the inter-generational aspect of the old-age insurance scheme — is pursued in Homburg (1990), Hu (1978), Breyer (1991), and Breyer and Straub (1993) as well.

Restricting attention to policy changes which hold *all* inter-generational transfers constant, appears to be rather problematic within the present framework. Conditions (1) and (2) noted in Section 4.2.4 introduce considerable difficulties: when the induced replacement ratio is smaller than unity, the possibility of accidental bequests must be taken into account when evaluating the inter-generational welfare effects of policy changes. This is demonstrated by Abel (1985) and Eckstein, Eichenbaum, and Peled (1985b) who show that the induced changes in the distribution of bequests generate ambiguous steady-state welfare effects in this case. Also, Abel (1986) and Hu (1986) add that this conclusion carries over to models with voluntary bequests, as long as lifetimes are uncertain and annuity coverage is incomplete. Thus, irrespective of the financing method and the bequest motive, uncertain lifetimes generally obscure the possibility to derive clearcut results concerning the inter-generational welfare effects of social security

---

[4]It suffices to show that a single consumer's welfare can be improved without affecting the welfare of others — including the members of subsequent generations.

[5]Peters focuses on pure capital-funded, pure pay-as-you-go, and mixed systems.

systems[6]. The inter-generational Pareto-comparisons carried out in the vast majority of the studies, noted in Sections 3.3 and 3.4.1, only apply to situations in which private savings and capital-funded pensions constitute perfect substitutes. However, in this respect the present study cannot provide a general solution either.

The scope of the present analysis is thus more limited to the extent that it focuses solely on the efficiency of the induced lifetime allocation. In doing so, the particular financing method implemented restricts the set of feasible policies, however. Pure capital funding of the pensions of a particular generation of workers — whether this occurs in private or in public plans — implies that intra-generational redistributions are limited to the extent that the expected discounted flow of contributions received from the members of this generation must equal the respective discounted flow of pension payments guaranteed. As far as pay-as-you-go financed public pension schemes are concerned, the implied (open) inter-generational transfers received by, or required from, the members of a generation must be ensured by the retirement policies under consideration. Hence, Pareto-comparisons of retirement policies are carried out assuming that the alternatives proposed are fiscally equivalent from the point of view of old-age insurance. This can be seen to represent a minimum restriction on the feasible policies, allowing one to address the (in)efficiency of the induced lifetime allocation sensibly[7]. Further, it will be seen that — even ignoring the inter-generational transfers induced by possible accidental bequests — the marginal fairness of the benefit schedule is generally insufficient for Pareto-efficient lifetime allocations.

6.2 DEFINING PARETO-EFFICIENT RETIREMENT POLICIES

In the studies noted above the particular means by which the consumers are induced to retire at a certain age, or provide a particular labor supply, are actually of minor importance. It suffices that the resulting lifetime allocation is efficient. In contrast, the present study will focus on the effects of variable retirement schemes inducing a retirement decision. A flexible retirement age program can thus be identified as a particular retirement policy among the possible policies inducing a lifetime allocation $\mathcal{A}(\Pi) = [\{z(t; p, R, x)\}, R]$. For groups of homogeneous consumers such policies can, therefore, more generally be described as follows:

---

[6]However, the specific results obtained in Abel (1985, 1986), Eckstein, Eichenbaum, and Peled (1985b), Hu (1986), and Schwödiauer and Wenig (1989, 1990) do not necessarily carry over, since these studies do not allow for varying retirement ages and the corresponding induced changes in the distribution of bequests.

[7]For all practical matters the 'fiscal neutrality', or 'fiscal improvements' which can be achieved via policy changes appear to be of sole importance anyway. Compare the discussion in Section 3.5. Also, Kruse and Söderström (1989), for instance, explicitly refer to 'fiscal neutrality' as a policy goal. The fact that this concept does not necessarily translate into corresponding inter-generational welfare gains hinges on Conditions (1) and (2) noted in Section 4.2.4. Hence, the resulting loss of generality can be associated with the attempt to introduce 'realism' in the sense of Crawford and Lilien (1981) and Kahn (1988).

Definition 1.   *A retirement policy is defined as*

$$\Pi \equiv [p, \mathcal{S}],$$

where p is the contribution rate required, and $\mathcal{S}$ denotes a set of rules which define a range of possible retirement ages, and relate attainable benefits x to retirement ages R chosen. The rules contained in $\mathcal{S}$ specify
  $\mathcal{S}(i): R \in [R_L, R_U]$, with $0 \leq R_L \leq R_U \leq T$,
  $\mathcal{S}(ii): x = \xi(R; \pi)$.

Here π is a vector of policy parameters—possibly including the contribution rate p again—which affect the calculation of benefits over the age interval $[R_L, R_U]$.

In terms of Definition 1, the marginal fair retirement policy analyzed in Chapter 5 can now be characterized by $R_L = 0$, $R_U = T$, $\pi = (p, B)$, and

$$\xi(R, \pi) = \xi^M(R; p, B) = \frac{-B + \displaystyle\int_0^R F(t)e^{-rt}dt\ pw}{\displaystyle\int_R^T F(t)e^{-rt}dt}. \tag{6.1}$$

However, it is obviously possible that a policy Π defines an alternative age interval of possible retirement ages and a benefit schedule which is not marginally fair. For example, $0 < R_L = R_U < T$ would imply mandatory retirement[8]. Given general benefit schedules ξ an interior solution to the maximization of the consumers' expected lifetime utility with respect to (x, R) yields the first-order conditions

$$\int_{R^*}^T U'(z(t; p, \xi(R^*, \pi), R^*))F(t)e^{-rt}dt\ \frac{\partial \xi(R^*, \pi)}{\partial R}$$

$$- \left(GF(R^*) - \lambda^*[(1 - p)w - \xi(R^*, \pi)]\right)e^{-rR^*} = 0, \tag{6.2}$$

if $w(1 - p) > \xi(R^*, \pi)$, or

$$\int_{R^*}^T F(t)e^{-rt}dt\ U'(\xi(R^*, \pi))\frac{\partial \xi(R^*, \pi)}{\partial R}$$

$$- \left(G + U(\xi(R^*, \pi)) - U((1 - p)w)\right)F(R^*)e^{-rR^*} = 0, \tag{6.3}$$

if $w(1 - p) \leq \xi(R^*, \pi)$.

Given that an interior solution exists, (6.2), or (6.3), respectively, characterize the optimal choice of the retirement age $R^* \in (R_L, R_U)$ and the benefit level

---

[8]Note that the set of rules $\mathcal{S}$ always consists of a 'forcing'-part (i) and an 'opportunity'-part (ii). Although the specified age R_L can be interpreted as an eligibility age, it should be clear that it also defines a minimum retirement age. It is assumed that realized retirement ages and the decision not to retire are publicly observed, so that enforcement of the policy constitutes no problem.

$x^* = \xi(R^*, \pi)$ conditional on the policy. Further, the consumers' optimization problem may yield the corner solutions $R^* = R_L$, or $R^* = R_U$. Thus, the insurance agency's budget plans must generally be contingent on correctly anticipating this retirement age. Whether the solution is interior, or a corner solution dominates — which appears to be of particular importance for policies specifying $0 < R_L \leq R_U < T$ — a policy Π always induces

- a lifetime allocation $\mathcal{A}(\Pi) = [\{z(t; p, R^*, \xi(R^*, \pi))\}, R^*]$,
- a flow of required contributions pw to be received over the age interval $[0, R^*]$, and a flow of benefits $x^* = \xi(R^*, \pi)$ guaranteed over the age interval $[R^*, T]$ by the insurance agency.

Again, comparing retirement policies with respect to the induced lifetime allocation requires a constraint to be imposed on the alternative policies. For the reasons discussed above feasible policy changes will be restricted to imply fiscal neutrality here.

Definition 2.   *Let $\bar{\Pi}$ denote a particular retirement policy and $\bar{R}^*$ the respective induced optimal retirement age. Further, the induced flow of contributions and benefits under this policy satisfies the insurance agency's budget requirement, given the financing method implemented. Then any policy change which guarantees that the insurance agency receives contributions $\bar{p}w$ over the age interval $[0, \bar{R}^*)$, while ensuring the benefit payments $\bar{\xi}(\bar{R}^*, \bar{\pi})$ over the age interval $[\bar{R}^*, T]$, is said to be feasible.*

Identifying a particular retirement policy as generating flows of contributions and benefits for individuals such that the pension system's budget can be balanced obviously hinges on the financing method implemented. At the same time, this does not bear implications for the feasibility of policy changes. Specifically, it is always possible to *add* new capital-funded pension accounts. Thus, the Pareto-efficiency of the retirement policy can be defined without reference to the financing method:

Definition 3.   *A retirement policy $\bar{\Pi}$ is said to be Pareto-efficient if there exist no feasible policy changes generating lifetime allocations which are preferred over the allocation $\mathcal{A}(\bar{\Pi}) = [\{z(t; \bar{p}, \bar{R}^*, \bar{\xi}(\bar{R}^*, \bar{\pi}))\}, \bar{R}^*]$ by the consumers covered under this policy.*

In the following the analysis will be pursued by applying this notion of Pareto-efficient retirement policies to the basic model outlined in Chapter 5. Given the qualifications noted above, it is at least clear that redesigning the retirement policy allows for additional inter-generational compensations to be extracted from generations of consumers facing an inefficient retirement policy in the sense of Definition 3.

6.3   MARGINAL FAIRNESS AS AN EFFICIENCY RULE

Given the definitions from above, particular retirement policies can now be evaluated according to the respective induced lifetime allocations. First, attention will be confined to policy changes maintaining that the fraction of labor income p devoted to obtaining old-age insurance is exogenously fixed. This obviously constitutes a rather arbitrary restriction. Nevertheless, focusing on such cases will prove to be of some virtue in the analysis to follow. It is rather easily obtained:

Proposition 7.   *Consider a sufficiently large group of identical consumers with expected lifetime utility functions defined in (5.3) and covered under a retirement policy* $\bar{\Pi}$. *This policy entails a fraction* $\bar{p}$ *of the labor income to be used for old-age insurance. Further, assume that the induced optimal retirement age* $\bar{R}^* \in (0, T)$. *If, and only if, the induced lifetime allocation* $\mathcal{A}(\bar{\Pi}) = [\{z(t; \bar{p}, \bar{R}^*, \bar{\xi}(\bar{R}^*, \bar{\pi})\}, \bar{R}^*]$ *satisfies:*

$$MRS^{x,R}\left(\bar{p}, \bar{R}^*, \bar{\xi}(\bar{R}^*, \bar{\pi})\right) = \frac{F(\bar{R}^*)e^{-r\bar{R}^*}\left[\bar{p}w + \bar{\xi}(\bar{R}^*, \bar{\pi})\right]}{\displaystyle\int_{\bar{R}^*}^{T} F(t)e^{-rt}dt},$$

where $MRS^{x,R}(\cdot)$ *is given by (5.30) above, the lifetime labor supply decision—given* $\bar{p}$—*is efficient.*

Proof.   The proof again follows by contradiction, but bears constructive elements indicating the directions of policy changes. First, define two cases as:

(I) $MRS^{x,R}\left(\bar{p}, \bar{R}^*, \bar{\xi}(\bar{R}^*, \bar{\pi})\right) > \dfrac{F(\bar{R}^*)e^{-r\bar{R}^*}[pw + \bar{\xi}(\bar{R}^*, \bar{\pi})]}{\displaystyle\int_{\bar{R}^*}^{T} F(t)e^{-rt}dt}$

(II) $MRS^{x,R}\left(\bar{p}, \bar{R}^*, \bar{\xi}(\bar{R}^*, \bar{\pi})\right) < \dfrac{F(\bar{R}^*)e^{-r\bar{R}^*}[pw + \bar{\xi}(\bar{R}^*, \bar{\pi})]}{\displaystyle\int_{\bar{R}^*}^{T} F(t)e^{-rt}dt}.$

Further, for each of these cases two sub-cases have to be distinguished according to the induced accumulation regime:

(1) $(1 - \bar{p})w > \bar{\xi}(\bar{R}^*, \bar{\pi})$
(2) $(1 - \bar{p})w \leq \bar{\xi}(\bar{R}^*, \bar{\pi})$.

Hence Cases I.1 and I.2 yield

$$\frac{\displaystyle\int_{\bar{R}^*}^{T} U'(z(t; \bar{p}, \bar{R}^*, \bar{\xi}(\bar{R}^*, \bar{\pi})))e^{-rt}dt}{\displaystyle\int_{\bar{R}^*}^{T} F(t)e^{-rt}dt}[\bar{p}w + \bar{\xi}(\bar{R}^*, \bar{\pi})]$$

$$+ U'(z(\bar{R}^*; \bar{p}, \bar{R}^*, \bar{\xi}(\bar{R}^*, \bar{\pi})))[(1 - \bar{p})w - \bar{\xi}(\bar{R}^*, \bar{\pi})] < G, \quad (6.4)$$

and

$$U'(\bar{\xi}(\bar{R}^*, \bar{\pi}))[\bar{p}w + \bar{\xi}(\bar{R}^*, \bar{\pi})] - U(\bar{\xi}(\bar{R}^*, \bar{\pi})) + U((1 - \bar{p})w) < G, \quad (6.5)$$

respectively. Similarly, Cases II.1 and II.2 are associated with the inequalities

$$\frac{\displaystyle\int_{\bar{R}^*}^{T} U'(z(t; \bar{p}, \bar{R}^*, \bar{\xi}(\bar{R}^*, \bar{\pi})))e^{-rt}dt}{\displaystyle\int_{\bar{R}^*}^{T} F(t)e^{-rt}dt}[\bar{p}w + \bar{\xi}(\bar{R}^*, \bar{\pi})]$$

$$+ U'(z(\bar{R}^*; \bar{p}, \bar{R}^*, \bar{\xi}(\bar{R}^*, \bar{\pi})))[(1 - \bar{p})w - \bar{\xi}(\bar{R}^*, \bar{\pi})] > G, \quad (6.6)$$

and

$$U'(\bar{\xi}(\bar{R}^*, \bar{\pi}))[\bar{p}w + \bar{\xi}(\bar{R}^*, \bar{\pi})] - U(\bar{\xi}(\bar{R}^*, \bar{\pi})) + U((1 - \bar{p})w) > G, \quad (6.7)$$

respectively.

For Cases I.1/I.2, assume now that the insurance agency allows for retirement at age $\check{R} = \bar{R}^* - \varepsilon$, with $\varepsilon \geq 0$. It then agrees to pay benefits $\check{x}$. Regardless of the financing method employed to guarantee the original pension flow over the age interval $[\bar{R}^*, T]$, conditional upon receiving contributions $\bar{p}w$ over the interval $[0, \bar{R}^*)$, it is clear that — with perfect capital markets — the agency can generate an expected profit equal to

$$\mathcal{P} = \int_{\bar{R}^*}^{T} F(t)e^{-rt}dt\, \bar{\xi}(\bar{R}^*, \bar{\pi}) - \int_{\check{R}}^{\bar{R}^*} F(t)e^{-rt}dt\, \bar{p}w - \int_{\check{R}}^{T} F(t)e^{-rt}dt\, \check{x}. \quad (6.8)$$

Obviously, $\mathcal{P} = 0$ and $\varepsilon = 0$ imply $\check{x} = \bar{\xi}(\bar{R}^*, \bar{\pi})$. Further,

$$\left.\frac{d\check{x}}{d\varepsilon}\right|_{\substack{\mathcal{P}=0 \\ \varepsilon=0}} = -\frac{F(\bar{R}^*)e^{-r\bar{R}^*}[\bar{p}w + \bar{\xi}(\bar{R}^*, \bar{\pi})]}{\displaystyle\int_{\bar{R}^*}^{T} F(t)e^{-rt}dt}. \quad (6.9)$$

For Case I.1 the respective change in the consumers' expected discounted lifetime utility can be derived as

$$-\left.\frac{dL_S^*(\bar{p}, \check{R}, \check{x})}{d\varepsilon}\right|_{\substack{\mathcal{P}=0 \\ \varepsilon=0}} \frac{1}{F(\bar{R}^*)e^{-r\bar{R}^*}}$$

$$= \frac{\displaystyle\int_{\bar{R}^*}^{T} U'(z(t; \bar{p}, \bar{R}^*, \bar{\xi}(\bar{R}^*, \bar{\pi})))e^{-rt}dt}{\displaystyle\int_{\bar{R}^*}^{T} F(t)e^{-rt}dt}[\bar{p}w + \bar{\xi}(\bar{R}^*, \bar{\pi})]$$

$$+ U'(z(\bar{R}^*; \bar{p}, \bar{R}^*, \bar{\xi}(\bar{R}^*, \bar{\pi})))[(1 - \bar{p})w - \bar{\xi}(\bar{R}^*, \bar{\pi})] - G. \qquad (6.10)$$

Here all first-order effects vanish again, since consumption is chosen optimally contingent on the insurance policy and the changes in the retirement age and benefits are assumed to be marginal. On the other hand, given Case I.2:

$$- \left. \frac{dL^*_{NS}(\bar{p}, \check{R}, \check{x})}{d\varepsilon} \right|_{\substack{\mathcal{P}=0 \\ \varepsilon=0}} \frac{1}{F(\bar{R}^*)e^{-r\bar{R}^*}}$$

$$= U'(\bar{\xi}(\bar{R}^*, \bar{\pi}))[\bar{p}w + \bar{\xi}(\bar{R}^*, \bar{\pi})] - U(\bar{\xi}(\bar{R}^*, \bar{\pi})) + U((1 - \bar{p})w) - G. \quad (6.11)$$

By definition of the cases, the RHSs of (6.10) and (6.11) are negative. This proves that $d\varepsilon > 0$ yields increases in the consumers' expected lifetime utility. Thus, it has been shown that marginal fiscally neutral decreases in the actual retirement age are welfare enhancing.

Turning to the Cases II.1/II.2, the new agreement negotiated between the consumers and the insurance agency takes on the following form: The consumers retire at age $\check{R} = \bar{R}^* + \varepsilon$, with $\varepsilon \geq 0$. They receive the benefits $\check{x}$ over the age interval $[\check{R}, T]$. Moreover, out of this income surviving consumers agree to pay the additional premium $\bar{p}w$ to the insurance company over the age interval $[\bar{R}^*, \check{R})$. The agency's expected, discounted profit can then be derived as:

$$\mathcal{P} = \int_{\bar{R}^*}^{\check{R}} F(t)e^{-rt}dt \, \bar{p}w + \int_{\check{R}}^{T} F(t)e^{-rt}dt \, \bar{\xi}(\bar{R}^*, \bar{\pi}) - \int_{\check{R}}^{T} F(t)e^{-rt}dt \, \check{x}. \quad (6.12)$$

Again, $\mathcal{P} = 0$ and $\varepsilon = 0$ imply $\check{x} = \bar{\xi}(\bar{R}^*, \bar{\pi})$. Thus, it can be obtained that

$$\left. \frac{d\check{x}}{d\varepsilon} \right|_{\substack{\mathcal{P}=0 \\ \varepsilon=0}} = \frac{F(\bar{R}^*)[\bar{p} + \bar{\xi}(\bar{R}^*, \bar{\pi})]}{\displaystyle\int_{\bar{R}^*}^{T} F(t)e^{-rt}dt}. \qquad (6.13)$$

The respective change in the consumers' expected lifetime utility equals

$$\left. \frac{dL^*_S(\bar{p}, \check{R}, \check{x})}{d\varepsilon} \right|_{\substack{\mathcal{P}=0 \\ \varepsilon=0}} \frac{1}{F(\bar{R}^*)e^{-r\bar{R}^*}}$$

$$= \frac{\displaystyle\int_{\bar{R}^*}^{T} U'(z(t; \bar{p}, \bar{R}^*, \bar{\xi}(\bar{R}^*, \bar{\pi})))e^{-rt}dt}{\displaystyle\int_{\bar{R}^*}^{T} F(t)e^{-rt}dt}[\bar{p}w + \bar{\xi}(\bar{R}^*, \bar{\pi})]$$

$$+ U'(z(\bar{R}^*; \bar{p}, \bar{R}^*, \bar{\xi}(\bar{R}^*, \bar{\pi})))[(1 - \bar{p})w - \bar{\xi}(\bar{R}^*, \bar{\pi})] - G \qquad (6.14)$$

for Case II.1. Similarly, given Case II.2:

$$\frac{dL^*_{NS}(\bar{p}, \check{R}, \check{x})}{d\varepsilon}\bigg|_{\substack{\mathcal{P}=0 \\ \varepsilon=0}} \frac{1}{F(\bar{R}^*)e^{-r\bar{R}^*}}$$

$$= U'(\bar{\xi}(\bar{R}^*, \bar{\pi}))[\bar{p}w + \bar{\xi}(\bar{R}^*, \bar{\pi})] - U(\bar{\xi}(\bar{R}^*, \bar{\pi})) + U((1-\bar{p})w) - G. \quad (6.15)$$

By definition of the cases, the RHSs of (6.14) and (6.15) are positive. Hence, marginal fiscally neutral increases of the actual retirement age ($d\varepsilon > 0$) are welfare enhancing.

Noting that the cases are exclusive, the proposition has been proved.
Q.E.D.

The cases introduced in the proof can now be utilized to state:

Definition 4.   *An induced lifetime allocation is said to entail 'inefficient early', or 'inefficient delayed' retirement according to whether Cases II.1/II.2, or Cases I.1/I.2, defined in the proof of Proposition 7, apply. This only refers to the fact that starting from an original retirement policy in the former cases (latter cases) marginal delays (marginal decreases) of the retirement age implemented fiscally neutral can be shown to be welfare enhancing.*

Turning to variable retirement policies and using this terminology, one can thus obtain

Corollary 5.   *Suppose the original retirement policy $\bar{\Pi}$ under consideration entails a flexible retirement age option within an age interval $[\bar{R}_L, \bar{R}_U]$. Given this policy, the consumers' optimal choice of the retirement age satisfies $\bar{R}^* \in (\bar{R}_L, \bar{R}_U)$. Then, if the benefit schedule $\bar{\xi}(R, \bar{\pi})$, $R \in [\bar{R}_L, \bar{R}_U]$, is characterized by*

$$\frac{\partial\bar{\xi}(\bar{R}^*, \bar{\pi})}{\partial R} \begin{Bmatrix} (a) > \\ (b) = \\ (c) < \end{Bmatrix} \frac{F(\bar{R}^*)e^{-r\bar{R}^*}[\bar{p} + \bar{\xi}(\bar{R}^*, \bar{\pi})]}{\displaystyle\int_{\bar{R}^*}^{T} F(t)e^{-rt}dt}$$

within a vicinity around $\bar{R}^*$, the resulting induced lifetime allocation is characterized by (a) inefficient delayed, (b) efficient, or (c) inefficient early retirement, respectively.

Now, consider the following 'adjustment to actuarial' fairness: Define a marginally fair flexible retirement age policy $\check{\Pi}$, with
    $\check{S}(i)$: $R \in [\check{R}_L, \check{R}_U]$, with $\check{R}_L < \bar{R}^* < \check{R}_U$, and

    $\check{S}(ii)$: $x = \check{\xi}^M(R; \bar{p}, \check{B})$, for $R \in [\check{R}_L, \check{R}_U]$, with $\check{\xi}(\bar{R}^*; \bar{p}, \check{B}) = \bar{x}^*$.
Then $\check{R}^* < [0, >] \bar{R}^*$, if the original policy is associated with Case (a) ((b),(c)) above. Moreover, the expected lifetime utility of the consumers increases given Cases (a) and (c).

Sketch of Proof. The proof follows directly from the definitions of the lifetime labor supply (in)efficiencies and the cases discussed in the proof of Proposition 7. It must only be noted that (a) implies Cases I.1/I.2, and (c) corresponds to Cases II.1/II.2. Hence,

$$MRS^{x,R}(\bar{p}, \bar{R}^*, \bar{x}^*) > [=, <] \frac{\partial \breve{\xi}^M(\bar{R}^*; \bar{p}, \breve{B})}{\partial R} \qquad (6.16)$$

in Cases (a) ((b),(c)). Then the proposed reaction of the optimal retirement age follows from $\partial MRS^{x,R}/\partial R > 0$ as exposed in the Appendix to Chapter 5. The welfare conclusions are obtained by noting that the choice $(\bar{R}^*, \bar{x}^*)$ remains possible after the adjustment of the benefit schedule.
Q.E.D.

The Corollary thus associates benefit schedules with labor supply inefficiencies as derived in Proposition 7. At the same time, it shows the directions of change in the optimal retirement age, if the benefit schedule is adjusted to 'actuarial fairness'. The fact that the welfare of the consumers is then increased if the original allocation is characterized by inefficiencies implies that it is also possible to decrease the attainable benefit levels corresponding to alternative choices of the retirement age and maintaining the expected lifetime utility level induced by the original policy. This is illustrated by Figure 6.1, which focuses on the situation with an originally inefficient early retirement decision. The original benefit schedule is indicated by the line denoted $\bar{\xi}$. Further, $\breve{\xi}_l^M$, with $l = 1, 2$, correspond to marginally fair benefit schedules. The schedule $\breve{\xi}_1^M$ is formulated according to the adjustment proposed in the Corollary. Hence, the welfare of the consumers is increased moving from the schedule $\bar{\xi}$ to $\breve{\xi}_1^M$ — as indicated by the shift in the respective indifference curves from $\bar{i}$ to $\breve{i}_1$. In contrast, $\breve{\xi}_2^M$ entails reduced benefits, while keeping the consumers' welfare constant at the level induced by the original retirement policy. The indifference curve $\bar{i}$ associated with the initial utility level is tangent to both the $\bar{\xi}$-curve at $R = \bar{R}^*$ and the $\breve{\xi}_2^M$-curve at $R = \breve{R}_2^*$.

Obviously, the welfare gains associated with shifts in the benefit schedule may require fundamental institutional changes. If the original pension flow is pay-as-you-go financed, movements from $\bar{\xi}$ to ξ_1^M can only be realized by establishing a supplementary capital-funded account. Over the additional working-life interval $[\bar{R}^*, \breve{R}_1^*]$ the surviving consumers then pay contributions $\bar{p}w$ into this account. The insurance agency invests these funds and the withheld pension payments, earning a return equal to the market rate of interest. Doing so, the agency can then guarantee the pension flow $\breve{x}_1^*$ beginning with age $\breve{R}_1^*$. However, even maintaining that all pensions must be purely pay-as-you-go financed, the existence of labor supply inefficiencies suggests that it may be possible to achieve fiscal improvements by simple 'adjustments' to actuarial fairness in the benefit rules.

Moving along the $\bar{i}$ indifference curve — hence, assuming welfare preserving adjustments in the attainable benefit/retirement age combinations — the necessary

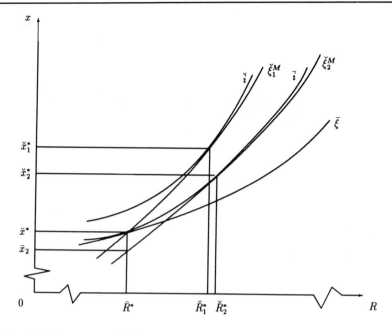

Figure 6.1   Adjusting to actuarial fairness

pension increment $(\check{x}_2^* - \bar{x}^*)$ falls short of a hypothetical actuarially fair adjusted increment $(\check{x}_2^* - \bar{x}_2)$. This is solely due to the fact that 'inefficient early' retirement arises when the slope of the indifference curve $\bar{i}$ evaluated at the offer $(\bar{x}^*, \bar{R}^*)$ is flatter than a marginally fair benefit schedule passing through this combination. Thus, even if the market rate of interest exceeds the 'biological' rate[9], it appears possible to achieve fiscal improvements, while holding the expected lifetime utility of the consumers constant. Nevertheless, this cannot be guaranteed. Clearly, if the difference between 'biological' and market rate of interest is relatively small, this result is more likely to hold. Similarly, rather significant labor supply inefficiencies — implying that the slope of the indifference curve is very flat compared to the slope of a marginally fair benefit schedule — also lend support to the hypothesis that fiscally favorable, welfare-preserving adjustments within a pure pay-as-you-go-system are possible.

Finally, it should be noted that corresponding conclusions carry over to the case of 'inefficient delayed' retirement. Maintaining pure pay-as-you-go financing, it may be possible to design a welfare-preserving, fiscally favorable alternative retirement policy. Again, this is not necessarily so, however. On the other hand, it is always possible to achieve welfare improvements by allowing earlier retirement,

---

[9]Assuming no real wage growth and a constant population growth rate n, pure pay-as-you-go financing implies $\int_0^R F(t)e^{-nt}\,dt\, p - \int_R^T F(t)e^{-nt}\,dt\, x = 0$.

specifying the new benefit level as actuarially fair reduced. Hence, fiscal neutrality can always be ensured by lending against the pay-as-you-go financed original benefit level.

Yet, so far it has been assumed that the contribution rate is exogenously fixed. Allowing for a complete conversion of the pension system into an annuity program then shows that efficient labor supply decisions are necessary, but not sufficient, for efficient lifetime allocations. Again, this hinges solely on the complementarity between self-protection and insurance coverage characterizing the current analytical framework. In particular, the following should be noted:

Proposition 8.   *Suppose an original retirement policy* $\bar{\Pi} = (\bar{p}, \bar{S})$ *induces/requires retirement age at* $\bar{R}^* \in (0, T)$ *and pays benefits* $\bar{x}^*$ *upon retirement at this age. Now, consider a fundamental institutional change in the old-age pension system which allows the consumers to annuitize their expected lifetime earnings.*
(a) The resulting expected, discounted lifetime utility maximizing allocation is $\tilde{A} = [\tilde{z}, \tilde{R}]$, *with* $\tilde{z}$ *defined by*

$$U'(\tilde{z})w = G ,$$

and $\tilde{R}$ *chosen such that*

$$\tilde{z} = \frac{\displaystyle\int_0^{\tilde{R}} F(t)\mathrm{e}^{-rt}\mathrm{d}t \, w}{\displaystyle\int_0^T F(t)\mathrm{e}^{-rt}\mathrm{d}t} + \frac{\displaystyle\int_{\bar{R}^*}^T F(t)\mathrm{e}^{-rt}\mathrm{d}t \, \bar{x}^* - \int_0^{\bar{R}^*} F(t)\mathrm{e}^{-rt}\mathrm{d}t \, \bar{p}w}{\displaystyle\int_0^T F(t)\mathrm{e}^{-rt}\mathrm{d}t} .$$

(b) This policy change yields a strictly Pareto-superior lifetime allocation unless $A(\bar{\Pi}) = \tilde{A}$.
(c) Hence, a Pareto-efficient retirement policy which intends to induce an optimal retirement age R^* *as an interior solution to the consumers' optimization problem*

$$\mathrm{Max}_{x,R} \ (5.27)$$
$$\text{subject to} \ (5.9)$$

by offering a flexible retirement age option, must entail $p = \tilde{p}$—*as defined in Proposition 4*—*and a benefit schedule*

$$x = \xi^M(R; \tilde{p}, \bar{B}^*) = \frac{-\bar{B}^* + \displaystyle\int_0^R F(t)\mathrm{e}^{-rt}\mathrm{d}t \, \tilde{p}w}{\displaystyle\int_R^T F(t)\mathrm{e}^{-rt}\mathrm{d}t} ,$$

for $R \in [R_L, R_U]$, *with* $R_L < \tilde{R} < R_U$. *Here*

$$\bar{B}^* = \int_0^{\bar{R}^*} F(t)\mathrm{e}^{-rt}\mathrm{d}t \, \tilde{p}w - \int_{\bar{R}^*}^T F(t)\mathrm{e}^{-rt}\mathrm{d}t \, \bar{x}^* .$$

Proof.   In order to prove Part (a) of the Proposition the following optimization problem can be set up:

$$\text{Max}_{\{c(t)\}, R} \quad \int_0^T U(c(t)) F(t) e^{-rt} dt - G \int_0^R F(t) e^{-rt} dt \qquad (6.17)$$

subject to

$$\int_0^T c(t) F(t) e^{-rt} dt \leq \int_0^R F(t) e^{-rt} dt\, w + \int_{\bar{R}^*}^T F(t) e^{-rt} dt\, \bar{x}^* - \int_0^{\bar{R}^*} F(t) e^{-rt} dt\, \bar{p}w.$$
$$(6.18)$$

The constraint reflects the fact that now the capital-funded accounts can function as a means to obtain income insurance, while the labor supply decision and the income flows generated by the original retirement policy determine the expected discounted lifetime income. The first-order condition with respect to the consumption path yields

$$U'(z(t)) = \tilde{\Lambda}\,, \quad \forall\, t \in [0, T]\,, \qquad (6.19)$$

where $\tilde{\Lambda}$ denotes the optimal value of the multiplier associated with constraint (6.18). Let $\tilde{z}$ denote the consumption value satisfying this equation. The first-order condition with respect to the actual retirement age R can be then be confirmed to determine $\tilde{z}$ by

$$G = U'(\tilde{z})w\,. \qquad (6.20)$$

Inserting for $c(t) = \tilde{z}, \forall\, t \in [0, T]$, in (6.18) can now be seen to prove Part (a) of the Proposition.

In order to verify Part (b), it must only be noted that the original allocation $\mathcal{A}(\bar{\Pi})$ satisfies the constraint (6.18). Further, Part (c) follows from Proposition 7 and Corollary 5 which can be seen to restrict the set of potentially Pareto-efficient retirement policies including a flexible retirement age option to those policies in which the benefit schedule is marginally fair. Then Proposition 2 implies that if, and only if, $p = \tilde{p}$, the induced replacement ratio equals unity. Further,

$$\int_{R^*}^T F(t) e^{-rt} dt\, x^* - \int_0^{R^*} F(t) e^{-rt} dt\, pw = -B \qquad (6.21)$$

for marginally fair policies. Then Part (c) can be proved as demonstrated for Proposition 4. The resulting induced lifetime allocation equals $\tilde{\mathcal{A}}$ in this case. *Q.E.D.*

Recalling Proposition 5, it should be obvious that the change in the optimal retirement age induced by implementing an institutional reform as proposed above is generally ambiguous. If the original retirement policy under consideration induces retirement by offering a marginally fair benefit schedule, but entails $p < \tilde{p}$, $R^*(p, B)$ can be greater, equal, or smaller than $\tilde{R}$. Further, the separation of income insurance and labor supply decisions restores the neutrality of the structure of received income payments with respect to the optimal choice of the retirement age as defined in Kahn (1988). The expected utility maximizing lifetime labor supply derived from the optimization problem (6.17)–(6.18) is contingent only on the expected, discounted value of the lifetime income flow. It follows that in this case the inter-generational welfare analysis provided in Peters (1988; 1989, Parts I,II) and the corresponding results derived in the two-period overlapping-generations models carry over. Thus, Part (c) of the Proposition also states that marginal fairness of the benefit schedule as such is insufficient in order to ensure that the lifetime allocation induced within a variable retirement scheme is efficient. Rather, this also requires the contribution rate $\tilde{p}$ to be imposed. Again, this reflects the impact of Conditions (A) and (B) discussed in Section 4.2.4.

Hence, Part (c) of Proposition 8 should be recognized as not merely restating the result noted in Proposition 4. It is true that for both results the possibility of improving the risk-shifting properties of the retirement policy is decisive. However, in Propositions 3 and 4 the focus was on the welfare impacts of changing the contribution rate, while *assuming* that this change is associated with corresponding marginally fair adjustments of the benefits attainable at every retirement age chosen. In particular, the changes in p are not absorbed by altering the budget parameter B. In contrast, Proposition 8 states that a flexible retirement age policy can only be Pareto-efficient, if the contribution rate is $\tilde{p}$ and the adjustments of benefits to alternative choices of the retirement age are calculated marginally fair. The former welfare analysis therefore refers to a particular policy change implemented within a flexible retirement age system. However, Part (c) of Proposition 8 implies that every policy change which does not result in requiring the contribution $\tilde{p}$ and — if inducing retirement via a variable retirement age plan — offering a marginally fair benefit schedule, does not maximize the consumers' expected lifetime utility among the set of fiscally neutral policy alternatives.

6.4 POLICY IMPLICATIONS

Focusing on the fundamental institutional change which has been proposed in the proof of Proposition 7 and in Proposition 8, the following can be noted: considering a social security agency, the policies would require to establish additional capital-funded accounts, while defining contribution flows and benefit guarantees for the generation under consideration. On the other hand, associating this institutional change with a role for private old-age insurance complementing a basic social insurance, the analysis reveals the benefits of 'integration'. However, the notion of 'integration' introduced here also differs fundamentally from the concepts discussed in the literature. The welfare improvements derived (partially) hinge on the fact that the additional insurance can counteract the liquidity constraint of the consumers by crediting future benefit payments. Hence, an 'integration' policy would have to ensure that private pension agreements can be written conditional on required contribution and guaranteed benefit flows, but allow for free borrowing and lending against these income flows.

More importantly, however, the institutional changes proposed separate the life-time labor supply decision from the determination of the expected lifetime income. Thus, the welfare gains can be captured by abolishing the requirement to retire at a certain age in order to receive the benefits associated with this retirement age. It should be noted that the proposed separation of the income and the labor supply decisions does not introduce an incentive problem. Since the policy must define a 'normal' retirement age (pay-out date) and the corresponding benefit level, the pensions actually received by the retirees depend on the retirement dates chosen. This aspect seems to correspond well with the respective policy conclusions drawn in Schmähl (1988, p. 25–33; 1989, p. 30–32), for instance: The studies stress that the decision on the retirement policy to be applied must be made in two steps. First, it has to be decided which retirement age should be regarded as 'normal', or as the 'reference age'. Accordingly, the policy defines a benefit level attainable at this age. In a second step, the respective deductions (increases) associated with earlier (delayed) retirement are specified.

However, this policy-oriented research maintains that all pension payments remain pay-as-you-go financed. Thus, Schmähl further suggests that increases in the actual retirement decisions should be induced by specifying an appropriate benefit schedule. Quinn and Burkhauser (1983) and Dye (1985) add that this can be achieved by adjusting to 'actuarial fairness'. Here Corollary 5 demonstrates that increases in the optimal retirement age can in fact be induced by 'restoring actuarial fairness', starting from an initial situation characterized by inefficient early retire-ment. Yet, implementing this adjustment policy fiscally neutrally and attempting to keep the consumers' utility level constant may conflict. If consumers must be compensated, the necessary increase in the benefits may actually be associated with further fiscal deteriorations. The amount of the necessary benefit increase can only be shown to fall short of an actuarially fair increment, taking the original benefit level as a reference. This hinges on the improved risk-shifting induced by marginally fair benefit schemes. Hence, simple comparisons of the situations before and after an 'adjustment to actuarial fairness' induces delayed retirement decisions holding the average benefit payments constant—as noted in Section 3.5 and Schmähl (1988, p. 28)—must be treated with great caution. Again, similar conclusions carry over to the case of initially 'inefficient delayed' withdrawals.

In this respect, the change in the institutional framework introduced above exhibits a fundamental difference. Here only the 'reference benefits' may essen-tially be pay-as-you-go financed. Given the fiscal impact of this decision, however, it is always possible to finance marginally fairly reduced or increased benefits by introducing additional capital-funded accounts. The present analysis therefore suggests that desired increases in the average retirement date should be carried out by appropriately specifying the 'reference age'. The additional capital-funded accounts then guarantee that (a) individual deviations from this 'reference age' are fiscally neutral, and (b) the resulting lifetime allocation is efficient. Here Proposition 7 and Corollary 5 characterize situations in which retirement policies can be associated with existing lifetime labor supply inefficiencies. They correspond to Breyer and Straub (1993, Theorem 1): the lifetime labor supply decision — given a contribution rate — is efficient if, and only if, transfers are implemented lump-sum, rather than generating deviations from marginal fairness. However, the risk-shifting properties of old-age insurance are important as well. Thus, Proposition 8 states that lifetime allocations are efficient only if they additionally entail perfect income insurance. Concentrating on retirement policies which incorporate a variable retirement option, Pareto-efficiency therefore also requires a particular contribution rate in addition to specifying a marginally fair benefit schedule[10].

There exist several objections which must be taken into account when focusing on the political implementability of such proposals. It may be questionable, for instance, whether the consumers will trust the social security agency to actually accumulate capital in order to finance the flexible retirement benefits. On the other hand, if left to private insurances, additional regulation may be required due to the problems noted in Section 3.2[11]. Such limitations imposed on the possibility of annuitizing social security pensions may then imply that Proposition 7 obtains greater significance. Yet, abstracting from such considerations, Proposition 8 defines a benchmark case: (1) if the old-age insurance is capital-funded, imposing the contribution rate $\tilde{p}$ and offering actuarially fair adjustments of the benefits to alternative choices of the individual retirement age are generally feasible policy options. This applies to both public and private pension systems. (2) Given pay-as-you-go financing of public pensions, the Pareto-efficient lifetime allocation could be implemented by converting all pension payments into pure annuities. Thus, regardless of the actual financing method employed there exist institutional arrangements which ensure that the induced lifetime allocation is efficient and the structure of the income flow is neutral with respect to the labor supply decisions. However, these results are obtained focusing on a group of identical consumers. In the following, the analysis will turn to Pareto-efficient retirement policies in the presence of consumer heterogeneity. It will be seen that the conclusions derived above carry over only if it is possible to implement separate, marginally fair variable retirement policies for each consumer-type. Due to institutional or informational constraints this may not be possible, however. Consequently, different consumer-types must be covered under a single retirement policy.

---

[10]It can now be speculated whether existing inefficient risk-shifting introduces additional possibilities of achieving an inter-generationally efficient transition path. As pointed out before, this question lies outside the scope of the present study, however.

[11]Yet, the argument that the computational burden in evaluating the fiscal effects of such policy changes may be excessive must be disputed. On the contrary, policy-oriented studies frequently note the extreme complexity of such calculations given that the basic 'pay-as-you-go'-scheme is maintained for all pensions paid out.

PART III

Heterogeneous populations and efficient retirement rules

CHAPTER 7

Variable retirement schemes and individual choices

7.1 THE SCOPE OF FLEXIBLE RETIREMENT AGE PROGRAMS

Despite the specific assumptions introduced in order to capture the impacts of uncertain lifetimes and liquidity constraints, the model outlined in Chapter 5 essentially analyzes the optimal retirement decision in terms of an income–leisure choice. The particular structure here only implies that this trade-off bears additional implications for both the realized degrees of self-protection and insurance against the old-age risk. Yet, income–leisure choices characterize the vast majority of related theoretical studies on retirement behavior[1]. Consequently, individual differences in retirement ages chosen are generally seen to depend on:

- health status;
- lifetime income opportunities;
- tastes for leisure;
- life-expectancies.

The 'induced retirement' literature almost exclusively focuses on the impact of the pension policy on the income structure and the expected value of the lifetime income flow. Moreover, the emphasis clearly lies on investigating a representative consumer's reaction to policy changes. As pointed out before, deviations from marginal fairness in calculating pension claims are most often associated with an increased 'generosity' of early retirement allowances. Thus, the retirement policies employed are seen to reflect an inter-generational transfer system[2]. However,

---

[1]With the exception of Hemming (1977), all of the approaches noted in Section 4.2.4 share this basic feature.

[2]Compare Genosko (1985, Ch. 5), Burkhauser and Quinn (1989), Reimers and Honig (1989), Börsch-Supan (1991), and Wildasin (1991), and many others.

Genosko (1985) and Wildasin (1991) also stress the group-interest approach in generating intra-generational transfers, which in turn influence the benefit schedule offered[3]. Similar to the debate on the role of inter-generational transfers in general[4], this view of the benefit provisions in flexible retirement age allowances competes with approaches based on risk-shifting arguments again.

Thus, studies incorporating random shocks, affecting the instantaneous preference structure, and/or the lifetime income opportunities, also constitute a predominant form of introducing consumer heterogeneity. Old-age pension systems are seen to provide an additional implicit insurance against the realizations of such shocks. Consequently, the 'disability insurance' models of Diamond and Mirrlees (1978, 1985, 1986), Nalebuff and Zeckhauser (1985), and Peters (1989, Part III) relate the aggregate labor supply of a cohort to a distribution of health shocks. At the same time, this distribution also determines *ex-post* differences in the individual lifetime labor supplies. Since the analyses do not require a particular financing method, they apply to both public and private old-age insurance plans. Similarly, Diamond, Helms and Mirrlees (1980), Gordon and Varian (1988), and Brunner (1990), for example, investigate intra-generational transfers as an implicit insurance against random realizations of individual productivities[5]. These arguments then also characterize the implicit contract view of private pension arrangements[6]. *Ex-post* differences in the individual incomes attained are related to incentive problems associated with providing perfect income insurance.

However, if the insurance is imperfect, the withdrawal ages realized by consumers facing variable retirement options will reflect the *ex-post* heterogeneity. Hence, in Genosko (1985) individual variations in the lifetime labor supplies are seen to correspond to differences in the lifetime income opportunities. The respective results are derived from pursuing a comparative static analysis — as demonstrated in Section 5.5 above as well. This can be verified to constitute the standard approach accounting for deterministic consumer heterogeneity throughout the respective literature. In particular, higher lifetime labor earnings and private wealth holdings are most often associated with earlier withdrawals. As is well known, the standard model of income–leisure choices yields ambiguous results in this respect — due to counteracting income and substitution effects. More specifically, Gustman and Steinmeier (1986), Fields and Mitchell (1984), and Mitchell and Fields (1984) therefore stress that income opportunities late in the consumers' life influence the retirement behavior more strongly than income attainable earlier. This again underlines that consumers are liquidity constrained. Gordon and Blinder

---

[3]Interestingly, Genosko's analysis utilizes the basic framework provided by Crawford and Lilien (1981) as well. However, the study exclusively discusses the case of certain lifetimes.

[4]See Section 3.3.

[5]In contrast, Laitner (1979a,b,c) focuses on the possibility to influence the economy-wide capital formation by adequate debt policies, given that income insurance is incomplete.

[6]Compare Section 4.2.3.

(1980) add that technological change may have resulted in a decline of (real) wages late in life relative to wages early in the consumers' life-cycle — thus contributing an additional tendency towards earlier withdrawal from the labor market. Further, Burtless and Moffitt (1984, 1985) note that the income redistribution implemented in the social security systems raises the attainable old-age income of low-income groups. Hence, these groups are additionally induced to retire earlier.

In contrast, the fact that consumers may differ with respect to their tastes for leisure or life-expectancies is only rarely noted in the respective literature. Gordon and Blinder (1980) and Schmähl (1988), for instance, point out that — within the given institutional framework — an overall increase in the consumers' preference for leisure may have contributed to the observed reduction in average retirement ages. Similarly, Quinn and Burkhauser (1983) state that this trend has been perceived as a natural by-product of an increasingly wealthy society. It reflects that some of this newly created wealth has been consumed as leisure. Uhlenberg (1988), however, warns that at the same time the increasing life-expectancies should have called for delayed retirement decisions. Thus, the study proposes a number of policy changes designed to cope with the demographic development holding the expected duration of the retirement period constant. Since old-age is not necessarily associated with decreased productivities and an increased hardship of labor, such changes need not yield decreases in the lifetime welfare.

Interestingly, however, flexible retirement age allowances are frequently claimed to have been introduced in order to provide the possibility for individuals to choose their retirement age according to their preferences[7]. Börsch-Supan (1991) states that the introduction of such schemes reflects the policy-makers' acceptance of 'consumer sovereignty'. Further, OECD (1988b) projects that 'future adjustments in the retirement arrangements should be accompanied by greater flexibility for the individual to choose the age [..] of withdrawal from the labor market'. This future development is seen to apply to both public and private pension provisions. In this context, OECD (1988b, 1992) also note that occupational pension plans have already introduced retirement age flexibility in countries in which the public old-age insurance does not offer general variable retirement options. From a theoretical point of view Nalebuff and Zeckhauser (1985) analyze the retirement behavior of individuals which differ with respect to tastes for leisure and life-expectancies. Here all consumers are covered under a single retirement policy. The benefit schedule is upward sloping — though not necessarily marginally fair. A first approach utilizes a comparative static analysis to demonstrate that consumers characterized by either (a) a stronger preference for leisure, or (b) lower life-expectancies, or (c) both retire earlier.

Referring to the institutional design again, Lupu (1984), Burkhauser and Quinn (1989), OECD (1988b, 1992), and many other policy-oriented studies further state that introducing the possibility of choice must be accompanied by adjustments to

---

[7]See Lupu (1984), Genosko (1985), OECD (1988b, 1992), Jacobs and Schmähl (1989) and Schmähl (1990), for instance.

actuarial fairness in the benefit schemes. This conclusion is obtained from the casual observance that otherwise particular consumer-types would derive additional benefits (losses) from the arrangement. Actuarially fair systems are seen to specify the opportunity costs of early withdrawals 'correctly'. Börsch-Supan (1991) again adds that, if the deductions made for early retirement were calculated actuarially fairly, the problem of providing additional work disincentives for older generations — associated with the fact that these individuals can currently increase their expected lifetime income by retiring earlier — vanishes. Lupu's (1984) conclusions correspond rather closely to the policy analysis provided in Chapter 6: '[..], if policy makers wanted to maximize freedom of choice with respect to work effort, they would simply convert all retirement programs into annuities, payable upon attaining a particular age, independent of an individual's choice whether to remain working or not'.

7.2   INDIVIDUAL DIFFERENCES IN RETIREMENT AGES

Turning back to the model introduced in Chapter 5, Section 5.5 has already derived reactions of the optimal retirement age to changes in the contribution rate p and the additional policy variable B. For contribution rates lower than the benchmark rate $\tilde{p}$, the results have been noted not to comply with the respective reactions derived from the standard model assuming certain lifetimes and the absence of liquidity constraints. Similarly, the focus will now be on the impacts of changes in the labor income, the instantaneous disutility of labor, and survival probabilities[8]. Hence, a first approach towards distinguishing individual withdrawal decisions considers the comparative statics of the basic model introduced above.

Proposition 9.   *For marginally fair benefit schedules, the effect of variations in the instantaneous labor income w on the optimal retirement age is generally ambiguous. In contrast, increases in the instantaneous disutility of labor are always associated with decreases in the optimal retirement age.*

Proof.   Assuming $p \geq \tilde{p}$ — hence, $(1 - p)w \leq x^*$ — (5.36) yields

$$-\frac{dR^*}{dw} \cdot U''(x^*) MRT^{x,R} =$$

$$U'((1 - p)w) + U''(x^*)[pw + x^*]\frac{\partial x^*}{\partial w} - p[U'((1 - p)w) - U'(x^*)] \, , \quad (7.1)$$

---

[8]Hence, no attention will be paid to differences in the non-labor lifetime wealth. It should be noted that marginal increases in $\omega(0)$ are treated quite easily. However, assuming more than just marginal differences in the initial wealth, or incorporating an age-contingent distribution of bequests requires a complete reformulation of the basic decision model. Further, changes in the instantaneous utility of consumption function are ignored as well. Here Corollaries 3 and 4 demonstrate that such variations may induce considerable qualitative differences in the induced retirement behavior.

with

$$\frac{\partial x^*}{\partial w} = \frac{\displaystyle\int_0^{R^*} F(t)e^{-rt}dt\, p}{\displaystyle\int_{R^*}^T F(t)e^{-rt}dt} > 0 , \tag{7.2}$$

as short-hand notation for the derivative of the marginally fair benefit schedule at $R = R^*$. The last two terms on the RHS of (7.1) can be observed to be negative. However, the first term is positive. Thus, the optimal retirement age actually increases, if this term dominates.

For $p < \tilde{p}$, (5.54) can be used to obtain

$$\frac{d\Delta W^*}{dw} = \frac{\dfrac{d\lambda^*}{dw}\displaystyle\int_{R^*}^{\theta_U} e^{-rt}dt + U''(x^*)\dfrac{\partial x^*}{\partial w}\displaystyle\int_{\theta_U}^T F(t)e^{-rt}dt}{\displaystyle\int_{R^*}^T F(t)e^{-rt}dt} - [pw + x^*]$$

$$+ \frac{\lambda^*\displaystyle\int_{R^*}^{\theta_U} e^{-rt}dt + U'(x^*)\displaystyle\int_{\theta_U}^T F(t)e^{-rt}dt}{\displaystyle\int_{R^*}^T F(t)e^{-rt}dt}\left(p + \frac{\partial x^*}{\partial w}\right)$$

$$+ \frac{d\lambda^*}{dw}\frac{1}{F(R^*)}[(1-p)w - x^*] + \frac{\lambda^*}{F(R^*)}\left[(1-p) - \frac{\partial x^*}{\partial w}\right]. \tag{7.3}$$

The income effect can be signed unambiguously again, since

$$\int_{\theta_L}^{\theta_U} H'\left(\frac{\lambda^*}{F(t)}\right)\frac{1}{F(t)}e^{-rt}dt\frac{d\lambda^*}{dw} = \int_{\theta_L}^{R^*} e^{-rt}dt(1-p) + \int_{R^*}^{\theta_U} e^{-rt}dt\frac{\partial x^*}{\partial w} \tag{7.4}$$

yields $d\lambda^*/dw < 0$. However, this only implies that the first and the third term in (7.3) are negative. The remaining positive terms must be associated with a counteracting substitution effect. Thus, $d\Delta W^*/dR < 0$ is insufficient to determine the qualitative response of the optimal retirement age to changes in the labor income.

As far as changes in the disutility of labor are concerned, it is easily obtained that

$$\frac{dR^*}{dG} = \frac{1}{U''(x^*)MRT^{x,R}} < 0 , \tag{7.5}$$

for cases with $p \geq \tilde{p}$. Also, for $p < \tilde{p}$,

$$\frac{dR^*}{dG} = \frac{1}{\dfrac{d\Delta W^*}{dR}} < 0 , \tag{7.6}$$

if the second-order sufficient condition for the maximization with respect to (R, x) is satisfied — as has been assumed before. (6.2) and (6.3) can be utilized to show that this conclusion can also be maintained for general benefit schedules. It must only be ensured that the choice of the retirement age implies an interior solution for the consumers' maximization problem.
Q.E.D.

Hence, increases in the labor income again yield counteracting income and substitution effects. In contrast to the respective results of Section 5.5, however, the existence of these effects does not hinge on the specific institutional structure imposed. On the one hand, an increasing instantaneous wage-income yields an incentive to prolong the working-life, in order to take advantage of the improved consumption possibilities. Since labor is normal in the instantaneous utility function, increases in the lifetime income always increase the demand for leisure as well, however. If the latter effect dominates, the consumers will therefore prefer to decrease the retirement age. Similarly, the results obtained for changes in the disutility of labor follow the standard economic intuition. The last statement then also confirms the respective findings in Nalebuff and Zeckhauser (1985). However, in order to analyze the reaction of the retirement age to changes in the labor income for more general benefit schedules, it would be necessary to specify the dependency of benefits on wages in such schemes. This is omitted, since the qualitative results do not change. There always exist income and substitution effects. The magnitudes of the effects depend on the particular assumptions made, though.

Focusing on variations in the consumers' life-expectancy, two problems arise. Technically, it is unclear whether this implies that the maximum life-span or the age-specific survival probabilities are subject to variations. In Nalebuff and Zeckhauser this distinction does not matter, since the consumers are assumed not to be liquidity constrained. Thus, they always choose constant income/consumption paths over working-life and old-age — contingent only on the expected lifetime. Within the present model individual savings are contingent on survival probabilities, however, if $p < \tilde{p}$. The second problem is associated with the fact that the particular form of the $F(t)$-function affects the benefit schedule as well. Maintaining marginal fairness implies that the pension scheme must be adjusted accordingly. Thus, age-specific changes in survival probabilities also determine whether the rate of return to contributions — given a retirement decision — increases, decreases, or remains constant. For general survival probability functions this cannot be determined easily. On the one hand, higher survival probabilities at every age must be associated with deteriorations in the annuity flow which can be derived from a given fund. Yet, by the same argument contributions are received with higher probabilities, implying that — holding the contribution rate and retirement age constant — a larger fund can be accumulated[9].

---

[9]A similar conclusion obviously carries over to pay-as-you go financed systems which offer a marginally fair benefit schedule.

Assuming that the survival probabilities are given by a function $F(t) = (1 - t/T)^\zeta$, with $\zeta \in [0, 1]$–as introduced in the Appendix to Chapter 5—it is possible to determine the cumulative effect of changes in ζ on attainable benefits. First, note that

$$\frac{\partial F(t)}{\partial \zeta} = \ln\left(1 - \frac{t}{T}\right) F(t) < 0; \ \forall \, t \in (0, T) \,. \tag{7.7}$$

The respective decrease in the expected lifetime can be obtained as

$$\frac{\partial \int_0^T F(t)dt}{\partial \zeta} = -\frac{T}{(1 + \zeta)^2} < 0. \tag{7.8}$$

For convenience—and in order to illustrate the arguments from above—let $B = 0$ and $r = 0$. Then, the attainable benefits associated with every retirement age chosen can be easily shown to increase when survival probabilities decrease:

$$\frac{\partial \xi^M(R; p, 0)}{\partial \zeta} = -\ln\left(1 - \frac{R}{T}\right)\left(1 - \frac{R}{T}\right)^{-(1+\zeta)} pw > 0 \,, \tag{7.9}$$

for $R \in (0, T)$, where ξ^M denotes the marginally fair benefit schedule. Yet, this specification of the survival probability function still does not suffice in order to determine the reaction of the optimal retirement age with respect to changes in ζ in general:

Proposition 10. *Assume $B = 0$, $r = 0$, and the survival probability function*

$$F(t) = \left(1 - \frac{t}{T}\right)^\zeta \,,$$

with $\zeta \in (0, 1)$. Regardless of whether the benefit schedule is adjusted to maintain actuarial fairness, the optimal retirement age decreases with increasing ζ within the regime characterized by $p \geq \tilde{p}$. For contribution rates $p < \tilde{p}$ this reaction cannot be determined unambiguously.

Proof. Assuming $p \geq \tilde{p}$ and an adjustment of the benefit schedule, such as to maintain actuarial fairness, (5.36) yields

$$\frac{dR^*}{d\zeta} = -\frac{\dfrac{\partial \xi^M(R^*; p, 0)}{\partial \zeta}}{MRT^{x,R}} < 0. \tag{7.10}$$

Given $p < \tilde{p}$, it follows from (5.54) that

$$
\frac{d\Delta W^*}{d\zeta} = \frac{\dfrac{d\lambda^*}{d\zeta}[\theta_U - R^*] + U''(x^*)\displaystyle\int_{\theta_U}^{T} F(t)dt \dfrac{\partial \xi^M(R^*; p, 0)}{\partial \zeta}}{\displaystyle\int_{R^*}^{T} F(t)dt} [pw + x^*]
$$

$$
+ \frac{d\lambda^*}{d\zeta}\frac{1}{F(R^*)}[(1 - p)w - x^*]
$$

$$
+ \frac{\lambda^*[\theta_U - R^*] + U'(x^*)\displaystyle\int_{\theta_U}^{T} F(t)dt}{\displaystyle\int_{R^*}^{T} F(t)dt}\frac{\partial \xi^M(R^*; p, 0)}{\partial \zeta} - \frac{\lambda^*}{F(R^*)}\frac{\partial \xi^M(R^*; p, 0)}{\partial \zeta}
$$

$$
+ \frac{\displaystyle\int_{\theta_U}^{T} \dfrac{\partial F(t)}{\partial \zeta}dt\, U'(x^*)}{\displaystyle\int_{R^*}^{T} F(t)dt}[pw + x^*]
$$

$$
- \frac{\displaystyle\int_{R^*}^{T} \dfrac{\partial F(t)}{\partial \zeta}dt}{\displaystyle\int_{R^*}^{T} F(t)dt}\frac{\lambda^*[\theta_U - R^*] + U'(x^*)\displaystyle\int_{\theta_U}^{T} F(t)dt}{\displaystyle\int_{R^*}^{T} F(t)dt}[pw + x^*]
$$

$$
- \frac{\partial F(R^*)}{\partial \zeta}\frac{\lambda^*}{[F(R^*)]^2}[(1 - p)w - x^*]. \tag{7.11}
$$

Further, it can be obtained that

$$
\int_{\theta_L}^{\theta_U} H'\left(\frac{\lambda^*}{F(t)}\right)\frac{1}{F(t)}dt\frac{d\lambda^*}{d\zeta} = [\theta_U - R^*]\frac{\partial \xi^M(R^*; p, 0)}{\partial \zeta}
$$

$$
+ \int_{\theta_L}^{\theta_U} H'\left(\frac{\lambda^*}{F(t)}\right)\frac{\lambda^*}{[F(t)]^2}\frac{\partial F(t)}{\partial \zeta}dt. \tag{7.12}
$$

Hence, $d\lambda^*/d\zeta < 0$. Thus, the first two lines in (7.11) can be observed to be negative. The third line then represents the counteracting substitution effect already discussed in Section 5.5. However, there are more positive terms in lines 5 and 6 of (7.11), while the expression in line 4 is negative again. Without further specification of the function $U(c)$ it is impossible to determine the sign of the derivative in (7.11).

If the benefit schedule is not adjusted for the change in the survival probabilities — thus, the scheme deviates from marginal fairness — (6.3) can be transformed into

$$\frac{T}{1+\zeta}\left(1 - \frac{R^*}{T}\right) U'(x^*) \frac{\partial \xi(R^*; \pi)}{\partial R} + U(1-p) - U(x^*) - G = 0. \quad (7.13)$$

Here $\xi(R^*; \pi)$ again denotes the benefit schedule. Assuming that this scheme is initially marginally fair, but remains unaltered now,

$$\frac{\mathrm{d}R^*}{\mathrm{d}\zeta} = -\frac{U'(x^*) \dfrac{\partial \xi^M(R^*; p, 0)}{\partial R}}{U'(x^*) \dfrac{1}{T} \dfrac{\partial \xi^M(R^*; p, 0)}{\partial R} - U''(x^*) \dfrac{\partial^2 \xi^M(R^*; p, 0)}{\partial R \partial R}} < 0. \quad (7.14)$$

Moreover, even if the initial situation is already characterized by a lack of marginal fairness in the benefit schedule, the optimal retirement always age decreases with lower survival probabilities–as long as the second-order sufficient condition for the consumers' maximization with respect to (x, R) is satisfied.

Focusing on the case $p < \tilde{p}$, (6.2) can be used to derive

$$\Delta W^* = \left(\lambda^*[\theta_U - R^*] + \int_{\theta_U}^T F(t)\mathrm{d}t\, U'(x^*)\right) \frac{\partial \xi(R^*; \pi)}{\partial R}$$

$$+\lambda^*[(1-p)w - x^*] - F(R^*)G = 0. \quad (7.15)$$

Again, the respective derivative with respect to ζ

$$\frac{\mathrm{d}\Delta W^*}{\mathrm{d}\zeta} = \left(\frac{\mathrm{d}\lambda^*}{\mathrm{d}\zeta}[\theta_U - R^*] + \int_{\theta_U}^T \frac{\partial F(t)}{\partial \zeta}\mathrm{d}t\, U'(x^*)\right) \frac{\partial \xi(R^*; \pi)}{\partial R}$$

$$+\frac{\mathrm{d}\lambda^*}{\mathrm{d}\zeta}[(1-p)w - x^*] - \frac{\partial F(R^*)}{\partial \zeta}G \quad (7.16)$$

cannot be signed. The term $\mathrm{d}\lambda^*/\mathrm{d}\zeta$ now only depends on partial derivatives of the $F(t)$-function. Compared to (7.12) the term multiplied by $\partial \xi^M/\partial \zeta$ vanishes. Hence, assuming a CRRA-function for the utility of consumption, for instance,

$$\frac{\mathrm{d}\lambda^*}{\mathrm{d}\zeta}\frac{1}{\lambda^*} = \frac{\displaystyle\int_{\theta_L}^{\theta_U} H\left(\frac{\lambda^*}{F(t)}\right) \ln\left(1 - \frac{t}{T}\right) \mathrm{d}t}{\displaystyle\int_{\theta_L}^{\theta_U} H\left(\frac{\lambda^*}{F(t)}\right) \mathrm{d}t} < 0. \quad (7.17)$$

However, (7.16) can again be seen to contain both positive and negative terms. Moreover, even assuming marginal deviations from an initially actuarially fair benefit schedule and inserting from (7.17) the sign of this expression cannot be determined without further specification of the $H(\cdot)$-function.
Q.E.D.

Of course, it would be possible to derive sufficient conditions for $dR^*/d\zeta < 0$ for the case $p < \tilde{p}$ again. This is not pursued further, since Proposition 10 already refers to a rather specific example. Hence, it should only be noted that the results reported in Nalebuff and Zeckhauser (1985) do not necessarily hold, if the induced replacement ratio is smaller than unity. This is solely due to the fact that—with private savings bearing the risk of involuntary bequests—the age-specific consumption decisions are contingent on the respective survival probabilities. The usual income and substitution effects only arise when the benefit schedule is adjusted for the change in survival probabilities. Regardless of whether this is done, however, lower remaining life-expectancies imply that old-age income—derived either from private savings or pensions—can only be consumed with lower probabilities. This tends to encourage early retirement and is reflected by the additional negative terms in (7.11) and (7.16). At the same time, the *ex-ante* probabilities to incur the opportunity costs of prolonged work are decreased as well—thus inducing a tendency to delay retirement. This effect shows up in the additional positive terms in these derivatives. For replacement rates smaller than unity the magnitudes of these effects hinge on the survival probabilities associated with dates in the private savings interval $[\theta_L, \theta_U]$, as well as on the shape of the marginal utility of consumption function.

On the other hand, for replacement ratios greater than or equal to unity the additional negative effects can always be shown to dominate the positive terms—given the survival probability function assumed. Hence, here there clearly exists an additional tendency towards earlier retirement. Nevertheless, it should be noted that in (7.10) the properties of the function $F(t) = (1 - t/T)^\zeta$ have been exploited. Thus, for more general functions and relative changes in the survival probabilities, the latter argument may not apply either. The structure of such variations of the survival probabilities more generally also influences the reaction of the optimal retirement age in cases where the replacement rate exceeds unity. The existence of the two counteracting effects noted above is determined only by the fact that consumers are liquidity constrained, which restricts the possibility of consumption smoothing and induces a complementarity between improved risk-shifting via insurance and self-protection.

7.3 STYLIZED FACTS AND EXPLANATORY LACUNAE

Chapter 6 suggests that in analyzing efficient variable retirement policies the focus should be confined to systems incorporating actuarially fair benefit schedules. This assumption also characterizes the 'benchmark' benefit schedule for the comparative static results obtained in Sections 5.5 and 7.2. The question remains whether the results obtained can be regarded as positive—given the actual retirement policies implemented. Table 4.2 reports average retirement ages for four OECD countries which—among others—have introduced a general flexible retirement age allowance in their public old-age insurance. The respective benefit formulas can be found in OECD (1988b, 1992). Perhaps the most simple and transparent rules exist in Canada. Here retirement can take place between ages 60 and 70. Every month of early or delayed withdrawal compared to the full benefit age 65 is associated with a 0.5% reduction, respectively increment, in the benefit. This system — only introduced in 1987 — has not undergone reform yet.

In France the normal age of retirement was 65 until 1982 and every year of early withdrawal was associated with a 5% reduction in the available benefit. Beginning in 1982, the 'normal' age was redefined as 60 years and — since 1983 — full bene-fits are available at this age for persons with $37\,^1/_2$ years of insurance coverage. This insurance coverage now generally characterizes the availability of full pensions. Every quarter of additional insurance after age 60 and prior to reaching $37\,^1/_2$ years of coverage yields a pension increment of 1/150 of the full pension[10]. Thus, a person with $37\,^1/_2$ years of coverage at age 65 — representing eligibility for the full pension under the old system — now experiences a deduction of 1/150 for each quarter of early withdrawal. This translates into 2.7% per year of early retirement. This insti-tutional change obviously attempts to encourage more insurance coverage — thus, increasing the contribution years. In doing so, early retirement decisions of persons who reach $37\,^1/_2$ years of coverage within the age interval 60 to 65 are associated with less pension deductions than under the old system, however.

In the US OASDI-system the pensions are currently reduced by 5/9 of 1% for every month of early retirement prior to age 65. Further, delaying retirement yields pension increments of 0.25% per month between ages 65 and 70. Retiring even later yields no additional increases in the available benefits. However, persons claiming benefits after age 70 are not subject to the so-called 'earnings-test'. This rule provides additional incentives to withdraw from labor market activities. In the US the receipt of the social security pension is not conditional upon actually retiring. The 'earnings test' reduces the pension by $1 for every $2 of additional earnings above $5760 for persons aged 62–65, however. The respective 'earnings-test' exempt income is $7800 for persons between ages 65 and 70[11].

In contrast, the benefit rules applied under current German laws are again contin-gent on insurance coverage. The eligibility for participating in the general flexible retirement age allowance requires a minimum of 35 years of insurance coverage, with at least 15 full years of actually contributing. For males early retirement can then occur between ages 63 and 65[12]. 40 years of insurance coverage entitle for the receipt of the full benefit. Every additional year of deferred retirement is associated with a benefit increase of 1.5% of 'assessed earnings'. These earnings are calcu-lated as the ratio of insured earnings over the national average of gross earnings

---

[10]'Régime Générale' — the respective rules under the 'Régimes Complémentaires' are similar.

[11]The work disincentive effects of the 'earnings-test' are extensively discussed in Blinder, Gordon and Wise (1980), Quinn and Burkhauser (1983), Dye (1985), and Reimers and Honig (1989).

[12]Women's early retirement options vary over the age interval 60–63. Moreover, disabled persons can retire as early as age 60 as well.

multiplied by a common computational base[13]. Prolonged work beyond age 65 is further rewarded by actuarial increments of 0.6% per month available for the next 24 months (age bracket 65–67). The maximum attainable actuarial increase of 14.4% for two years thus imposes a cap on the financial incentives to delay retirement. Further, increasing the insurance coverage always adds to the pensions in the way described above until age 67. Hence, the 'standard' 40 years of insurance coverage yielding the full pension do not define a maximum attainable pension level.

This brief account highlights two stylized facts. First, actual benefit schedules are highly complex and involve discontinuities. The systems attempt to influence retirement behavior by offering additional income opportunities associated with delayed withdrawals, while also imposing upper bounds on the incentives to retire late. Casual observance — as illustrated in Tables 4.1 and 4.2, for instance — suggests that the consumers' reactions have been more unanimous than the complexity of the benefit rules and the differences in the institutional settings — whether deductions are calculated actuarial, or are related to insurance coverage — would suggest. Focusing on the US and German situation in more detail, Table 4.4 further shows that the largest increase in the fraction of individuals fully retired occurs between ages 60–64. Börsch-Supan (1991) adds that the vast majority of delayed retirement decisions take place immediately after age 65 is reached. This underlines that the financial incentives to defer retirement beyond the normal age have been rather ineffective.

Second — but closely related — the benefit schedules appear to lack actuarial fairness. For Germany, Genosko (1985, p. 36) stresses that this applies to both early and late retirement options. The deductions (increments) associated with early (delayed) retirement are smaller than actuarially fair. Similar conclusions are obtained by Börsch-Supan (1991), Jacobs and Schmähl (1989), and Schmähl (1988, 1990). This is seen to contribute to the general trend towards earlier retirement — corresponding to the analysis summarized as Corollary 5 above. In contrast, the US benefit scheme is noted to be approximately actuarially fair within an interval around age 65 by Börsch-Supan (1991) and Reimers and Honig (1989)[14]. This must obviously be based on particular assumptions concerning life-expectancies and interest rates and cannot apply to the benefit schedule as a whole. The top half of Table 7.1 contrasts (average) actual pension accruals in % of the benefit available at age 65 with actuarially fair deductions/increments. The assumed interest rate is 3% and the life-expectancy 77 years. Hence, the calculations sketch out a reference system, rather than describing the actually necessary actuarial adjustments[15]. The actual

---

[13]Formally — though not factually — this separates the calculation of benefits from the contributions paid. For more details see Genosko (1985, Ch. 2), and the respective parts in Casmir (1989) and VDR (1988), and OECD (1988).

[14]Interestingly, the latter therefore also conclude that the benefit provisions are neutral with respect to lifetime labor supply decisions for individuals planning to retire at the normal age. The statement is noted to require the absence of liquidity constraints, however.

[15]For example, Casmir (1989, p. 478) suggests that fair adjustments would require 7.5% deductions in Germany. Also, compare the discussion in Genosko (1985, Ch. 2).

Table 7.1   Actual pension accruals and actuarial fairness

Pensions as % of benefit attainable at the 'normal' retirement age

US OASDI as of 1989
German system as of 1990

Age	United States	Actuarially fair	Germany[a]
60	—	59.8	87.5
61	—	65.8	90.0
62	80.0	72.6	92.5
63	86.7	80.4	95.0
64	94.4	89.5	97.5
65	100.0	100.0	100.0
66	103.0	112.5	109.9
67	106.0	127.5	120.1
68	109.0	145.9	123.0
69	112.0	168.9	125.8
70	115.0	198.5	128.7

After full implementation of reforms[b]

Age	United States	Actuarially fair 67=100	Actuarially fair 65=100	Germany[c]
62	70.0	56.9	72.6	89.2
63	75.0	63.1	80.4	92.8
64	80.0	70.0	89.5	96.4
65	86.5	78.4	100.0	100.0
66	93.3	88.2	112.5	106.0
67	100.0	100.0	127.5	112.0
68	108.0	114.4	145.9	118.0
69	116.0	132.5	168.9	124.0
70	124.0	155.7	198.5	130.0

Sources: Adapted by permission of Economic Policy from Börsch-Supan (1991), and by permission of Springer-Verlag from Reimers and Honig (1989), with calculations by the author.
[a] Ages 60–62 only available for women and workers who cannot find appropriate employment due to health deficits and labor market conditions.
[b] US social security amendments of 1983; German 'Rentenreformgesetze' of 1992.
[c] Benefits at age 62 only available for persons currently entitled to retire prior to age 63.

pension accruals refer to the US OASDI-system as of 1989 and the German general public scheme[16] as of 1990—thus, before the reform amendments/laws introduced effective changes for retirees.

---

[16] 'Gesetzliche Rentenversicherung'.

As noted before, both systems have undergone significant reforms by now. The 1992 reform in Germany will maintain the 'normal' retirement age 65, but raise the age-brackets of early withdrawals. Early retirement will be possible up to three years prior to the 'normal' age — explicitly excluding the possibility of retiring earlier than under the current scheme. The benefits will then be actuarially reduced by 0.3% for every month of earlier retirement (3.6% per year). Delaying retirement beyond age 65 is associated with pension increments of 0.5% per month (6% per year). In addition, gradual retirement options have already been introduced as partial benefits are available for part-time employed persons. It is frequently noted that the benefit schedule — once completely installed — will still considerably lack actuarial fairness. This is illustrated by the lower half of Table 7.1. If the actuarial fair calculations are accepted, there exists no reason to claim that the schedule will even approach fairness in the future. Further, given that life-expectancies will continue to increase as well, the early retirement deductions would have to be larger than those reported. Thus, Börsch-Supan (1991) estimates that strong financial incentives encouraging considerable early retirement will be preserved. Yet, Jacobs and Schmähl (1989) and Schmähl (1988, 1990) indicate that the induced delays in the average retirement age — combined with the decrease in the full pension level and the gradual retirement options — constitute effective measures to reduce the fiscal burden. Tentatively, it is suggested that the induced change in the average retirement age alone yields a 3% reduction of the required contribution rate as of 2030.

The 1983 amendments to the US Social Security Act will result in a gradual increase of the 'normal' retirement age from 65 to 67. Upon full implementation, the respective benefit reductions associated with earlier pension receipts will be maintained at 5/9 of 1% for the first 36 months prior to age 67, and increased to 2/3 of 1% for each month during the preceding 24 months (age bracket 62–64). Delaying retirement beyond the normal age will yield pension increments of 2/3 of 1% for each month then. Beginning in 1990 the benefits associated with late retirement are increased by an additional 1/24 of 1% per month every two years — at the same time accounting for the gradual increase in the retirement age. Hence, the full 8% per year increase in the benefit, if postponing retirement until age 70, will be available for the generation born in 1943. Moreover, also starting in 1990 already the 'earnings-test' has been adjusted. The deductions now amount to $1 for every $3 of additional earnings above the exempt levels. This is intended to encourage part-time work. However, since 1986 social security benefits are subject to income taxes. The combined implicit tax on old-age income is thus estimated to actually increase for individuals in the middle-income range. Dye (1985) therefore doubts that this change will induce more employment of older persons[17]. Yet, Dye (1985), Quinn and Burkhauser (1983), and Reimers and Honig (1989) agree that the package of new benefit rules will induce an increase in the average retirement

---

[17] Also, see Sanmartino and Kasten (1985).

age. Again, as illustrated in the lower half of Table 7.1 there is little reason to believe, however, that the proposed adjustments will introduce actuarial fairness into the benefit schedule.

Moreover, Lupu (1984) and Burkhauser and Quinn (1989) stress that the actual retirement behavior cannot be forecast without explicitly taking account of the retirement incentives contained in private insurance plans. Current regulation in the US requires that early retirement pensions cannot be reduced more than actuarially fairly. Most private pension plans today are of the 'defined-benefit'-type. They specify benefit flows available upon retiring at certain ages. Many studies — including Lazear (1983), Lupu (1984), Burkhauser and Quinn (1989), Fields and Mitchell (1984), and Nalebuff and Zeckhauser (1985), for example — note that the actual deductions of the benefits are less than fair. The latter observe that benefit formulas — ranging from 'exceedingly simple to [..] bewilderingly complex' — usually relate attainable pensions to income, years of service, and social security payments to be received. All plans surveyed entail an early retirement option. The deductions specified usually range between 3 and 7%' per year — a large percentage reduces the benefit uniformly by 4 to 5%. Fields and Mitchell (1984, p. 55) report the following average adjustments found in 14 major pension plans: delaying retirement from age 60 to 61 decreases the present discounted value of the pension payments by 1%; between 62 and 63 this value is increased by 5%; all subsequent delays until age 65 are associated with further decreases of 2% in the present value. Most private pension plans do not reward delays of the retirement decision beyond social security's 'normal' age of 65 years.

A very similar picture arises considering the German situation again. Here four basic forms of providing old-age income-support can be distinguished[18]. If the employing firm itself guarantees the pension payments by building up reserves, the funds accumulated must be sufficient to cover the future claims by actuarial standards. It is also possible to establish separate insurance subsidiaries, however. Here general 'support schemes' differ from 'pension schemes', since the former do not specify entitlements for particular payments to be received by the employees. Due to the increased regulation of private pension plans, the significance of such arrangements has deteriorated strongly compared to 'pension schemes', however. In the latter, the employees possess legally enforceable pension claims. Regulation here requires the use of actuarial methods in calculating contributions and benefits. Finally, firms can turn to private insurers in order to purchase pension coverage for individuals or groups of employees. Focusing on benefit formulas, 'integrated pensions' are very common. Here the employer guarantees an old-age income — consisting of both public and private pensions — calculated as a particular fraction of the last yearly income. Contributions generally only vary over

---

[18]The following account corresponds to the so-called 'Direktzusagen', 'Unterstützungskassen', 'Pensionskassen', and 'Direktversicherung', respectively.

income groups. Further, there also exist plans which specify a fixed payment to be received upon retirement. Moreover, the employees are legally entitled to receive an early pension from the occupational plan, if the respective requirements for early retirement under the public system are fulfilled. Unless specified otherwise in the private pension plan, deductions can only be based on the contribution years realized. These deduction rules will obviously lack actuarial fairness. Additional actuarial reductions must be prespecified in the plan. However, even in plans in which actuarially fair deductions would therefore be possible, the benefits are in practice decreased by rates ranging between only 0.4 and 0.7% per month[19].

Hence, although both the US ERISA and the German 'Betriebsrentengesetz' have introduced a tendency towards the use of actuarial methods in calculating the benefits for worker cohorts, the benefit schedules associated with early withdrawals lack actuarial fairness. In most economic studies this is attributed to the incentive role of private pensions, given that mandatory retirement rules are precluded. The detailed investigations provided by Lazear (1983) and Fields and Mitchell (1984) lend some support for this hypothesis. However, the latter also find that 'firms and workers may sort themselves according to their preferences for continued work'. This conclusion is derived from the observance of a significant (negative) correlation between a proxy measuring tastes for leisure and early retirement incomes provided in the different plans. This suggests that the mix of worker-types may differ between pension plans. Similarly, Lazear (1983) agrees that simple comparisons of the present discounted values of pension payments cannot generally be utilized in order to evaluate the implied work-disincentives. Such evaluations would have to account for the preference structure of the workers as well. In turn, it must be concluded that different worker-types' reactions to the benefit provisions vary.

Summing up, lack of actuarial fairness clearly seems to constitute a common feature of flexible retirement age allowances. Abstracting from arguments relating this phenomenon to efficient separations in long-term labor contracts, the analysis of Chapter 6 thus suggests that efficiency gains are possible by transforming pension agreements into annuities. Moreover, deriving the reactions of the optimal retirement age to changes in the policy variables (Section 5.5), or the individual lifetime preference structure and income opportunities (Section 7.2), the benefit schedule has been taken as exogenous. Since the attention has been largely confined to marginally fair benefit schemes, the discussion above suggests that the positive implications of this analysis may be rather limited. This conclusion finds additional support, since the benefit schedules appear to entail 'kinks'. Accounting for the even more complex structure of early retirement options, including disability- and employment-related allowances, further renders the simple comparative static analysis subject to doubts. Hence, Nalebuff and Zeckhauser (1985) already propose that the benefit rules specified in the retirement policy reflect an optimal policy given consumer heterogeneity. Applying a common retirement policy to different

---

[19]Genosko (1985, p. 59).

consumer-types induces deviations from the type-contingent best policies. An optimal policy — defined as maximizing the weighted sum of lifetime utilities, with weights equal to the relative frequencies of consumer-types in the population under consideration — balances the utility losses associated with a necessarily second-best policy. The study proposes three reasons why retirement policies cannot explicitly account for consumer heterogeneity:

- Events affecting the instantaneous preference structure and life-expectancies are *ex-ante* random and realized only after the individuals have entered the insurance arrangement.
- Consumer-types are not observable for the insurance agency.
- Legal restrictions prevent differential treatment of individuals.

In the following, the present research focuses on the latter two of these issues[20]. It derives efficient institutional arrangements, under which retirement decisions take place. Thus, in contrast to the analysis pursued in Section 7.2, the individuals' reaction to the flexible retirement age allowance cannot be derived as comparative static results from an 'induced retirement' model. Rather, the rules under which retirement takes place reflect intra-generational efficiency, given consumer-heterogeneity. Consequently, pension provisions are also determined endogenously. It can be shown that such schemes generally lack actuarial fairness. Although clearly motivated by the previous research of Nalebuff and Zeckhauser (1985), the present approach is also quite distinct. In particular, the following two chapters distinguish the impacts of institutional and informational constraints on the design of efficient benefit rules. This allows emphasis of the roles of efficient transfer systems, as opposed to assumed differences in the consumers' risk-classification, in generating deviations from actuarial fairness.

---

[20]The case in which consumer heterogeneity manifests randomly again yields an implicit insurance argument. Nalebuff and Zeckhauser (1985) thus pursue this analysis following the disability insurance model of Diamond and Mirrlees (1978, 1985, 1986).

CHAPTER 8

The common contribution rate

8.1 INTRODUCTORY COMMENTS

This section focuses on the distortions induced by the fact that old-age insurance imposes an identical contribution rate on all employed workers covered under a policy. Hence, the emphasis lies on analyzing an effective institutional constraint. Identical contribution rates obviously characterize social security schemes. Yet, it can be argued that the possibility of accumulating additional claims in private pension plans, or an effective opting-out policy, may re-introduce the possibility of realizing individually different premium/coverage relationships. As noted by Nalebuff and Zeckhauser (1985), however, most occupational pension plans in the US do not offer choices with respect to the premium either. This reflects the legal restriction that such differential treatment can only be negotiated in collective bargaining agreements. Although the firms sometimes offer choices regarding the particular benefit formula to be applied, these formulas differ almost exclusively as far as relating benefits to income and tenure is concerned.

The ERISA legislation has additionally introduced significantly more conformity. In Germany this tendency was even stronger after the enactment of the 'Private Pension Act[1]' in 1974. Thus, the self-selection of worker-types among different plans can be assumed to be imperfect. Further, an effective 'contracting-out' option only exists in the UK. Here this option can be seen to provide additional opportunities for selecting the individual insurance coverage. As far as contracting-out of the public into an occupational pension scheme is concerned, similar qualifications to those noted above apply. Contracted-in contributions only vary over certain income groups, for instance[2]. Since 1988 this may have changed though. Today employees can also opt out of occupational pension plans, if purchasing adequate

---

[1] 'Betriebsrentengesetz'.

[2] Details are provided in OECD (1988b).

private annuity insurance ('personal pensions') — a possibility which before has been confined to self-employed persons[3]. However, there exists no OECD member country in which 'contracting-out' and variable retirement options in the public pension scheme coexist.

As far as this analysis is concerned, the rates may actually vary with the labor income obtained, but are not adjusted for differences in the disutility of labor. Since the welfare-maximizing premium is known to depend on this parameter, the institutional requirement to impose identical premium rates induces second-best solutions. In terms of the discussion above, the policies cannot attain Pareto-efficient lifetime allocations as described in Proposition 8. In general, second-best policies will be seen to involve efficient intra-generational redistribution. Given the transfers between consumer-types, retirement policies then deviate from offering a single marginally fair benefit schedule. In particular, early retirement benefits are calculated better than actuarially fair if the policy-maker maximizes the average lifetime utility in the population. Moreover, the second-best policy — subject to the institutional constraint — may be associated with the existence of an additional moral hazard problem, if consumer-types cannot be observed by the insurance agency. However, the present study untangles the effects of redistribution and moral hazard on the design of the benefit schedule[4]. Here, the focus is more generally on efficient policies — some of which would even require late benefits to be better than fair. A particular efficient policy can also be shown to be implementable by offering a single actuarially fair benefit schedule. Which of the efficient policies will be chosen as 'optimal' depends on the preferences of the policy-maker.

Moreover, since individuals only differ with respect to their disutility of labor, it can be shown that there exists an implementable policy which achieves the best by offering options with respect to premiums. Hence, the existence of a moral hazard problem hinges on the fact that the retirement policy is already second-best, due to the institutional constraint. The common contribution rate requirement is necessary — though not sufficient — for moral hazard when consumer-types are not observable. Further, deviations from marginal fairness are only 'seeming' — they reflect the intra-generational transfers. In absence of moral hazard the induced life-time labor supplies are efficient in the sense of Proposition 7. Given the contribution rate specified, the consumer-types cannot improve their well-being by annuitizing the pension flow. Moral hazard — if effective — can then further be demonstrated to yield inefficient retirement decisions. The subsidized consumer-type could achieve welfare improvements by annuitizing the pension claims, if there were no incentive problem.

---

[3] Atkinson (1991); Brugiavini (1993).

[4] This also distinguishes the present study from the previous research by Nalebuff and Zeckhauser (1985).

8.2   ADDITIONAL ASSUMPTIONS

In order to illustrate the basic arguments, the model presented below is kept rather simple. In particular, it will be assumed that there exist only two types of consumers — denoted types H and L — with expected lifetime utility functions

$$V_k \equiv \int_0^T U(c(t))F(t)\mathrm{d}t \; - \; G_k \int_0^R F(t)\mathrm{d}t \; , \qquad k = H, L \; . \qquad (8.1)$$

For convenience, the interest/discount rates have been set equal to zero here. Apart from this (8.1) obviously reflects the assumptions noted in Section 5.1. The two consumer-types only differ with respect to the disutility of labor. Specifically, it will be assumed that

$$G_H > G_L \; . \qquad (8.2)$$

Given a contribution rate, a benefit level, and a retirement age the consumers always choose an optimal consumption path. The additive-separability of the expected lifetime utility in consumption and labor supply implies that optimal consumption paths are contingent only on these policy variables. This can easily be verified by noting that the results reported in Lemma 1, Proposition 1, and Corollary 1 of Section 5.2 only depend on the utility of consumption function. Thus, the optimal consumption paths satisfy[5]

$$\{z_k(t; \bar{p}, \bar{R}, \bar{x})\} = \{z(t; \bar{p}, \bar{R}, \bar{x})\} \; , \qquad (8.3)$$

for $k = H, L$, and arbitrary combinations $(\bar{p}, \bar{x}, \bar{R})$. Hence, also,

$$V_k^* = \beta(p, R_k, x_k)L_S^*(p, R_k, x_k) \; + \; [1 - \beta(p, R_k, x_k)]L_{NS}^*(p, R_k, x_k)$$

$$-G_k \int_0^R F(t)\mathrm{d}t \; , \qquad (8.4)$$

with L_S^*, L_{NS}^*, and β defined in Section 5.2 as well. Again, $\beta = 1$ ($\beta = 0$), if the replacement rate falls short of (is greater than or equal to) unity. Finally, the respective marginal rates of substitutions can be derived as in (5.30) and (5.31). Again it is easily seen that only the marginal rate of substitution $MRS^{x,R}$ reflects the differences in the disutility of labor between the two consumer-types — if evaluated for identical policy offers.

Merely for convenience, it will from now on also be assumed that the labor income equals unity[6]. Further, let m and $(1 - m)$, $0 < m < 1$, be the fractions of H-type and L-type consumers in the population, respectively. Then, given that both

---

[5]This property and the relationship expressed in Proposition 10 constitute the main reasons for focusing on differences in the disutility of labor.

[6]The assumptions $r = 0$ and $w = 1$ are utilized by Crawford and Lilien (1981) as well. They only serve to simplify the notation.

consumer-types are required to pay an identical contribution (rate) p, the feasibility of a retirement policy is assumed to imply:

$$\left[m \int_0^{R_H} F(t)dt + (1-m) \int_0^{R_L} F(t)dt \right] p$$

$$- m \int_{R_H}^T F(t)dt \, x_H - (1-m) \int_{R_L}^T F(t)dt \, x_L \geq B. \tag{8.5}$$

Obviously, $B = 0$ implies full capital-funding in either a public, or a private insurance, for instance. However, the analysis is not necessarily limited to such insurance arrangements. The results generated in the subsequent sections carry over to situations with $B \neq 0$ as well. $B > 0$ corresponds to the case when the insurance agency accumulates capital in excess of the fund just needed to finance the benefits for the group of consumers under consideration. This may reflect either an inter-generational efficiency condition, or simply the fact that the agency earns positive expected profits. As long as the benefit payments are covered by accumulated funds (8.5) obviously defines the set of feasible policies, given that B is held constant. Pure pay-as-you-go financing can generally be associated with $B > (=, <) 0$ according to whether the population growth rate falls short of (equals, exceeds) zero. Then (8.5) can again be identified with maintaining fiscal neutrality, if—following Lupu (1984), for instance—the pension system is transformed into an annuity insurance. Generally, let

$$B_k \equiv \int_0^{R_k} F(t)dt \, p - \int_{R_k}^T F(t)dt \, x_k . \tag{8.6}$$

(8.5) can then be restated as

$$m B_H + (1-m) B_L \geq B. \tag{8.7}$$

Again, if the system operates pay-as-you-go finance, a reference retirement policy can be defined as follows: assume $B_H = B_L = B$ and values for p, R_k, and x_k such that the flows of contributions received from and the benefit flows guaranteed for the consumer-types satisfy the agency's budget requirement. Then transforming the benefits x_k into annuities available upon reaching the age R_k and contributing p over the age interval $[0, R_k]$, changes in (p, R_k, x_k) can in principle be implemented fiscally neutrally as long as the expected value of contributions actually received in excess of the expected value of benefits to be paid out remains constant.

Regardless of the actual financing method, the analysis will therefore very generally address the issue whether $B_H = B_L = B$ characterizes efficient retirement policies requiring a common contribution rate p from both consumer-types. For convenience and without loss of generality with respect to the qualitative results, it will in the following be assumed that $B = 0$. Correspondingly, if Pareto-efficient policies yield $m B_H = -(1-m) B_L \neq 0$, the assumption $B = 0$ stresses that intra-generational redistribution may be welfare-enhancing even in fully funded social security systems, or private pension schemes generating zero expected profits. As will be seen, this will in turn also affect the design of the benefit rules.

To begin with, consumer-types will be assumed to be publicly observable, thus, isolating the effects of the common contribution requirement. Hence, the retirement policy can offer different benefit schedules for each consumer-type. It must only ensure that (8.7) is satisfied. In terms of Definition 1, the policies under consideration can thus be characterized as $\Pi = (p, \mathcal{S}_k)$, with $k = H, L$ and

$$\mathcal{S}_k(\mathrm{i}): R_k \in [0, T];$$

$$\mathcal{S}_k(\mathrm{ii}): x_k = \xi_k^M(R_k; p, B_k) \equiv \frac{-B_k + \displaystyle\int_0^{R_k} F(t)\mathrm{d}t \; p}{\displaystyle\int_{R_k}^T F(t)\mathrm{d}t}.$$

Later, the retirement policies will also be required to entail common benefit rules as well. For the time being, however, the schedules may actually differ. Following Proposition 7, this ensures that the search for Pareto-efficient policies can first be restricted to those policies which are marginally fair for each consumer-type. A single, marginally fair benefit schedule then arises as a special case — associated with the fact that $B_k = 0$, for $k = H, L$, implies that the two schedules defined in the policy are identical. While requiring an identical contribution rate p, the particular value of this rate will be determined by the fact that the resulting policy must be intra-generational Pareto-efficient. Intra-generational Pareto-efficiency is defined in accordance with the discussion in Chapter 6 above:

Definition 5.   *Consider the set of feasible retirement policies* $\Pi = (p, \mathcal{S}_k)$. *Then a policy* $\bar{\Pi} = (\bar{p}, \bar{\mathcal{S}}_k)$ *is said to be intra-generational Pareto-efficient, if there exists no other policy in this set which yields a higher expected lifetime utility for one consumer-type, while the expected lifetime utility for the respective other consumer-type is at least as high as under the policy* $\bar{\Pi}$.

8.3   THE CONTRIBUTION-TRANSFER TRADE-OFF

As in the basic model of Chapter 5, each consumer of type-k, $k = H, L$, chooses an optimal retirement date and benefit level given the contribution rate p and a value B_k specified in the policy. Using the notation introduced before, let $W_k^* = W_k^*(p, B_k)$, $k = H, L$, denote the respective value of the objective function after optimization with respect to (R, x). Correspondingly, $R_k^* = R_k^*(p, B_k)$ and $x_k^* = x_k^*(p, B_k)$ denote the optimal retirement dates and pension flows. Finally, $\psi_k^* = \psi_k^*(p, B_k)$ refers to the optimal value of the multiplier associated with the constraint that the difference between the expected values of contributions and benefits equals B_k for type-k consumers.

Utilizing the envelope theorem again, it can be derived that

$$
MRS_k^*[\beta_k^* = 1] \equiv \left.\frac{dB_k}{dp}\right|_{dW_k^*=0} = -\frac{\dfrac{\partial W_k^*}{\partial p}}{\dfrac{\partial W_k^*}{\partial B}}
$$

$$
= \frac{-\displaystyle\int_0^{R_k^*} U'(z(t))F(t)dt + \psi_k^* \int_0^{R_k^*} F(t)dt}{\psi_k^*}
$$

$$
= -\int_{R_k^*}^{T} F(t)dt \left[\frac{\displaystyle\int_0^{R_k^*} U'(z(t))F(t)dt}{\displaystyle\int_{R_k^*}^{T} U'(z(t))F(t)dt} - \frac{\displaystyle\int_0^{R_k^*} F(t)dt}{\displaystyle\int_{R_k^*}^{T} F(t)dt}\right] , \qquad (8.8)
$$

if $(1 - p) > x_k^*$. Since the optimal consumption path is non-increasing and strictly decreasing over a non-trivial subinterval, it is easily checked that the term in brackets is negative. Hence, the expression in (8.8) must be positive. Similarly,

$$
MRS_k^*[\beta_k^* = 0] = -\int_0^{R_k^*} F(t)dt \left[\frac{U'(1-p)}{U'(x_k^*)} - 1\right] , \qquad (8.9)
$$

if $(1 - p) \leq x_k^*$. This expression can be verified to be non-positive. Further, it is equal to zero if, and only if, $(1 - p) = x_k^*$.

Now, Propositions 2 and 3 imply that (8.8) applies when $p < \tilde{p}_k$, and (8.9) corresponds to the case where $p \geq \tilde{p}_k$, with $\tilde{p}_k$, for $k = H, L$, defined by the equations

$$
U'(1 - \tilde{p}_k) = G_k . \qquad (8.10)
$$

(8.2) yields

$$
\tilde{p}_H > \tilde{p}_L . \qquad (8.11)
$$

It should be noted that as long as the consumers' optimization problems entail interior solutions (given B_k), the value of this transfer is irrelevant for the definition of the welfare-maximizing contribution $\tilde{p}_k$. More importantly yet, assuming B_k equals zero, for $k = H, L$, (8.8) and (8.9) characterize the respective trade-offs between changes in the contribution rate and transfers B_k which keep the individual welfare constant — starting from an arbitrarily chosen common contribution rate and identical marginally fair benefit schedules.

Further, the regime $p \geq \tilde{p}_k$ implies

$$
\frac{\partial^2 W_k^*}{\partial p \partial p} = \int_0^{R_k^*} F(t)dt \, [U''(1 - p) + U''(x^*)] < 0 , \qquad (8.12)
$$

$$\frac{\partial^2 W_k^*}{\partial B \partial B} = -U''(x^*) \frac{\partial \xi_k^M (R_k^*; p, B_k)}{\partial B_k} < 0 , \qquad (8.13)$$

$$\frac{\partial^2 W_k^*}{\partial p \partial B} = -U''(x^*) \frac{\displaystyle\int_0^{R_k^*} F(t)dt}{\displaystyle\int_{R_k^*}^T F(t)dt} > 0 , \qquad (8.14)$$

and thus

$$\frac{\partial^2 W_k^*}{\partial p \partial p} \frac{\partial^2 W_k^*}{\partial B \partial B} - \left[\frac{\partial^2 W_k^*}{\partial p \partial B} \right]^2 = \frac{\displaystyle\int_0^{R_k^*} F(t)dt}{\displaystyle\int_{R_k^*}^T F(t)dt} U''(1-p)U''(x^*) > 0 . \qquad (8.15)$$

For the range of contributions $p \in (0, \tilde{p}_k)$ the strict concavity of the W_k^*-functions cannot be shown as easily. There exist second-order effects on the optimal accumulation paths which obscure the possibility of signing the respective expressions. Hence, for these cases it will be *assumed* that W_k^* is concave as well. This obviously simplifies the analysis considerably. The implied loss of generality should not be overrated here, since the analysis only serves to exemplify some basic arguments.

Hence, the trade-offs between contributions and transfers can be illustrated as shown in Figure 8.1. Contribution (rates) are depicted on the horizontal and transfers B_k on the vertical axis. The I_k-curves thus represent (p, B_k)-combinations such that W_k^* is held constant. It is clear that higher values of B_k *ceteris paribus* induce welfare losses. Hence, the expected lifetime utility of the consumers decreases moving from a lower to a higher indifference curve. Further, Figure 8.1 illustrates the result stated as Part (c) of Proposition 8. For each B_k-value exogenously specified, type-k consumers expected lifetime utility is maximized, if the contribution rate is $\tilde{p}_k$.

Policies with $B_k = 0$—hence, $x_k = \xi^M(R_k; p, 0)$, for $k = H, L$—are characterized by points on the horizontal axis. The different slopes of the indifference curves I_k already suggest that starting from such policies there may exist Pareto-improvements which can be captured by implementing intra-generational transfers. Thus, an equal division of the 'financial burden'—$B_H = B_L = 0$—may not be intra-generational Pareto-efficient. However, whether or not this will be the case depends on the contribution rate specified.

For the illustrations to be presented in the subsequent sections it is convenient to insert the feasibility constraint

$$m B_H = -(1 - m)B_L \iff B_H = -\frac{(1 - m)}{m} B_L \qquad (8.16)$$

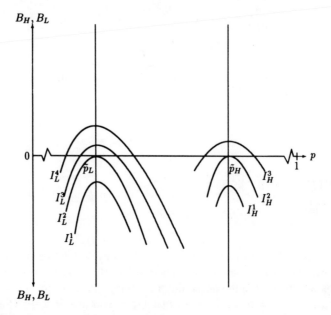

Figure 8.1   The trade-off between contributions and transfers

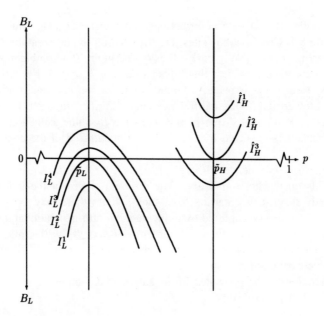

Figure 8.2   Inserting the feasibility constraint

in order to define

$$\widehat{W}_H^*(p, B_L) \equiv W_H^*\left(p, -\frac{(1-m)}{m} B_L\right) . \tag{8.17}$$

The respective trade-offs between contributions and transfers B_L for type-H consumers can then be graphed as illustrated in Figure 8.2. Here the $\hat{I}_H$ curves represent type-H consumers' 'indifference' curves between contribution rates and per-capita transfers B_L to be received by type-L consumers. Obviously, these curves are upward sloping for $p > \tilde{p}_H$ and downward sloping for $p < \tilde{p}_H$.

8.4   PARETO-IMPROVING TRANSFERS

Given the discussion above, two issues arise immediately:

(1) Since for each B_k — thus, also for $B_k = 0$ — $p = \tilde{p}_k$ and $x_k = \xi_k^M(R_k; \tilde{p}_k, B_k)$, for $R_k \in [0, T]$, maximizes type-k consumers' expected lifetime utility, the problem of determining a common intra-generational efficient contribution rate must be addressed.

(2) The fact that at least one consumer-type cannot realize the contribution rate $\tilde{p}_k$ may induce intra-generational redistribution.

With respect to point (1) above, the following preliminary result is rather easily obtained:

Proposition 11.   *If Π^E is an intra-generational efficient retirement policy with contribution (rate) p^E, then $p^E \in (\tilde{p}_L, \tilde{p}_H)$.*

Proof.   Suppose $p^E < \tilde{p}_L$. Then holding B_k^E constant

$$\left.\frac{dW_k^*(p^E, B_k^E)}{dp}\right|_{dB_k^E=0} > 0 , \tag{8.18}$$

for $k = H, L$, by Proposition 3. Here it must only be noted that $p^E < \tilde{p}_L$ implies $(1 - p) > x_k^*(p^E, B_k^E)$ for both consumer-types k. Similarly, Proposition 3 yields

$$\left.\frac{dW_k^*(p^E, B_k^E)}{dp}\right|_{dB_k^E=0} < 0 , \tag{8.19}$$

for $k = H, L$, if $p^E > \tilde{p}_H$. In this case the induced retirement behavior is associated with $(1 - p) < x_k^*(p^E, B_k^E)$. Moreover, since $dB_k^E = 0$ obviously implies $dB = 0$, these changes in the contribution are feasible. Thus, $p^E \in [0, \tilde{p}_L)$ and $p^E \in (\tilde{p}_H, 1]$ can be contradicted.

Next, consider the case $p^E = \tilde{p}_L$. The change in type-L consumers' expected lifetime utility associated with further marginal increases in the contribution and changes in the transfer B_L can be obtained as

$$dW_L^*(\tilde{p}_L, B_L) = \frac{\partial W_L^*(\tilde{p}_L, B_L)}{\partial p}dp + \frac{\partial W_L^*(\tilde{p}_L, B_L)}{\partial B}dB_L = -\psi_L^*(\tilde{p}_L, B_L)dB_L.$$
(8.20)

This expression is positive for all $dB_L < 0$. However, the respective differential for type-H consumers can be derived as

$$dW_H^*(\tilde{p}_L, B_H) = \frac{\partial W_H^*(\tilde{p}_L, B_H)}{\partial p}dp + \frac{\partial W_H^*(\tilde{p}_L, B_H)}{\partial B}dB_H$$

$$= \left[-\int_0^{R_H^*} U'(z(t; \tilde{p}_L, R_H^*, x_H^*))F(t)dt + \psi_H^* \int_0^{R_H^*} F(t)dt \right]dp - \psi_H^* dB_H. \quad (8.21)$$

Inserting for ψ_H^*, the first term in this expression is positive for $dp > 0$. It is easily obtained now that it is possible to achieve Pareto-improvements by increasing the contribution and allowing for a marginal positive transfer from type-H consumers to type-L individuals. A similar analysis shows that $p^E = \tilde{p}_H$ cannot be intra-generational Pareto-efficient either. In this case improvements could always be realized by lowering the contribution and implementing a transfer from type-L consumers to type-H consumers.
Q.E.D.

The proposition restates that, given a retirement age, both consumer-types always prefer more (less) insurance in situations characterized by underinsurance (overinsurance). In Figure 8.2 this is reflected by the fact that type-H consumers' 'indifference' curves $\hat{I}_H$ slope upward (downward), while type-L consumers' indifference curves possess a negative (positive) slope for $p < \tilde{p}_L$ ($p > \tilde{p}_H$). Hence, both consumer-types would be willing to pay an additional 'transfer' in order to improve on the desired income/consumption smoothing. Moreover, marginal deviations from the welfare maximizing contribution rate can always be associated with a utility gain, if the consumers receive a positive transfer.

Proposition 11 thus identifies a range for possible intra-generational efficient contribution rates. Further, the following is now clear:

Corollary 6.   *An intra-generational Pareto-efficient retirement policy* $\Pi^E = (p^E, \mathcal{S}_k^E)$ *induces* $(1 - p^E) > x_H^*$ *and* $(1 - p^E) < x_L^*$.

Sketch of Proof.   The corollary follows directly from Proposition 2. For H-type (L-type) consumers $p^E < \tilde{p}_H$ ($p^E > \tilde{p}_L$) induces replacement ratios greater (smaller) than unity.
Q.E.D.

Thus, requiring an identical contribution rate will always induce deviations from perfect risk-shifting for both consumer-types. In particular, H-type consumers will be underinsured and, therefore, save privately in addition to accumulating claims in the insurance system. On the other hand, L-type consumers will turn out to be overinsured. The non-negativity constraint on private wealth is binding for this consumer-type over the whole length of their lifetime. It follows that $MRS_H^* = MRS_H^*[\beta_H^* = 1]$ and $MRS_L^* = MRS_L^*[\beta_L^* = 0]$ for contributions $p \in (\tilde{p}_L, \tilde{p}_H)$. This is utilized in order to derive the following:

Proposition 12.   *Let Π^F denote a feasible retirement policy with identical, marginally fair benefit schedules $\xi_k^M(R_k; p^F, 0)$ for both consumer-types. Further, $\tilde{p}_L < p^F < \tilde{p}_H$.*

$$
If \quad -\frac{m}{(1-m)} \frac{MRS_H^*(p^F, 0)}{MRS_L^*(p^F, 0)} \begin{Bmatrix} (a) & > \\ (b) & = \\ (c) & < \end{Bmatrix} 1, \quad then
$$

(a)   there exists a Pareto-dominant retirement policy Π^E which entails different marginally fair benefit schedules $\xi_k^M(R_k; p^E, B_k^E)$ for the two consumer-types, with $B_L^E < 0 \Rightarrow B_H^E = -((1-m)/m)B_L^E > 0$ and $\tilde{p}_H > p^E > p^F > \tilde{p}_L$;

(b)   the policy Π^F is intra-generational Pareto-efficient;

(c)   there exists a Pareto-dominant retirement policy Π^E which entails different marginally fair benefit schedules $\xi_k^M(R_k; p^E, B_k^E)$ for the two consumer-types, with $B_L^E > 0 \Rightarrow B_H^E = -((1-m)/m)B_L^E < 0$ and $\tilde{p}_H > p^F > p^E > \tilde{p}_L$.

Proof.   Consider the following optimization problem:

$$
\text{Max}_{p, B_H, B_L} \quad W_H^*(p, B_H) \tag{8.22}
$$

subject to

$$
mB_H + (1-m)B_L \geq 0 \tag{8.23}
$$

$$
W_L^*(p, B_L) \geq W_L^*(p^F, 0) \tag{8.24}
$$

$$
B_H \geq 0. \tag{8.25}
$$

It has been assumed that W_H^* is strictly concave. By virtue of Corollary 6, $\partial W_H^*/\partial p > 0$ and $\partial W_L^*/\partial p < 0$. Further, $\partial W_k^*/\partial B < 0$, for $k = H, L$. Hence, some simple rearrangements yield

$$
-MRS_H^* = \frac{(1-m)}{m} MRS_L^* - \frac{\Upsilon_H(1-m)MRS_L^*}{m\dfrac{\partial W_H^*}{\partial B}}, \tag{8.26}
$$

with $\Upsilon_H \geq 0$ denoting the multiplier associated with constraint (8.25). This can now be utilized to derive a necessary condition for $B_H = 0$ in the optimum as

$$-\frac{m}{(1-m)}\frac{MRS_H^*(p^F, 0)}{MRS_L^*(p^F, 0)} \leq 1 . \tag{8.27}$$

Intuitively, it is clear that—starting from the initial policy Π^F—type-H consumers' expected lifetime utility can only be increased by increasing the contribution. Holding B_H constant and equal to zero, this would decrease the expected lifetime utility of type-L consumers and therefore violate (8.24). Similarly to the arguments utilized in the proof of Proposition 11 it can then also be obtained that

$$-\frac{m}{(1-m)}\frac{MRS_H^*(p^F, 0)}{MRS_L^*(p^F, 0)} > 1 \tag{8.28}$$

is sufficient for the existence of a Pareto-dominant policy Π^E as described in Part (a) of Proposition 12. It must only be noted that (8.28) implies that H-type consumers would be willing to pay a transfer in order to obtain a marginal increase in the contribution which exceeds the one necessary to just compensate type-L consumers.

In contrast, considering the optimization problem

$$\text{Max}_{p, B_L, B_H} \quad W_L^*(p, B_L) \tag{8.29}$$

subject to

$$mB_H + (1-m)B_L \geq 0 \tag{8.30}$$

$$W_H^*(p, B_H) \geq W_H^*(p^F, 0) \tag{8.31}$$

$$B_L \geq 0 \tag{8.32}$$

the respective first-order conditions can be transformed to yield

$$-MRS_L^* = \frac{m}{(1-m)}MRS_H^* - \frac{m\Upsilon_L MRS_H^*}{(1-m)\frac{\partial W_L^*}{\partial B}} . \tag{8.33}$$

Here $\Upsilon_L \geq 0$ constitutes the multiplier associated with constraint (8.32). Following the same line of arguments exposed above,

$$-\frac{m}{(1-m)}\frac{MRS_H^*(p^F, 0)}{MRS_L^*(p^F, 0)} < 1 \tag{8.34}$$

can here be shown to constitute a sufficient condition for $B_L^E > 0$ in the optimum. Since $MRS_H^* > 0$, $MRS_L^* < 0$, $\partial W_L^*/\partial B < 0$, the necessary condition for $B_L^E = 0$ can be obtained as

$$-\frac{m}{(1-m)}\frac{MRS_H^*(p^F, 0)}{MRS_L^*(p^F, 0)} \geq 1. \tag{8.35}$$

Part (c) of the Proposition is thus proved rather easily as well.

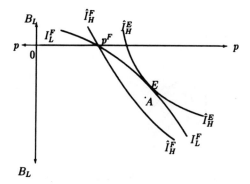

Figure 8.3   Pareto-improving transfers to L-types

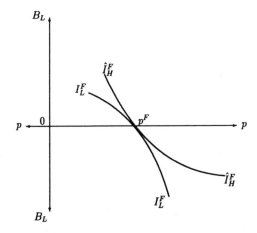

Figure 8.4   Pareto-efficiency without transfers

Obviously, the cases associated with the optimization problems (8.22)–(8.25) and (8.29)–(8.32), respectively, are exclusive. Hence, the necessary conditions (8.35) and (8.27) also prove Part (b)[7].
Q.E.D.

The three cases noted in Proposition 12 can be illustrated graphically as shown in Figures 8.3–8.5. In Figure 8.3 type-L consumers' indifference curve $I_L^F I_L^F$ is less steep than the respective curve $\hat{I}_H^F \hat{I}_H^F$ — both passing through point $(p^F, 0)$ on the horizontal axis. Point $E = (p^E, B_L^E)$ then indicates the solution to the

---

[7] In order to prove the existence of Pareto-improving transfer/contribution combinations for situations characterized as in Parts (a) and (c), it is obviously not necessary to assume the concavity of W_H^*. However, Part (b) can only be ensured, if this is guaranteed.

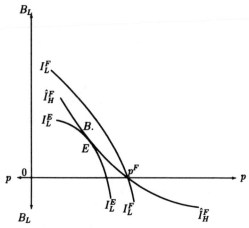

Figure 8.5　Pareto-improving transfers to H-types

maximization problem (8.22)–(8.25). $\Upsilon_H = 0$ implies that the maximum occurs at a point of tangency. Moreover, by virtue of (8.24) type-L consumers' expected utility remains constant at the level associated with the contribution p^F and the transfer $B_L^F = 0$.

Similarly, Figure 8.5 depicts the situation characterized in Part (c) of the Proposition. Here point E again indicates the solution to the optimization problem (8.29)–(8.32). Finally, Figure 8.4 corresponds to case (b) in Proposition 12. Here the initial combination $(p^F, 0)$ also solves the two maximization problems set up in the proof above.

8.5　DETERMINING OPTIMAL CONTRIBUTION/TRANSFER COMBINATIONS

8.5.1　THE CASE OF A MARGINALLY FAIR REFERENCE SCHEDULE

The two maximization problems defined in the proof of Proposition 12 not only demonstrate the possible existence of Pareto-improving transfer systems. Rather, they also generate particular solutions (p^E, B_k^E). First, a reference policy with $B_k = 0$ and contribution rate p^F defines reservation utility levels here. In addition, the solutions are characterized by the implicit assumption made that all welfare gains — arising due to the intra-generational redistribution — are captured by the consumer-type which finances the transfer. However, there obviously may exist other (p, B_L)-combinations which are intra-generational Pareto-efficient as well. This is illustrated by points A in Figure 8.3 and B in Figure 8.5. Given the respective contributions and transfers, both consumer-types are better off than under the original reference policy.

More generally, an intra-generational Pareto-efficient policy — given the alternative is Π^F as defined above — can be found by solving

$$\text{Max}_{p, B_H, B_L} \quad \delta W_H^*(p, B_H) + (1 - \delta) W_L^*(p, B_L) \tag{8.36}$$

$$W_H^*(p, B_H) \geq W_H^*(p^F, 0) \tag{8.37}$$

$$W_L^*(p, B_L) \geq W_L^*(p^F, 0) \tag{8.38}$$

$$m B_H + (1 - m) B_L \geq 0. \tag{8.39}$$

Here δ $((1 - \delta))$ represents a weight attached to type-H (type-L) consumers' expected lifetime utility in the objective function. This objective function could express the policy-makers preferences, for instance. The concavity of the W_k^*-functions again ensure that a unique maximum exists. Rearranging the first-order conditions yields the following characterization:

$$- \frac{MRS_H^*}{MRS_L^*} \frac{m}{(1 - m)} = 1. \tag{8.40}$$

Note that, if either $B_H > 0$ and $p^E < p^F$, or $B_L > 0$ and $p^E > p^F$, $W_H^*(p^E, B_H) < W_H^*(p^F, 0)$, or $W_L^*(p^E, B_L) < W_L^*(p^F, 0)$, respectively. This — and the concavity properties once more — then imply that the solution to the maximization problem above always entails $B_H > 0$, if the initial situation is described as in Part (a) of Proposition 12. Also, $B_L > 0$ in the optimum, given that Part (c) of this Proposition applies. Finally, the optimum is characterized by $B_H = B_L = 0$, if the reference policy Π^F satisfies (8.40) — thus, reflecting Part (b). This demonstrates the directions of the efficient transfers — starting from an arbitrarily chosen reference retirement policy with identical, marginally fair benefit schedules for both consumer-types. Here the weight δ only governs the distribution of the welfare gains between the consumer-types. It does not determine the direction of the transfers, however.

Figure 8.6 illustrates these arguments for the Case (c) defined in Proposition 12. Point E_0 here corresponds to point E in Figure 8.5 above. The optimization problems (8.36)–(8.39) and (8.29)–(8.32) obviously yield identical solutions if $\delta = 0$ in (8.36). Similarly, Point E_1 is associated with $\delta = 1$, and E_δ corresponds to some $\delta \in (0, 1)$. The contract curve $\overline{E_0 E_\delta E_1}$ then depicts all intra-generational efficient combinations (p^E, B_L^E) for this case. Note that the respective indifference curves sketched out imply that (8.37) and (8.38) are always satisfied.

Focusing on the situations described in Parts (a) and (c) of Proposition 12 — where (8.37) and (8.38) are not binding — it can be obtained that

$$\frac{dp^E}{d\delta} \cdot |J| = - \left[\frac{\partial W_H^*}{\partial p} - \frac{\partial W_L^*}{\partial p} \right] \left[\left(\frac{(1 - m)}{m} \right)^2 \delta \frac{\partial^2 W_H^*}{\partial B \partial B} + (1 - \delta) \frac{\partial^2 W_L^*}{\partial B \partial B} \right]$$

$$- \left[\frac{(1 - m)}{m} \frac{\partial W_H^*}{\partial B} + \frac{\partial W_L^*}{\partial B} \right] \left[-\frac{(1 - m)}{m} \delta \frac{\partial^2 W_H^*}{\partial p \partial B} + (1 - \delta) \frac{\partial^2 W_L^*}{\partial p \partial B} \right] \tag{8.41}$$

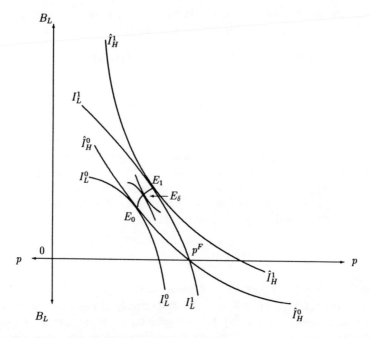

Figure 8.6   The contract curve assuming an exogenous reference policy

$$\frac{\mathrm{d}B_L^E}{\mathrm{d}\delta} \cdot |J| = \left[\frac{(1-m)}{m}\frac{\partial W_H^*}{\partial B} + \frac{\partial W_L^*}{\partial B}\right]\left[\delta\frac{\partial^2 W_H^*}{\partial p\partial p} + (1-\delta)\frac{\partial^2 W_L^*}{\partial p\partial p}\right]$$

$$+ \left[\frac{\partial W_H^*}{\partial p} - \frac{\partial W_L^*}{\partial p}\right]\left[-\frac{(1-m)}{m}\delta\frac{\partial^2 W_H^*}{\partial p\partial B} + (1-\delta)\frac{\partial^2 W_L^*}{\partial p\partial B}\right]. \qquad (8.42)$$

Here

$$|J| = \left[\delta\frac{\partial^2 W_H^*}{\partial p\partial p} + (1-\delta)\frac{\partial^2 W_L^*}{\partial p\partial p}\right]\left[\left(\frac{(1-m)}{m}\right)^2\delta\frac{\partial^2 W_H^*}{\partial B\partial B} + (1-\delta)\frac{\partial^2 W_L^*}{\partial B\partial B}\right]$$

$$- \left[-\frac{(1-m)}{m}\delta\frac{\partial^2 W_H^*}{\partial p\partial B} + (1-\delta)\frac{\partial^2 W_L^*}{\partial p\partial B}\right]^2. \qquad (8.43)$$

By assumption $|J| > 0$. Further, the first terms in (8.41) and (8.42) are positive. A sufficient condition for both $\mathrm{d}p^E/\mathrm{d}\delta > 0$ and $\mathrm{d}B_L^E/\mathrm{d}\delta > 0$ can therefore be derived as

$$-\frac{(1-m)}{m}\delta\frac{\partial^2 W_H^*}{\partial p \partial B} + (1-\delta)\frac{\partial^2 W_L^*}{\partial p \partial B} > 0. \tag{8.44}$$

In general, the sign of this expression cannot be determined unambiguously. This is explained by the fact that increasing the contribution *ceteris paribus* induces welfare gains (losses) for type-H (type-L) consumers. Assuming, for instance, that (p, B_L) are both 'normal goods' in the policy-maker's objective function (8.36) therefore gives rise to counteracting effects. However, for $\delta = 0$ (8.14) ensures that (8.44) is satisfied. Starting from $\delta = 0$, both the contribution and the transfer B_L^E therefore always increase as more weight is attached to H-type consumers' expected lifetime utility in the objective function (8.36). Thus, this consumer-type benefits in two ways. First, the contribution rate is increased, providing for better risk-shifting. Second, the transfer received from (or paid to) type-L consumers is increased (decreased).

Obviously, the next step must be to check whether the results obtained can be used to characterize 'optimal' policies. Here the main problem is to determine the policy-maker's objectives. If it can be agreed that such choices always yield Pareto-efficient policies, then it can be assumed that an optimal policy must maximize (8.36) for some δ characterizing the preferences for consumer-types. The respective literature then identifies a prominent case. Setting $\delta = m$ implies that the policy-makers are interested in maximizing the average welfare attained by the members of the group under consideration. The following can be derived now:

Proposition 13.   *Consider the following two-stage problem: First, solve*

$$\text{Max}_p \quad \delta W_H^*(p, 0) + (1-\delta)W_L^*(p, 0) \, .$$

Let the solution — denoted p^F — determine reservation utility levels $W_k^*(p^F, 0)$. In a second step, (p^E, B_k^E), $k = H, L$, then characterize the optimal policy found by maximizing (8.36) subject to (8.37)–(8.39).
  Setting $\delta = m$ will always induce $B_H^E < 0$ — thus $B_L^E = -(m/(1-m))B_H^E > 0$. An optimal policy with $B_L^E = B_H^E = 0$ therefore requires $\delta < m$.

Proof. $\partial^2 W_k^*/\partial p \partial p < 0$, for $k = H, L$, ensures the existence of a unique interior maximum $p^F \in (\tilde{p}_L, \tilde{p}_H)$. for the optimization problem spelled out. The contribution rate p^F is characterized by

$$-\frac{\displaystyle\int_0^{R_H^*} U'(z_H(t))F(t)\mathrm{d}t - \psi_H^* \int_0^{R_H^*} F(t)\mathrm{d}t}{\displaystyle\int_0^{R_L^*} F(t)\mathrm{d}t\,[U'(1-p) - \psi_L^*]}\frac{\delta}{(1-\delta)} = 1 \,. \tag{8.45}$$

Inserting $\delta = m$ and assuming that the solution is Pareto-efficient, it follows from (8.40) that

$$\frac{\dfrac{\partial W_L^*}{\partial B}}{\dfrac{\partial W_H^*}{\partial B}} = \frac{\psi_L^*}{\psi_H^*} = \frac{U'(x_L^*)}{\left(\dfrac{\displaystyle\int_{R_H^*}^{T} U'(z_H(t))F(t)dt}{\displaystyle\int_{R_H^*}^{T} F(t)dt}\right)} = 1. \tag{8.46}$$

Since $z_H(t) < (1-p)$, $\forall t \in [R_H^*, T]$, this would imply

$$\frac{U'(x_L^*)}{U'(1-p)} > \frac{U'(x_L^*)}{\left(\dfrac{\displaystyle\int_{R_H^*}^{T} U'(z_H(t))F(t)dt}{\displaystyle\int_{R_H^*}^{T} F(t)dt}\right)} = 1. \tag{8.47}$$

(8.47) can be contradicted by noting that $1-p < x_L^*$. Hence it is clear that arranging for transfers between consumer-types is intra-generational Pareto-dominant. $B_H^E < 0$, if $\delta = m$, then follows from the fact that (8.45) implies (8.34). Finally, (8.45) and (8.40) yield

$$\frac{\dfrac{\partial W_H^*}{\partial B}}{\dfrac{\partial W_L^*}{\partial B}} \frac{(1-m)}{m} \frac{\delta}{(1-\delta)} = 1, \tag{8.48}$$

if a retirement policy incorporating identical marginally fair benefit schedules should be Pareto-efficiency. Thus,

$$\frac{(1-m)}{m} \frac{\delta}{(1-\delta)} < 1 \Rightarrow m > \delta. \tag{8.49}$$

Q.E.D.

Of course, this proposition is particularly noteworthy, since reference policies are restricted to those which offer a single marginally fair benefit schedule. Hence, it explains why policies originally proposed to achieve this goal may be renegotiated to deviate from this rule. No intra-generational redistribution is optimal only if the policy-maker attaches a weight to L-type consumers' utility exceeding this consumer-type's relative frequency in the total population $(1-m)$. In other words, if the policy maker's preferences are such as to maximize the average lifetime utility in the population, L-types will subsidize H-types.

On first sight, the result seems to correspond to the respective finding in Nalebuff and Zeckhauser (1985). Yet, it can be verified that the previous research derives the conclusion from assuming a moral hazard problem associated with the fact that late retirees always prefer to retire earlier, if benefits are calculated actuarially fairly. In contrast, within the current framework this phenomenon can again be attributed solely to the liquidity constraints imposed. Underinsurance can be compensated to some extent by accumulating privately. On the other hand, overinsured individuals cannot transfer old-age income to the working life. Thus, H-type consumers are less affected by deviations from their welfare maximizing contribution than L-types. Consequently, L-type consumers' willingness to accept the payment of a positive transfer dominates the respective acceptance of further increases in the contribution. The latter would clearly induce additional deteriorations of the risk-shifting properties associated with the second-best policy for this consumer-type, which cannot be offset by decumulation during the working-life.

8.5.2   THE CASE OF 'VOLUNTARY PARTICIPATION'

The problem remains to motivate the restriction imposed on the search for optimal policies in Proposition 12. In general, it would only be necessary to define reservation utility levels — not necessarily by reference to an initial policy incorporating a single, marginally fair benefit schedule though. This would suffice to preclude the solutions $p^E = \tilde{p}_L$ and $B_L^E = -\infty$ for $\delta = 0$, or $p^E = \tilde{p}_H$ and $B_H^E = -\infty$ for $\delta = 1$, which would otherwise trivially solve (8.36) subject only to feasibility. Such solutions are clearly not politically implementable. One consumer-type would always be better off by not participating in the pension system at all.

Note that all (p^E, B_H^E, B_L^E)-combinations derived above involve mutual gains from intra-generational redistribution (for $\delta \in (0, 1)$) — if this in fact occurs. Since attention has been confined to reference policies with contributions $p^F \in (\tilde{p}_L, \tilde{p}_H)$, it is clear that

$$W_H^*(p^E, B_H^E) \geq W_H^*(\tilde{p}_L, 0) \qquad (8.50)$$

and

$$W_L^*(p^E, B_L^E) \geq W_L^*(\tilde{p}_H, 0) , \qquad (8.51)$$

with equality if, and only if, $\delta = 0$ and $\delta = 1$, respectively. Obviously, a violation of (8.50) ((8.51)) implies that type-H (type-L) individuals would prefer to set up their own insurance scheme — accepting whatever contribution is determined in the scheme designed exclusively for the respective other type and offering free entry. Thus, these inequalities can be associated with 'voluntary participation' in a single old-age insurance plan, given that all consumer-groups are in principle free to establish separate programs subject to the requirement that all old-insurances must levy the same contribution (rate). Focusing on (8.50) and (8.51) as defining reservation utility levels, it can in fact be shown that there exists a one-to-one correspondence between reference policies as utilized in Propositions 12 and 13 and particular choices of weights δ.

Proposition 14.   *Assume that the policy-maker's objective is to maximize (8.36) subject to (8.50), (8.51), and feasibility.*

(a) *Constraint (8.50) is binding, if, and only if, $\delta = 0$. Similarly, constraint (8.51) is binding, if, and only if, $\delta = 1$.*

(b) *If (8.41) and (8.42) imply $\mathrm{d}p^E/\mathrm{d}\delta > 0$ and $\mathrm{d}B_L^E/\mathrm{d}\delta > 0$, then:*

  (i) *There exists a unique value $\tilde{\delta} \in (0, m)$ such that the optimal contribution $p^E(\tilde{\delta}) \equiv \tilde{p}^F$ yields $B_L^E(\tilde{\delta}) = B_H^E(\tilde{\delta}) = 0$.*

  (ii) *Moreover, there exists $\delta_L < \tilde{\delta}$ such that $W_L^*(p^E, B_L^E) \geq W^*(\tilde{p}_L, 0)$ for weights within the range $[0, \delta_L]$, with strict inequality unless $\delta = \delta_L$.*

  (iii) *Similarly, one can find $\delta_H > \tilde{\delta}$ such that $W_H^*(p^E, B_H^E) \geq W_L^*(\tilde{p}_H, 0)$ for weights within the range $[\delta_H, 1]$, with strict inequality unless $\delta = \delta_H$.*

  (iv) *For weights in the range (δ_L, δ_H), $W_H^*(p^E, B_H^E) < W_H^*(\tilde{p}_H, 0)$ and $W_L^*(p^E, B_L^E) < W_L^*(\tilde{p}_L, 0)$.*

Sketch of proof.   First note that constraints (8.50) and (8.51) cannot both be binding at the same time. This is so, since there clearly exists a policy, with $p^F \in (\tilde{p}_L, \tilde{p}_H)$ and $B_L = B_H = 0$, which ensures that both consumer-types' expected lifetime utilities exceed the respective reservation utility levels. Next, suppose $\delta = 1$ and (8.51) non-binding. Investigating the first-order conditions of the optimization problem spelled out in the proposition reveals that $p^E(1) = \tilde{p}_H$ in this case. By virtue of the voluntary participation constraint it then follows that $B_H^E = B_L^E = 0$. Recalling Proposition 11, this cannot be optimal. Similarly, $\delta = 0$ necessarily implies that (8.50) must be binding. Yet, whenever (8.51) is binding $p^E(\delta) = p^E(1)$ and $B_L^E(\delta) = B_L^E(1)$. Differentiating the first-order conditions at $\delta = 1$, however, shows that the constraint cannot remain binding. Again, analyzing the respective other 'corner' solution completes the proof of Part (a). Further, $\delta = 1$ ($\delta = 0$) implies $W_H^*(p^E(1), B_H^E(1)) > W_H^*(\tilde{p}_H, 0)$ ($W_L^*(p^E(0), B_L^E(0)) > W_L^*(\tilde{p}_L, 0)$). Hence, $B_H^E(1) < 0$ and $B_L^E(0) < 0$. The assumed reactions of the optimal contribution and transfers to changes δ and Proposition 12 then suffice to prove Part (b) (i)–(iv).
Q.E.D.

The contract curve can now be illustrated as depicted in Figure 8.7. Here index '0' refers to the case with $\delta = 0$. The 'indifference' curve $\hat{I}_H^0$ represents the (p, B_L)-combinations such that $\hat{W}_H^*(p, B_L) = W_H^*(\tilde{p}_L, 0)$. Setting the weight $\delta = 0$ then implies that type-H consumers remain indifferent between the combinations $(\tilde{p}_L, 0)$ and $(p_0^E, B_{L,0}^E)$ which maximizes (8.36) subject to feasibility and participation of H-types. It can be seen that all contribution and transfer combinations which are

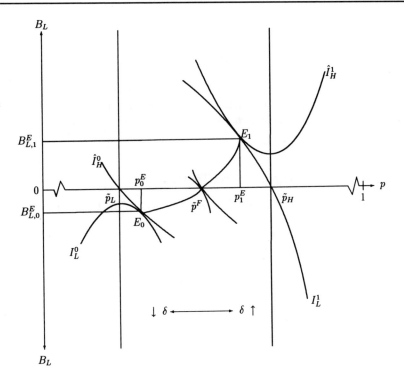

Figure 8.7 A possible contract curve

located to the right of I_L^0 involve utility losses of type-L consumers. Further, all combinations to the left of the $\hat{I}_H^0$ curve yield $W_H^*(p, B_L) < W_H^*(\tilde{p}_L, 0)$ and therefore violate the participation constraint. Similarly, indices '1' refer to the case with $\delta = 1$. Here $(p_1^E, B_{L,1}^E)$ maximizes (8.36) subject to feasibility and voluntary participation of L-types.

For $\delta \in (0, 1)$ the 'voluntary participation' constraints are not binding. Here welfare gains are always mutual — regardless of which consumer-type must finance the transfer. The line $\overline{E_0 E_1}$ thus characterizes the location of a possible contract curve. Its positive slope has been assumed in Part (b) of Proposition 13. Interestingly, type-H (type-L) consumers' welfare actually exceeds the respective best utility level for sufficiently high (low) values of δ. Hence, the second-best policy, which must be arranged for given the institutional constraint imposed, does not necessarily yield welfare losses for both consumer-types. This can be attributed to the fact that, as one consumer-type gains more political influence, the respective no-transfer solution becomes less attractive for the other consumer-type. In the extreme cases $\delta = 1$, or $\delta = 0$, the decisive consumer-type sells off its right to impose its welfare-maximizing contribution.

Hence, it should also be noted that, introducing (8.50) and (8.51), every point on the contract curve corresponds to the respective solution obtained under the conditions spelled out in Proposition 12. If $\delta = 1$ ($\delta = 0$) the reference policy generated by maximizing with respect to contributions — holding $B_k^E = 0$, for $k = H, L$ — is characterized by $p^F = \tilde{p}_H$ ($p^F = \tilde{p}_L$). For $\delta \in (0, 1)$, neither (8.50) nor (8.51) is binding. At the same time, the reference policy $(p^F, 0)$ — derived from the first-stage maximization problem in Proposition 12 — can be verified to impose no binding restrictions.

8.6   EFFICIENT BENEFIT 'SCHEDULES'

8.6.1   THE BENEFIT RULES UNDER SECOND-BEST POLICIES

The preceding sections have dealt with deriving efficient transfer systems, given that a common contribution rate must be agreed upon. Figures 8.8 and 8.9 illustrate how these results translate into the calculation of the respective efficient benefit/retirement age combinations. It should be recalled that it has been assumed that the consumer-type can be observed by the insurance agency. The retirement policy proposed in Section 8.2 thus offers two marginally fair benefit schedules. The consumers then choose their optimal retirement age and benefit level according to the schedule which has been assigned to their type.

Figure 8.8 depicts a situation in which the efficient policy entails $B_H^E < 0$. Hence, it corresponds to the case $\delta > \tilde{\delta}$ as defined in Proposition 14, for instance. The $\xi^M(p^E, 0)$-line represents a reference benefit schedule assuming the contribution is fixed at p^E. Thus, $R_k^*(p^E, 0)$, $k = H, L$, denote 'hypothetical' optimal retirement ages given the retirement policy would entail no intra-generational transfers. In contrast, the $\xi^M(p^E, B_k^E)$-curves depict the marginally fair benefit schedules for the two consumer-types accounting for the efficient transfer system. Thus, $R_k^*(p^E, B_k^E)$, $k = H, L$, refer to the actual optimal retirement ages induced by the efficient policy. It is clear that type-H consumers' welfare under this policy is higher than under the reference policy involving no transfers. The reverse holds for type-L individuals. This is illustrated by the fact that the indifference curve i_H^B lies above i_H^0 and i_L^B below i_H^0. The superscripts 'B' and '0' indicate utility levels associated with optimal retirement under the efficient policy and under the reference policy, respectively.

It follows from Proposition 2 that, regardless of the transfer systems, interior solutions to the individual optimization problems imply $x_H^*(p^E, B_H^E) < (1 - p^E) < x_L^*(p^E, B_L^E)$. Yet, it can clearly be seen that the deduction associated with earlier retirement is less than fair. Taking the benefit level $x_H^*(p^E, B_H^E)$ as a reference, for instance, H-types could receive a pension exceeding $x_L^*(p^E, B_L^E)$, if deciding to retire at age $R_L^*(p^E, B_L^E)$. Similarly, starting from $x_L^*(p^E, B_L^E)$ marginally fair deductions would require benefits lower than $x_H^*(p^E, B_H^E)$, if L-types would decide to retire at age $R_H^*(p^E, B_H^E)$.

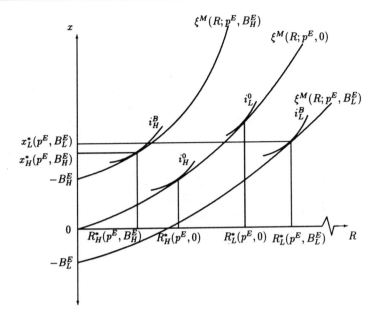

Figure 8.8   Optimal retirement with subsidized H-types

Next, consider the case where an efficient policy entails $B_L^E < 0$ — thus $\delta < \tilde{\delta}$ in Proposition 14, for example. Figure 8.9 shows the respective type-specific benefit schedules $\xi^M(R; p^E, B_k^E)$ and a reference schedule $\xi^M(R; p^E, 0)$ again. Optimal retirement of the two consumer-types under each of these benefit schedules is indicated by points of tangency with indifference curves again. In this case, type-L consumers, welfare, given optimal retirement under the benefit schedule $\xi^M(R; p^E, B_L^E)$, exceeds the welfare obtained given the reference schedule involving no transfers. The reverse obviously holds for type-H consumers. It can easily be seen now that late benefits seem better than fair here. Again, this is due to the implied intra-generational transfers.

The two figures thus illustrate that — observing only the realizations of optimal retirement dates and benefit levels under an efficient policy — the benefit rules seem to lack actuarial fairness. Yet, given the efficient transfers, the two schedules offered actually are marginally fair. However, only if the efficient policy yields identical benefit schedules — involving no intra-generational transfers — is the relationship between observed early and late benefits characterized by marginal fairness. This is illustrated in either Figure 8.8 or Figure 8.9, letting $\xi^M(R; p^E, 0)$ denote the actual efficient policy. Hence, the explanatory virtue of comparative static results derived within an 'induced retirement' approach — as in Chapter 7 and the bulk of related literature — can now be seen to be confined to a very specific situation.

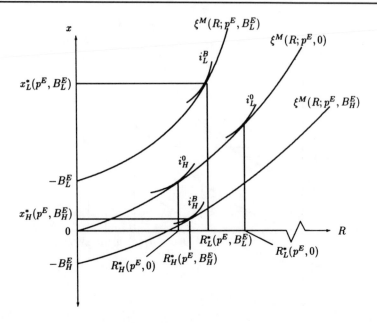

Figure 8.9 Optimal retirement with subsidized L-types

Two further points should be noted. First, taking a positive perspective, the transfer system defines intercepts $-B_k^E$, for $k = H, L$. As noted above, actual benefit schedules are usually characterized as involving a lack of marginal fairness by calculating actuarially fair deductions with respect to a common reference benefit level. In Table 7.1 this is the benefit level attainable at the 'normal' retirement age, for instance. If the system entails non-trivial intra-generational transfers, such comparisons can now be verified to be generally invalid. Rather, investigating deviations from marginal fairness it is necessary to calculate hypothetical marginal rates of transformation $MRT^{x,R}$ given the implied intra-generational transfers. Such calculations can proceed in three steps. (1) The expected present value of the total pension payments realized by the members of a cohort must be derived. (2) Given the distribution of actual retirement dates and the respective present values of realized benefit flows, it is possible to calculate the intra-generational transfers between consumer-types. (3) Finally, these transfers and information from life-tables can be used to derive the marginal rates of transformation at different retirement ages conditional on the transfer system. These calculated values are then to be compared with the realized pension flows.

A second remark—closely related, however—concerns the efficiency of the induced retirement decisions. Obviously, Proposition 8 cannot apply to the cases discussed here, since it has been assumed that there exists a single insurance agency which levies a common contribution (rate). Yet, the consumers' optimal retirement ages are efficient in the sense of Proposition 7. The institutional constraint imposes a limit (requirement) to use no more (no less) than a fraction p of labor income in order to obtain old-age insurance. Given this constraint and the efficient transfers both consumer-types cannot improve their well-being by choosing to retire earlier or later ensuring fiscal neutrality.

However, the retirement policies discussed so far crucially require the observability of consumer-types by the insurance agency. If this cannot be taken for granted, it is clear that, offered two different marginally fair benefit schedules, both consumer-types would opt for the subsidized benefit scheme. This always holds unless the schedules offered are identical. Enforceability therefore requires that the consumers must choose between the efficient (x_k^*, R_k^*)-combinations. Observable benefit schedules will therefore be specified such as to achieve a separation of consumer-types — hence, possibly also involving 'kinks' or 'steps'. However, such arrangements are still not necessarily incentive-compatible.

8.6.2   THE IMPACT OF ADDITIONAL MORAL HAZARD

Focusing on the efficient policies derived above, incentive compatibility further requires

$$V_H^*(p^E, R_H^*(p^E, B_H^E), x_H^*(p^E, B_H^E)) \geq V_H^*(p^E, R_L^*(p^E, B_L^E), x_L^*(p^E, B_L^E)) \quad (8.52)$$

and

$$V_L^*(p^E, R_L^*(p^E, B_L^E), x_L^*(p^E, B_L^E)) \geq V_L^*(p^E, R_H^*(p^E, B_H^E), x_H^*(p^E, B_H^E)).$$
$$(8.53)$$

Without explicit proof, it can easily be obtained that a necessary condition for (8.52) to be violated is $B_H^E > 0$. Turning back to Figure 8.8, the type-H consumers' indifference curve lies strictly above the $\xi^M(R; p^E, B_L^E)$-curve. Hence, subsidized H-types would never opt for the combination $(x_L^*(p^E, B_L^E), R_L^*(p^E, B_L^E))$. Similarly, if $B_L^E > 0$, it is only possible that (8.53) may be violated. Further, recalling that the optimal consumption paths only depend on the (p, R, x)-combinations, not on consumer-types, a simple addition of (8.52) and (8.53) reveals that $R_H^* > R_L^*$ is sufficient for the existence of a moral hazard problem. However, due to $x_L^* > 1 - p^E > x_H^*$, this can only occur when $B_L^E < 0$. Comparing Figures 8.8 and 8.9, it can generally be obtained that moral hazard is more likely to occur when the efficient policy requires a subsidization of L-types. Assuming $\partial R_k^*/\partial B > 0$ for both consumer-types the optimal retirement ages move closer together when L-types receive a positive transfer. As differences in the retirement ages vanish, the impact of the transfer system on the benefit levels becomes more important.

Yet, a possible moral hazard problem can obviously go either way, depending on the transfer to be received/paid. Clearly, if H-types are subsidized strongly, L-types may wish to obtain the benefits x_H^* at age R_H^* as well. Whether or not an incentive compatibility constraint turns out to be binding depends on the consumers' preference structure and the magnitude of the transfer. In the following the interest will therefore be confined to investigating the qualitative impact of existing moral hazard on the efficiency of the retirement decisions. Hence, consider the following 'representative' problem of determining an optimal policy:

$$\text{Max}_{p,\{x_k,R_k\}|_{k=H,L}} \delta V_H^*(p, x_H, R_H) + (1 - \delta)V_L^*(p, x_L, R_L). \tag{8.54}$$

Subject to the constraints

$$V_L^*(p, x_L, R_L) \geq W_L^*(p^F, 0) \tag{8.55}$$

$$V_H^*(p, x_H, R_H) \geq W_H^*(p^F, 0) \tag{8.56}$$

$$V_L^*(p, x_L, R_L) \geq V_L^*(p, x_H, R_H) \tag{8.57}$$

$$V_H^*(p, x_H, R_H) \geq V_H^*(p, x_L, R_L) \tag{8.58}$$

$$\left[m \int_0^{R_H} F(t)\mathrm{d}t + (1 - m) \int_0^{R_L} F(t)\mathrm{d}t \right] p$$

$$-m \int_{R_H}^T F(t)\mathrm{d}t \, x_H - (1 - m) \int_{R_L}^T F(t)\mathrm{d}t \, x_L \geq 0. \tag{8.59}$$

For simplicity, reservation utility levels are again defined by an exogenous no-transfer reference policy with contribution p^F. The following can now be shown:

Proposition 15.   *Recall the classifications of Definition 4. If (8.57) constitutes a binding restriction in the optimization problem (8.54)–(8.59), type-H consumers retire inefficiently early. The optimal retirement date specified for type-L consumers remains efficient. In contrast, if (8.58) is binding, type-L consumers retire inefficiently late. In this case, the optimal retirement date for type-H consumers is efficient.*

Sketch of proof.   Let the solution of optimization problem (8.54)–(8.59) be indicated by the superscript 'I'. It is easily seen that, if the incentive compatibility constraints are not binding, the solution can be characterized as discussed in the previous sections. Hence, it must be checked whether (8.52) and (8.53) are satisfied. Following the arguments above both constraints cannot be binding at the same time. Thus, Part (a) of Proposition 11 can be verified to constitute a necessary condition for (8.58) to be binding in the optimum. Similarly, the situation described by Part (c) of this proposition is necessary for (8.57) to be binding. The first-order conditions can then be rearranged to yield

$$U'(x_L^I)[p^I + x_L^I] + U(1 - p^I) - U(x_L^I) - G_L = \Gamma_H^I \frac{[G_L - G_H]U'(x_L^I)}{\Lambda^I(1 - m)} \tag{8.60}$$

$$\frac{\int_{R_H^I}^{T} U'(z(t; p^I, x_H^I, R_H^I)) F(t) dt}{\int_{R_H^I}^{T} F(t) dt} [p^I + x_H^I]$$

$$+ U'(z(R_H^I; p^I, x_H^I, R_H^I))[(1 - p^I) - x_H^I] - G_H =$$

$$\Gamma_L^I \frac{[G_H - G_L] \int_{R_H^I}^{T} U'(z(t; p^I, x_H^I, R_H^I)) F(t) dt}{\Lambda^I m \int_{R_H^I}^{T} F(t) dt}. \tag{8.61}$$

Here Γ_L^I, Γ_H^I, and Λ^I denote the optimal values of the multipliers associated with the incentive-compatibility constraints (8.57) and (8.58), and the budget constraint (8.59), respectively. Recalling the cases defined in Proposition 7 now confirms the assertion stated above.
Q.E.D.

The conclusion reported in this proposition hinges on the fact that the consumers' indifference curves i_k — depicted in Figures 8.8 and 8.9, for instance — exhibit a *single crossing property* (SCP)[8]. In particular,

$$MRS_H^{x,R}(p, x, R) > MRS_L^{x,R}(p, x, R), \forall (p, x, R) \tag{8.62}$$

for all identical $(\bar{p}, \bar{x}, \bar{R})$-combinations.

Hence, the incentive compatible choices of (x_k^I, R_k^I), $k = H, L$, must be characterized as illustrated in Figures 8.10 and 8.11, respectively. Consider the situation depicted in Figure 8.10, for example. Given the contribution p^I, the point of intersection of the $\xi^M(R; p^I, B_H^I)$ and the type-L consumers' indifference curve i_L^I identifies the incentive compatible (x_H, R_H)-combination. Benefit/retirement age offers to the left of this combination — such as the one indicated by point A — are incentive-compatible, but yield a lower expected lifetime utility for H-types as well. On the other hand, combinations such as those indicated by points B and C are preferred by type-L consumers and, thus, are not incentive-compatible. Clearly, a second feasible and incentive-compatible offer exists. It must be located to the right of point C, however. Such benefit/retirement age combinations yield a lower expected lifetime utility for H-types than (x_H^I, R_H^I). Given (x_H^I, R_H^I) the slope of the type-H consumers' indifference curve i_H^I is flatter than the slope of the benefit schedule. Hence,

$$MRS_H^{x,R}(p^I, x_H^I, R_H^I) < MRT_H^{x,R}(p^I, x_H^I, R_H^I) \tag{8.63}$$

---

[8]Compare Nalebuff and Zeckhauser (1985), again.

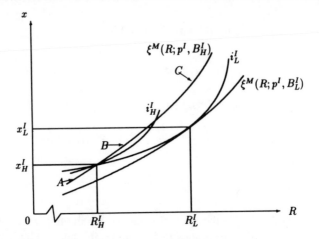

Figure 8.10   Incentive compatibility with subsidized H-types

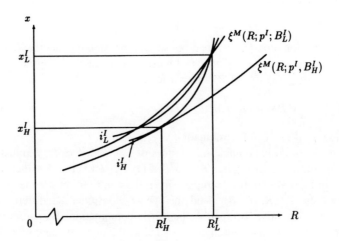

Figure 8.11   Incentive compatibility with subsidized L-types

$$\Longleftarrow$$

$$\frac{\displaystyle\int_{R_H^I}^{T} U'(z(t; p^I, x_H^I, R_H^I)) F(t)\,\mathrm{d}t}{\displaystyle\int_{R_H^I}^{T} F(t)\,\mathrm{d}t}[p^I + x_H^I]$$

$$+U'(z(R_H^I; p^I, x_H^I, R_H^I))[(1 - p^I) - x_H^I] > G_H \qquad (8.64)$$

as stated in the proposition.

On the other hand, if the optimal policy entails a subsidization of L-types and induces a moral hazard problem as illustrated in Figure 8.11, the incentive-compatible (x_L^I, R_L^I)-combination satisfies

$$MRS_L^{x,R}\left(p^I, x_L^I, R_L^I\right) > MRT_L^{x,R}\left(p^I, x_L^I, R_L^I\right) . \tag{8.65}$$

This can be rearranged to confirm that L-types retire inefficiently late in the sense of Definition 4. Thus, the inefficiencies generated due to an existing moral hazard problem can be interpreted as follows: Type-H (type-L) consumers' welfare could *ceteris paribus* be increased by marginally raising (lowering) the retirement age, if there were no incentive problem involved. Although the inefficiencies reported can be classified as in Definition 4, the interpretation is dramatically different. In the present context, establishing additional capital-funded accounts does not suffice to remove the labor supply inefficiencies. In fact, the optimal policy only achieves a separation of consumer-types by tying certain benefit flows to particular retirement ages chosen. Unless the information structure is altered — if the agency possesses some *ex-ante* information allowing for a classification of consumer-types, for instance — effective moral hazard must always be associated with *ex-post* inefficiencies. Nevertheless, considering survey responses, individuals who retire inefficiently early would indicate their preference for prolonged work, if offered hypothetical actuarially fair adjustments in the attainable pensions.

Moreover, the first-order conditions of the optimization problem (8.54)–(8.59) can always be rearranged to yield

$$-m\int_{R_H^I}^{T} F(t)\mathrm{d}t \left[\frac{\int_0^{R_H^I} U'(z(t; p^I, x_H^I, R_H^I))F(t)\mathrm{d}t}{\int_{R_H^I}^{T} U'(z(t; p^I, x_H^I, R_H^I))F(t)\mathrm{d}t} - \frac{\int_0^{R_H^I} F(t)\mathrm{d}t}{\int_{R_H^I}^{T} F(t)\mathrm{d}t} \right]$$

$$= (1-m)\int_0^{R_L^I} F(t)\mathrm{d}t \left[\frac{U'(1-p^I)}{U'(x_L^I)} - 1 \right]. \tag{8.66}$$

This condition is identically equal to (8.40) above, if, and only if, the incentive-compatibility constraints are not binding. Thus, existing moral hazard also induces deviations from the efficient contribution/transfer system derived under perfect information. The interpretation of (8.66) is very similar, however: holding retirement ages constant at (R_H^I, R_L^I), type-H (type-L) consumers' welfare cannot be improved further by increasing (decreasing) p^I and decreasing (increasing) B_L^I, without either violating feasibility, or lowering type-L (type-H) consumers' welfare. Obviously, the optimal policy remains intra-generational Pareto-efficient. Since this must be associated with changes in the contribution/transfer system, direct comparisons between the realized optimal retirement ages under perfect information and those assuming an existing moral hazard problem cannot be drawn. It is only true that $R_H^I < R_H^*(p^I, B_H^I)$, if (8.58) is binding. Similarly, $R_L^I > R_L^*(p^I, B_L^I)$.

8.7   SUMMARY

Picking up the discussion of the preceding section, it should be noted that the possible existence of a moral hazard problem actually hinges on the fact that common contribution (rates) induce second-best solutions with intra-generational transfers. This is best illustrated by considering the following example: Suppose that the population under consideration is originally homogeneous. Then Proposition 8 applies and a contribution rate levied will be defined accordingly. Now, assume that preferences change such that H- and L-type consumers can be distinguished, but consumer-types can opt for insurance policies with different contribution requirements. Efficient policies would in this case always define contributions $\tilde{p}_k$, for $k = H, L$. Given that the policy-makers preferences do not induce transfers from one consumer-type to the other, offering two marginally fair benefit schedules $\xi^M(R; \tilde{p}_k, 0)$ can easily be verified to be incentive-compatible. This can be contrasted with the results obtained in Proposition 13. Here reference policies are defined which initially do not involve transfers. These policies must balance the welfare losses associated with necessarily second-best insurance arrangements. However, intra-generational efficient policies normally entail some redistribution between consumer-types. Moral hazard therefore only arises as a possible consequence of efficient redistributions.

Primarily, the preceding analysis highlights, however, that intra-generational redistribution can occur due to the fact that policies incorporating a common contribution (rate) are second-best. Hence, it untangles the effects of efficient redistribution and moral hazard. Further, the resulting common benefit rules have been noted to lack actuarial fairness. The implementability of the policies may also require discontinuities in the benefit schedule and/or the use of eligibility rules. Realized benefits always appear to lack actuarial fairness when an efficient policy entails non-trivial transfers. Three basic settings have been distinguished in an attempt to formulate optimal policies:

(1) Given an arbitrarily chosen reference policy characterized by a particular contribution and incorporating a single marginally fair benefit schedule, intra-generational transfers may be welfare enhancing. In turn, realigning an efficient benefit system to restore actuarial fairness, while maintaining the contribution, yields welfare losses for one consumer-type. Weights expressing the policy-maker's preferences for consumer-types do not determine the direction of the transfers here. Rather, they only govern the distribution of the welfare benefits associated with deviating from the reference policy — hence, the magnitudes of the transfers and changes in the contribution.

(2) The reference policy has also been derived as an optimal choice among the set of policies with common contributions and offering single marginally fair benefit schedules. In a second step the optimal policy is then found allowing for additional transfer/contribution trade-offs. In this case it is interesting to note that, if the weights attached to the type-specific expected lifetime

utilities equal the relative frequencies of the consumer-types in the population, this reference policy can always be Pareto-dominated by subsidizing the consumer-type which experiences a high disutility of labor. Consequently, early benefits appear better than fair in the optimal policy.

(3) Finally, the policy-makers have been assumed to maximize a weighted average of type-specific lifetime utilities subject to voluntary participation constraints. Here the main problem is to define the respective reservation utility levels. A particular case has been identified such that the contract curve obtained corresponds to solutions of the two-step problem described above. Again this specification of the participation constraints ensures that the transfer system reflects mutual gains for the two consumer-types.

The preceding analysis has therefore demonstrated quite clearly that deviations from actuarial fairness in the calculation of pensions can be viewed as a natural by-product of such second-best insurance policies. On the other hand, if the consumers are allowed to opt for individually different contributions, the best policy is implementable by inducing the self-selection of consumer-types over a menu of old-age insurances. Thus, the non-observability of consumer-types alone is not 'responsible' for the effects discussed above. In contrast, the analysis will now turn to an approach which relates the observed deviations from marginal fairness directly to an existing moral hazard problem.

CHAPTER 9

Adverse selection and benefit rules

9.1 MOTIVATION

Whereas the previous chapter focused on differences in the instantaneous preference structure, while maintaining identical survival risks, the analysis now turns to models in which consumer heterogeneity is solely manifested in differing survival probability functions. With perfect and public information concerning an individual's risk-classification, intra-generational efficient policies always entail an identical contribution and benefit flow for all consumer-types. Only the retirement ages depend on the survival risk and intra-generational transfers. In particular, with no *a priori* transfers, 'good' risk-types retire earlier than 'bad' risk individuals. Hence, this best policy is not implementable under private information of the consumers with respect to their survival risk. 'Bad' risk consumers would always claim to constitute 'good' risks in order to benefit from the early retirement option.

The analysis pursued in the following suggests that this 'adverse selection' problem is overcome by designing benefit/retirement age combinations which induce a self-selection of consumer-types. Whereas under best conditions intra-generational transfers raise one consumer-type's expected lifetime utility at the expense of another type, private information is seen to introduce a possibility for a mutually welfare-enhancing transfer system. This obviously contrasts sharply with the results obtained in the preceding chapter. Regardless of whether a non-trivial efficient transfer system exists, however, adverse selection always induces seemingly actuarially unfair benefit rules. Self-selection must be achieved by specifying pensions which increase with the retirement age chosen. Yet, since the order of retirement is not reversed, 'good' risk-types still retire earlier than 'bad' risks. Early benefits thus appear to be better than fair, utilizing the average survival risk in the cohort as a point of reference.

Following the work of Pauly (1974), Rothschild and Stiglitz (1976), Wilson (1977), and Leland (1978), adverse selection arguments have been applied to old-age insurance problems before. Eckstein, Eichenbaum, and Peled (1985a) and Eichenbaum and Peled (1987) focus on competitive annuity markets. Here the self-selection of consumers is achieved via offering different premium/benefit combinations. Implicitly, it is therefore assumed that all consumers retire at the same date. As argued before, neither social security nor private pension plans offer choices with respect to contributions, however. At the same time, flexible retirement age allowances constitute a very common feature. Moreover, within the current framework, requiring an identical contribution does not impose a binding constraint on the design of best policies. Hence, differences in the retirement ages chosen in fact give rise to the existence of an adverse selection problem here. Townley and Boadway (1988) analyze markets for term-insured annuities. Self-selection is achieved by varying the amount of wealth invested in purchasing the annuity and the pay-out period. Again, social security and private pension plans generally require a common contribution payable over the entire length of an individual's working-life, rather than a one-time investment of wealth accumulated privately. Further, although private pension plans sometimes entail the option to choose a one-time pay-out instead of receiving an annuity flow, the dominant form of varying the term of insurance coverage is generally associated with offering choices with respect to the retirement age. Thus, attainable pension flows are again tied to particular lifetime labor supply decisions.

While these stylized facts obviously do not render the previous research invalid, they clearly motivate the analysis of flexible retirement age programs in the light of possibly existing adverse selection. Interestingly, however, all of the work noted above[1] assumes that a compulsory social security system is not subject to adverse selection. Given the institutional constraint of requiring a common contribution rate, this in fact appears to be plausible, when self-selection must be achieved via variations of premium/benefit combinations. Townley and Boadway (1988) add an explicit analysis of the goals pursued by the social security agency by considering social welfare functions. It is shown that there exist particular functions implying that social welfare is maximized by pooling individuals under a single offer. Thus, adverse selection does not hinder the implementation of the socially optimal policy in these cases. Yet, if a flexible retirement age program exists and informed consumers choose their retirement age according to their survival risk, then maintaining feasibility always implies that policy-makers must be aware of adverse selection, when designing the benefit rules. Thus, the main question — only to be addressed on empirical grounds, however — remains whether it is plausible to assume that consumers possess private information concerning their survival risk.

Although generally supporting this hypothesis, Nalebuff and Zeckhauser (1985) are careful to state that 'individuals are not likely to have substantial information about their life-expectancies early in life, at the time pension benefits start to be accrued'. This qualification obviously applies to the present study as well. Hence, focusing on *ex-ante* efficient benefit rules in the following, mainly intends to keep the analysis simple and traceable again. This exercise appears to be worth pursuing, since the framework can be seen to provide an interesting alternative

---

[1] This also applies to Abel (1986).

view of seemingly unfair benefit rules[2]. Implicitly, Hammermesh (1985) provides some empirical support for the private information assumption. The study reports that individuals utilize information about their family background, personal health history, and health-related consumption behavior in order to estimate their survival risk, relative to the general development of longevity in society. In particular, the consumers seem to be well aware of the adverse effect of a 'smoking' habit on life-expectancies, for instance. This information is not available for an insurance agency.

More directly, but again focusing on private annuity markets, Friedman and Warshawsky (1988, 1990) find support for the adverse selection approach. The prices for annuities actually traded are shown to be calculated actuarially fairly for consumer groups exhibiting significantly higher than average survival risks. Thus, the research supports the hypothesis of market failure due to adverse selection. Moreover, Wolfe (1983) specifically addresses the issue of self-selection via choices of the retirement age directly. In a first step, the study presents actuarial calculations demonstrating that the early retirement benefits in the US OASDI system provide a maximum discounted lifetime pension flow, if the consumer dies before a threshold age is reached. This suggests that, if the individuals base their retirement decision on life-cycle considerations, those with low remaining life-expectancies should retire earlier. A second step then shows that actual mortality differences between consumer-groups can be predicted very well utilizing the information about individual retirement decisions. The author concludes that 'adverse selection [...] is probably a more important element in life-cycle decision-making than has been previously recognized'. While this strongly supports the current approach, Wolfe's theoretical model is restricted to consumers maximizing their expected lifetime income. Consequently, the qualitative results obtained are rather limited in focus here.

Further, as discussed in Section 4.3, there exists strong evidence that health deficits perceived by the individuals are associated with earlier retirement. Here the standard approach has been to analyze benefit rules as providing some implicit health insurance. Yet, an individual's personal health history can also be viewed as generating information about longevity. Even maintaining the assumption that the instantaneous preferences are unaffected by health-related events, the consumers will then use this information to form expectations concerning their remaining life-expectancy and choose their retirement age accordingly. Unless the health-status is directly associated with the entitlement for early retirement and the consumers must therefore document 'poor health', the old-age insurance agency does not possess this information. This corresponds to Packard and Reno (1988) again, who show that a large fraction of individuals with self-reported 'poor health' do not claim disability benefits. Nevertheless, these consumers may possess private information

---

[2]Nevertheless, introducing the possibility of learning about the survival risk — as recently proposed by Brugiavini (1993) — and updating the retirement plans accordingly, may open interesting new perspectives.

concerning their survival risk influencing their retirement decision within a general variable retirement scheme.

A first application of the adverse selection argument to retirement issues can again be found in Nalebuff and Zeckhauser (1985). As noted before, however, this study does not distinguish the effects of differences in the instantaneous preference structure and the survival risk. Thus, the current approach can be verified to contribute by isolating these different aspects. Interestingly, both Wolfe (1983) and Nalebuff and Zeckhauser (1985) associate lower survival risks with existing health deficits. In a second step, it will therefore be assumed that the insurance agency can observe some aspects associated with a consumer's health status. It can be shown that, if the observed health status provides an informative, but imperfect, signal with respect to a consumer's risk-classification, the model is capable of generating co-existing health-related variable retirement programs. Thus, Boskin's (1977) argument that, due to improvements in the overall health condition of the population, the increased use of disability programs can only be explained by the 'generosity' of the benefits provided in such schemes, cannot be shared in this context. Rather, once it is accepted that flexible retirement plans face adverse selection problems, the value of health-contingent schemes depends on the additional information about longevity revealed by observing a particular health status.

9.2   INTRODUCING THE ANALYSIS

9.2.1   A BASIC SETTING

In order to concentrate on the fundamental arguments, the model presented in the following will be kept very simple again. Particularly, there exist only two risk-classes in the population under consideration, identified by subscripts 'b' and 'g'. Type-g individuals exhibit a comparative advantage in accumulating pension claims. Recalling the discussion of Section 7.2, the impact of different survival probability functions on the attainable pension flow, given a contribution, cannot be determined unambiguously. To begin with, it will therefore be *assumed* that

$$\frac{F_g(R)}{\int_R^T F_g(t)\mathrm{d}t} > \frac{F_b(R)}{\int_R^T F_b(t)\mathrm{d}t}, \ \forall \ R \in (0, T) . \tag{9.1}$$

Defining[3]

$$\xi_k^M(R; p, 0) \equiv \frac{\int_0^R F_k(t)\mathrm{d}t \ p}{\int_R^T F_k(t)\mathrm{d}t} , k = g, b , \tag{9.2}$$

---

[3]For convenience, labor income equals unity and the interest rate is set equal to zero again.

this implies

$$MRT_g^{x,R}\left(\bar{p}, \bar{R}, \bar{x}\right) > MRT_b^{x,R}\left(\bar{p}, \bar{R}, \bar{x}\right), \qquad (9.3)$$

for a given combination $(\bar{p}, \bar{R}, \bar{x})$. Here ξ_k^M, $k = g, b$, as usual refers to marginally fair benefit schedules designed separately for the two consumer-types. By virtue of (9.1) type-g individuals obtain larger pension increments when delaying their retirement decisions. Given a contribution (rate) and assuming no intra-generational transfers, they can therefore attain a more favorable pension flow at every retirement age chosen. Of course, this corresponds to the classification of individual-types as 'good' and 'bad' risks from the point of view of the insurance agency. For stylized survival probability functions $F(t) = (1 - (t/T))^{\zeta_k}$ — as introduced before — (9.1) can easily be verified to hold for $\zeta_g > \zeta_b$. Thus, following the standard intuition 'good' risk consumers are characterized by lower survival probabilities in this case.

Obviously, it is maintained that all individuals are characterized by an identical maximum life-span T. It should also be noted that date 0 is not necessarily associated with the actual date of entrance to the labor market. Rather, it represents a date at which the consumers possess accurate information concerning their risk classification. The expected lifetime utility, assuming that the individuals choose an optimal consumption path, can then be obtained as

$$V_k^* = \beta(p, R, x)L_{S,k}^*(p, R, x) + [1 - \beta(p, R, x)]L_{NS,k}^*(p, R, x) - G \int_0^R F_k(t)\mathrm{d}t ,$$
$$(9.4)$$

with

$$L_{S,k}^*(p, R, x) = \int_0^T U(z_k(t; p, R, x))F_k(t)\mathrm{d}t , \qquad (9.5)$$

and

$$L_{NS,k}^*(p, R, x) = \int_0^R F_k(t)\mathrm{d}t\, U(1 - p) + \int_R^T F_k(t)\mathrm{d}t\, U(x) , \qquad (9.6)$$

for $k = g, b$. Thus, the instantaneous utility functions are identical for the two consumer-types. This allows isolation of the effects which stem from the assumption of different survival probability functions. As before, accumulation regimes are determined by the replacement rate — $\beta = 1$ ($\beta = 0$), if $(1 - p) > x$ $((1 - p) \leq x)$. However, in contrast to the model presented in the preceding chapter, the optimal consumption path is not identical for the two consumer-types when the replacement rate exceeds unity.

The marginal rates of substitution between pensions x and retirement ages R exhibit a *single crossing property* (SCP) again. For the accumulation regime with replacement rates greater or equal to unity, (9.1) suffices to state

$$MRS_g^{x,R}(\bar{p}, \bar{R}, \bar{x}|\beta = 0) > MRS_b^{x,R}(\bar{p}, \bar{R}, \bar{x}|\beta = 0) , \qquad (9.7)$$

where $(\bar{p}, \bar{R}, \bar{x})$ denotes an arbitrary combination with $(1 - \bar{p}) \leq \bar{x}$. As shown in the Appendix to Chapter 5 and stressed again in Section 7.2, (9.1) is insufficient to determine such properties of indifference curves within the accumulation regime characterized by $(1 - p) > x$. Here there exist second-order effects on the optimal consumption paths, which generally obscure the possibility of deriving clearcut conclusions concerning the slopes of indifference curves. For this regime it will therefore be *assumed* that

$$MRS_g^{x,R}(\bar{p}, \bar{R}, \bar{x}|\beta = 1) > MRS_b^{x,R}(\bar{p}, \bar{R}, \bar{x}|\beta = 1) . \qquad (9.8)$$

These additional assumptions characterize a basic setting which serves well to illustrate the qualitative aspects of adverse selection. Although they appear to be rather restrictive, it should be noted that (9.1) only ensures that the situation of comparative advantage can be identified unambiguously for all retirement ages chosen. Further, the SCP-assumption will be seen to simplify the analysis considerably[4]. Together these qualifications ensure that the standard adverse selection model discussed in the literature can be applied.

9.2.2   BEST WITH OBSERVABLE CONSUMER-TYPES

As before, let

$$B_k \equiv \int_0^{R_k} F_k(t)\mathrm{d}t\ p - \int_{R_k}^T F_k(t)\mathrm{d}t\ x_k , \qquad (9.9)$$

for $k = g, b$. Consequently, feasibility is again assumed to require

$$B \equiv [\mu \int_0^{R_g} F_g(t)\mathrm{d}t + (1 - \mu) \int_0^{R_b} F_b(t)\mathrm{d}t]p$$

$$-\mu \int_{R_g}^T F_g(t)\mathrm{d}t\ x_g - (1 - \mu) \int_{R_b}^T F_b(t)\mathrm{d}t\ x_b \geq 0 , \qquad (9.10)$$

where μ $((1 - \mu))$ refers to the fraction of type-g (type-b) individuals in the cohort under consideration. As a point of reference, assume first that consumer-types are publicly observable. Then it is rather easily shown that:

(1)   Requiring a common contribution in the insurance system does not distort the possibility of inducing efficient lifetime allocations in the sense of Proposition 8 by specifying an adequate retirement policy.

(2)   Consequently, there exists no mutually beneficial transfer system, with $B_k \neq 0$, if the contribution is specified so as to allow for efficient lifetime allocations.

---

[4]Cooper (1984) provides a detailed discussion of the assumption that the consumers' preferences can be ordered as proposed above.

Since all necessary arguments have been provided before, formal proofs of these statements can be omitted. Recall only that — since the instantaneous preference structure is identical for the two consumer-types — efficient lifetime allocations can be induced by specifying the contribution to equal $\tilde{p}$, with $U'(1 - \tilde{p}) = G$. Then define two marginally fair benefit schedules

$$\xi_k^M (R; \tilde{p}, B_k) \equiv \frac{-B_k + \int_0^R F_k(t)\mathrm{d}t\ \tilde{p}}{\int_R^T F_k(t)\mathrm{d}t} . \tag{9.11}$$

With observable consumer-types, it is possible to assign consumers to either of the two schedules — depending on their risk-classification. The resulting induced, optimal benefit level equals $x_k^*(\tilde{p}, B_k) = \tilde{x}$, while the retirement ages chosen satisfy $R_k^*(\tilde{p}, B_k) = \tilde{R}_k(B_k)$, and are defined by the equations

$$H(G) = \tilde{x} = \frac{\int_0^{\tilde{R}_k(B_k)} F_k(t)\mathrm{d}t}{\int_0^T F_k(t)\mathrm{d}t} - \frac{B_k}{\int_0^T F_k(t)\mathrm{d}t} , \tag{9.12}$$

for $k = g, b$. Interior solutions can be ensured for $B_k = 0$ and G sufficiently large[5]. Hence, let $\tilde{W}_k(B_k) = V_k^*(\tilde{p}, \tilde{x}, \tilde{R}_k(B_k))$. Note that (9.12) implies

$$\frac{\partial \tilde{R}_k(B_k)}{\partial B_k} = \frac{1}{F_k(\tilde{R}_k(B_k))} . \tag{9.13}$$

Thus,

$$\frac{\partial \tilde{W}_k(B_k)}{\partial B_k} = -G F_k(\tilde{R}_k(B_k)) \frac{\partial \tilde{R}_k(B_k)}{\partial B_k} = -G . \tag{9.14}$$

This demonstrates that transfers from one consumer-type to the other cannot be mutually welfare-enhancing under symmetric — and public — information, if instantaneous preferences are identical. For $p = \tilde{p}$, Figure 9.1 illustrates the benchmark situation with $B_k = 0$. Due to (9.1) type-g consumers' benefit schedule is always steeper than the respective schedule specified for type-b individuals. Consequently, $\tilde{R}_g(0) < \tilde{R}_b(0)$, reflecting type-$g$ consumers' comparative advantage in accumulating pension claims. Any increase in B_g and corresponding, fiscally neutral, decrease in B_b will shift the $\xi_g^M(R; \tilde{p}, B_g)$-curve ($\xi_b^M(R; \tilde{p}, B_b)$-curve) to the right (left). Thus, $\tilde{R}_g(B_g)$ ($\tilde{R}_b(B_b)$) increases (decreases). Moreover, since — given any transfer system (B_g, B_b) — both consumer-types can still realize the consumption

---

[5] Again, it must be guaranteed that (9.12) can be realized for $\tilde{R}_k < T$ and requires $\tilde{R}_k > 0$.

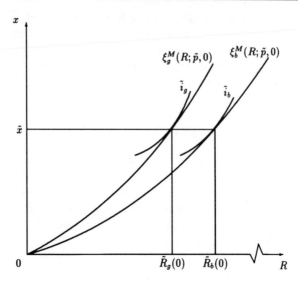

Figure 9.1   First-best policy with no transfers

path $z_k(t) = \tilde{z}$, $\forall\, t \in [0, T]$, as derived in Proposition 8, it is obvious that in the present case there exists no welfare-preserving trade-off between contributions and transfers incurred by each consumer-type — unless the contribution is arbitrarily specified to deviate from $\tilde{p}$. However, if this should be the case, both individual types would agree to adjust to $\tilde{p}$ — maintaining the existing transfer system.

Figure 9.1 also illustrates that best policies incorporating no *a priori* transfers are not implementable, when the consumers possess private information concerning their risk-classification. In order to be able to benefit from earlier retirement, type-b consumers would always claim to be of type g. In contrast to the model presented in the previous chapter, the moral hazard problem is generally not associated with the fact that this best allocation is induced utilizing a particular retirement policy — namely offering two marginally fair benefit schedules and a free choice of the pension age. Rather, it always arises when the insurance agency attempts to implement the corresponding best allocation.

Although $B_k = 0$, for $k = g, b$, has been shown to be intra-generational Pareto-efficient under complete information, the question of determining a socially optimal policy is rather problematic within the current framework. By virtue of (9.14) maximizing a social welfare function calculated as a weighted sum of the type-specific lifetime utilities does not sensibly determine an optimal transfer system here[6].

---

[6]This notion of a social optimum constitutes one of the possible concepts proposed by Townley and Boadway (1988) in a related context, for instance. However, it should be noted that this problem of determining a socially optimal best policy also applies to the case of the preceding section, when the policy allows one to opt for contribution rates.

Yet, accepting that an optimal policy must satisfy 'voluntary participation' of both consumer-types — as argued before — clearly identifies $B_k = 0$ as the sole candidate for an optimal policy here. Again, 'voluntary participation' can be defined by reference to the restriction that no consumer-type would prefer to establish a separate, feasible insurance scheme, maintaining the contribution and allowing for free entry assigning different offers to each observable consumer-type. Throughout the remaining parts of this analysis, an optimal policy will consequently be assumed to choose a common contribution p and two offers $\{(x_k, R_k)\}$, such as to maximize

$$V_g^*(p, x_g, R_g) \, , \tag{9.15}$$

subject to

$$V_b^*(p, x_b, R_b) \geq \widetilde{W}_b(0) \, , \tag{9.16}$$

$$V_k^*(p, x_k, R_k) \geq V_k^*(p, x_l, R_l) \, , \quad k, l = g, b \, , \tag{9.17}$$

and feasibility expressed by (9.10).

Here (9.17) reflects the need to design incentive-compatible benefit rules, assuming that the individuals possess private information concerning their risk-classification. The constraints ensure a self-selection of consumer-types over the type-specific offers $\{(x_k, R_k)\}$. Moreover, if the consumer-types were publicly observable and the necessity to induce self-selection could therefore be ignored, maximizing (9.15), subject only to (9.16) and (9.10), yields the benchmark case $B_g = B_b = 0$. Thus, the individuals attain the best expected utility $\widetilde{W}_k(0)$. Hence, defining the optimality of a retirement policy as proposed above, again reflects the intention to isolate the impact of the asymmetric information assumption on the design of benefit rules. In particular, if a non-trivial transfer system arises under asymmetric information, this must be mutually welfare enhancing.

9.3   OPTIMAL POLICIES UNDER ADVERSE SELECTION

9.3.1   SELF-SELECTION WITHOUT TRANSFERS

The analysis to follow has been decomposed into three steps. To begin with, the contribution will be exogenously fixed at $\tilde{p}$. This section will then focus on the case in which no additional transfer system arises. It will serve as a reference case for the discussion concerning the possible existence of welfare-enhancing transfers to be pursued in the subsequent section. In a final step, the optimal contribution will then be determined as well.

Proposition 16.   *Consider an optimal policy with contribution $\tilde{p}$ and offers $\{(x_k^I, R_k^I)\}$. Then (9.17) does not impose a binding constraint for type-g consumers. Assuming (9.16) is binding in the optimum, $B_k^I = 0$, for $k = g, b$. Further, $x_b^I = \tilde{x}$,*

$R_b^I = \tilde{R}_b(0)$, $x_g^I < \tilde{x}$, and $R_g^I < \tilde{R}_g(0)$. *Hence, type-g consumers are under-insured* $((1 - \tilde{p}) > x_g^I)$ *and save privately in addition to accumulating insurance claims. Moreover, this consumer-type's lifetime labor supply decision entails inefficient early retirement in the sense of Definition 4.*

Proof.   From the discussion above, it is clear that at least one of the incentive-compatibility constraints (9.17) must be binding. Thus, suppose both constraints would be binding — implying that both consumer-types are indifferent between the combinations (x_g^I, R_g^I) and (x_b^I, R_b^I). Feasibility guarantees that the funds accumulated are greater than or equal to the expected value of the pension flows paid out. In the optimum (9.10) must be binding. Assuming that both consumer-types are indifferent between offers, this implies that the respective pension/retirement age combinations must be identical. Otherwise it would always be possible to relax the budget constraint by reassigning consumer-types to different offers. Investigating the first-order conditions, assuming that all consumers receive identical pensions and retire at a common age R^I, reveals that in this case the marginal rates of substitution $MRS_k^{x,R}(\tilde{p}, x^I, R^I)$ would have to be equalized between the consumer-types. This contradicts the SCP-assumptions made in (9.7) and (9.8) above and establishes that both constraints cannot be binding at the same time. In a second step, it is then rather easily shown that (9.17) must constitute a binding constraint for type-b individuals in the optimum.

Consequently, the first order-conditions can be obtained as

$$\frac{\partial V_g^*(x_g^I, R_g^I, \tilde{p})}{\partial x} - \Lambda^I \mu \int_{R_g^I}^{T} F_g(t)\mathrm{d}t = \Phi^I \frac{\partial V_b^*(x_g^I, R_g^I, \tilde{p})}{\partial x} \tag{9.18}$$

$$[\Psi^I + \Phi^I]\frac{\partial V_b^*(x_g^I, R_g^I, \tilde{p})}{\partial x} - \Lambda^I(1 - \mu) \int_{R^I}^{T} F_b(t)\mathrm{d}t = 0 \tag{9.19}$$

$$\frac{\partial V_g^*(x_g^I, R_g^I, \tilde{p})}{\partial R} + \Lambda^I \mu F_g(R_g^I)[\tilde{p} + x_g^I] = \Phi^I \frac{\partial V_b^*(x_g^I, R_g^I, \tilde{p})}{\partial R} \tag{9.20}$$

$$[\Psi^I + \Phi^I]\frac{\partial V_b^*(x_g^I, R_g^I, \tilde{p})}{\partial R} + \Lambda^I(1 - \mu)F_b(R_b^I)[\tilde{p} + x_b^I] = 0. \tag{9.21}$$

Here Λ^I, Ψ^I, and Φ^I —all non-negative—denote the optimal values of the multipliers associated with constraints (9.10), (9.16), and (9.17), respectively[7].

Investigating conditions (9.19) and (9.21) reveals that

$$MRS_b^{x,R}\left(\tilde{p}, x_b^I, R_b^I\right) = MRT_b^{x,R}\left(\tilde{p}, x_b^I, R_b^I\right). \tag{9.22}$$

---

[7]Following the arguments above, the multiplier, associated with the constraint that offers must be incentive-compatible for g-types as well, has been set equal to zero.

Recalling Proposition 2, this can only be satisfied for $x_b^I = \tilde{x}$. If (9.16) is binding — as stated in the Proposition — it can now be seen that $B_g^I = B_b^I = 0$. Rearranging conditions (9.18) and (9.20), it follows that:

$$MRS_g^{x,R}\left(\tilde{p}, x_g^I, R_g^I\right) - MRT_g^{x,R}\left(\tilde{p}, x_g^I, R_g^I\right)$$

$$= \frac{\Phi^I \dfrac{\partial V_b^*(x_g^I, R_g^I, \tilde{p})}{\partial x}}{\dfrac{\partial V_g^*(x_g^I, R_g^I, \tilde{p})}{\partial x}} \left[MRS_b^{x,R}\left(\tilde{p}, x_g^I, R_g^I\right) - MRT_g^{x,R}\left(\tilde{p}, x_g^I, R_g^I\right)\right]. \quad (9.23)$$

Now $\Phi^I > 0$ and $\partial V_k^*/\partial x > 0$, for $k = g, b$, reveals that the two differences on the LHS and the RHS of (9.23) must possess identical signs. Further, (9.7) and (9.8) assure that both terms cannot be equal to zero at the same time.

For notational convenience, let $MRS_{kl}^{x,R}$ denote the marginal rate of substitution for consumer-type k evaluated at the policy offer (x_l^I, R_l^I), with $k, l = \{g, b\}$. Similarly, V_{kl}^* shall refer to the expected lifetime utility of consumer-type k given (x_l^I, R_l^I). Finally, $MRT_{kl}^{x,R}$, $k, l = \{g, b\}$, corresponds to the slope of a benefit schedule ξ_k^M evaluated at type-l's offer. Now, assume $MRS_{kg}^{x,R} > MRT_{gg}^{x,R}$, for $k = g, b$. Then suppose the policy is altered such that

$$\frac{dx_g^I}{dR_g^I} = MRS_{bg}^{x,R}. \quad (9.24)$$

Obviously, type-b consumers' welfare associated with choosing a combination (x_g^I, R_g^I) remains constant. However, type-g individuals' welfare changes according to

$$dV_{gg}^* = \left[MRS_{bg}^{x,R} - MRS_{gg}^{x,R}\right] \frac{\partial V_{gg}^*}{\partial x} dR_g^I. \quad (9.25)$$

This expression is positive for all $dR_g^I < 0$ — due to (9.7) and (9.8). Further

$$dB_g^I = -\left[MRS_{bg}^{x,R} - MRT_{gg}^{x,R}\right] \int_{R_g^I}^T F_g(t)dt\, dR_g^I, \quad (9.26)$$

which is clearly positive as well for $dR_g^I < 0$ in this case. Hence, $MRS_{kg}^{x,R} > MRT_{gg}^{x,R}$ in (9.23) can be contradicted by noting that there exists a policy change which could generate an increase in type-g consumers' welfare without violating either incentive compatibility, or feasibility. Consequently, it must be true that

$$MRS_{kg}^{x,R} - MRT_{gg}^{x,R} < 0. \quad (9.27)$$

Recalling the cases discussed in Proposition 7 and Definition 4 confirms that type-g consumers retire inefficiently early. Moreover, assuming $(1 - \tilde{p}) < x_g^I$ and inserting into (9.27), gives rise to the inequality

$$\frac{G + U(x_g^I) - U(1 - \tilde{p})}{U'(x_g^I)} < \tilde{p} + x_g^I . \tag{9.28}$$

Similar to the arguments exploited in the proof of Proposition 2, this can be contradicted by noting that (9.28) would imply

$$\frac{G}{U'(x_g^I)} - 1 < 0 , \tag{9.29}$$

since $U(c)$ is concave. However, by assumption $(1 - \tilde{p}) < x_g^I$ and — by definition — $U'(1 - \tilde{p}) = G$. Hence, it has been proved that $x_g^I < (1 - \tilde{p}) = \tilde{x}$. The remaining inequalities reported in the Proposition follow from the fact that $B_k^I = 0$, for $k = g, b$.
Q.E.D.

Again, the results can be illustrated graphically as well: in Figure 9.2 type-b consumers are indifferent between their best offer $(\tilde{x}, \tilde{R}_b(0))$ and the offer (x_g^I, R_g^I).

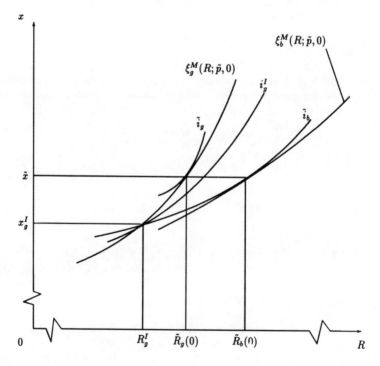

Figure 9.2   An optimal policy without transfers

This reflects the assumption that constraint (9.16) is binding in the optimum. In this case it is assumed that type-b consumers choose the offer $(\tilde{x}, \tilde{R}_b(0))$. Since $B_g^I = 0$, the optimal offer (x_g^I, R_g^I) available for type-g individuals must be located on the $\xi_g^M(R; \tilde{p}, 0)$-curve. It can now be easily verified that type-g individuals prefer (x_g^I, R_g^I) over all offers to the left on this benefit schedule. Further, all offers located to the right of (x_g^I, R_g^I) are either preferred by both consumer-types and, therefore, violate incentive-compatibility, or yield a lower expected lifetime utility for type-g consumers.

Summing up, the following can be noted already:

(1) Asymmetric information can generate benefit rules in which attainable pension levels increase with retirement ages chosen. In contrast, symmetric — and public — information always yields pension payments which are invariant with respect to the individual lifetime labor supply decisions.

(2) Although early pensions x_g^I fall short of late pensions $\tilde{x}$, they appear to be better than actuarially fair. This is so, since early (late) pensions are calculated fairly for better (worse) risk-classes. Hence, if investigations of actual benefit rules utilize information from life-tables calculated for the 'average' individual in the population, the deductions associated with earlier withdrawals appear to be less than fair.

(3) Adverse selection yields a decrease in the average lifetime labor supply of the cohort under consideration. Also, type-g consumers retire inefficiently early, while type-b individuals' lifetime labor supply decision is efficient.

Again, the inefficiency result reported in (3) above must be interpreted as follows: in the absence of an incentive problem, type-g consumers welfare could be increased by delaying retirement. Given the benchmark case defined here, this can also be identified with the fact that, under asymmetric information, this consumer-type retires earlier than under best conditions. Since type-b consumers still retire at date $\tilde{R}_b(0)$, it is therefore clear that the labor supply of the cohort decreases, given second-best conditions. In the following, it will now be checked whether (1)–(3) constitute artifacts created by the specific assumptions introduced, or possess a more general virtue. This is pursued by relaxing the assumptions one at a time.

9.3.2   SELF-SELECTION WITH OPTIMAL TRANSFERS

As pointed out above, Uhlenberg (1988) addresses the question whether a social old-age insurance should account for individual differences in life-expectancies. On the one hand, such differentiation is associated with increased 'equity' in the system, as low-risk types are not required to subsidize higher-risk groups. Yet, the author concludes that treating all consumers alike appears to be the only 'workable' policy option. Obviously, the present analysis takes a quite different route. In fact, it has already been shown that, if consumer-groups only differ with respect to their life-expectancies, a policy which allows for the self-selection of individual-types may explain the existence of variable retirement schemes incorporating seemingly actuarially unfair benefit rules. However, so far the possibility of optimal intra-generational transfers has been excluded by assumption. Moreover, following Akerlof (1970) and Rothschild and Stiglitz (1976), it can be shown that under certain conditions a policy in which all consumers are treated equally may Pareto-dominate this no-transfer self-selection solution. Consequently, it must also be asked whether such policies are optimal within the present framework.

As is well known, though, optimal policies in the sense defined above will never entail an identical offer for both consumer-types. This has been shown by Pauly (1974) and Wilson (1977) and applied to old-age insurances which offer choices between contribution/benefit combinations by Eckstein, Eichenbaum and Peled (1985a) and Eichenbaum and Peled (1987)[8]. Since the same basic arguments can be repeated for the present case — and, in fact, have been utilized in the preceding section already — it suffices to provide an illustration. Hence, suppose that the policy would maximize (9.15), subject to (9.16), and the constraint that both consumer-types must choose an identical pension/retirement age combination (x, R) which satisfies

$$\int_0^R [\mu F_g(t) + (1 - \mu)F_b(t)]dt \ \tilde{p} - \int_R^T [\mu F_g(t) + (1 - \mu)F_b(t)]dt \ x \geq 0. \quad (9.30)$$

Let the corresponding 'marginally fair' benefit schedule be denoted

$$\xi_P^M (R; \tilde{p}, 0) = \frac{\int_0^R [\mu F_g(t) + (1 - \mu)F_b(t)]dt \ \tilde{p}}{\int_R^T [\mu F_g(t) + (1 - \mu)F_b(t)]dt}. \quad (9.31)$$

Using the notation introduced before, it can easily be obtained that

$$MRS_{gP}^{x,R} = MRT_{PP}^{x,R} , \quad (9.32)$$

in the optimum. Here $MRT_{PP}^{x,R}$ is the respective marginal rate of substitution given (9.31) — evaluated at the solution (x_P, R_P). Then $MRT_{gP}^{x,R} > MRT_{PP}^{x,R}$ implies $x_P < \tilde{x} = (1 - \tilde{p})$ and $\tilde{R}_g(0) < R_P < \tilde{R}_b(0)$. Due to (9.7) and (9.8) it follows:

$$MRS_{bP}^{x,R} < MRT_{PP}^{x,R}. \quad (9.33)$$

Moreover, it is easily shown that (9.16) is not binding in the optimum.

---

[8] In contrast, Townley and Boadway's (1988) analysis of adverse selection in markets for term-insured annuities generates the possibility of a Pareto-optimal non-selective policy. Here low-risk types are characterized by lower survival probabilities *and* a shorter maximum life-span. Hence, this consumer-type may not benefit from a separation of risk-types, if this can only be achieved by extending the insurance-term beyond its maximum life-span.

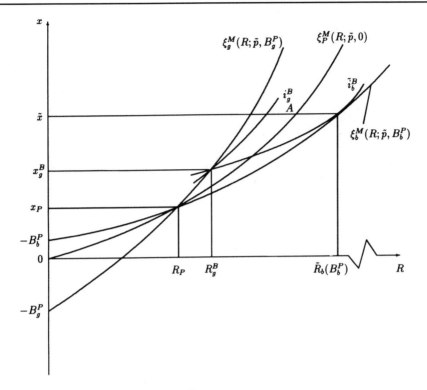

Figure 9.3   The optimality of self-selection

Figure 9.3 depicts the situation described above. The ξ_P^M-curve refers to a 'marginally fair' benefit schedule as defined by (9.31). For expositional clarity, the two consumer-types' indifference curves passing through point (x_P, R_P) have been omitted. The respective slopes are characterized by (9.32) and (9.33). It should be clear that (x_P, R_P) involves a subsidization of type-b consumers. Hence, let the corresponding per-capita transfer from type-g consumers to type-b individuals be denoted $B_g^P = -(B_b^P(1-\mu)/\mu) > 0$. Given this transfer system, it is possible to calculate two marginally fair benefit schedules $\xi_k^M(R; \tilde{p}, B_k^P)$ again. By definition, these two schedules must intersect in point (x_P, R_P). It can rather easily be seen now that offering (x_g^B, R_g^B) to type-g consumers and $(\tilde{x}, \tilde{R}_b(B_b^P))$ to type-b consumers strictly Pareto-dominates the policy in which both consumers receive (x_P, R_P). The indifference curve i_g^B must be located above the type-g indifference curve passing through (x_P, R_P) due to (9.32). Similarly, all points on $\tilde{i}_B$ are preferred by type-b consumers over (x_P, R_P). As shown before, complete income insurance and a corresponding adjustment of the retirement age is welfare-maximizing for every transfer B_b received by this consumer-type, if the contribution equals $\tilde{p}$.

The fact that non-selective policies can never be optimal is also reflected in the first-order conditions (9.18)–(9.21) above. Note that $\Psi^I = 0$ and $\Phi^I = 0$—as would be the case for an offer (x_P, R_P)—generates $x_g^I = \tilde{x}$ and $R_g^I = \tilde{R}_g(B_g)$. The only incentive-compatible and possibly optimal transfer system would then be such that benefits $\tilde{x}$ can be financed given the benefit schedule $\xi_P^M(R; \tilde{p}, 0)$—as indicated by point A in Figure 9.3. It is rather easily shown that this cannot constitute a solution for the optimization problem formulated above. The question remains under which conditions an optimal policy will entail transfers. So far, it has only been stated that optimal transfers equal zero if (9.16) constitutes a binding constraint. A more detailed investigation of the optimization problems now reveals the following:

Proposition 17.   *An optimal policy will entail transfers $B_g^I > 0$ from type-g to type-b consumers, if*

$$\left[\frac{MRT_{g0}^{x,R} - MRS_{g0}^{x,R}}{MRT_{g0}^{x,R} - MRS_{b0}^{x,R}}\right]$$

$$\times \left(1 + \frac{\mu}{(1-\mu)} \frac{\displaystyle\int_{R_g^0}^T F_g(t)\mathrm{d}t\ G}{\displaystyle\int_{R_g^0}^T U'(z_b(t; \tilde{p}, x_g^0, R_g^0)) F_b(t)\mathrm{d}t}\right) > 1 .$$

Here subscripts 'k0' refer to marginal rates of substitution/transformation evaluated at (x_g^0, R_g^0), where $\{(x_g^0, R_g^0), (\tilde{x}, \tilde{R}_b(0))\}$ characterizes the optimal policy if transfers were restricted to equal zero. Given this condition is met, the optimal policy entails offers $\{(x_g^I, R_g^I), (\tilde{x}, \tilde{R}_b(B_b^I))\}$ for the two consumer-types, with

$$x_g^0 < x_g^I < \tilde{x}$$

and

$$R_g^0 < R_g^I < \tilde{R}_b(B_b^I) < \tilde{R}_b(0) .$$

Type-g consumers again retire inefficiently early.

Proof.   From (9.19) and (9.21) it is clear that type-b consumers always receive an undistorted offer: $x_b^I = \tilde{x}$ and $R_b^I = \tilde{R}_b(B_b^I)$. Hence the problem of determining the optimal policy can be rewritten as

$$\text{Max}_{x_g, R_g, B_g, B_b} \quad V_g^*(x_g, R_g, \tilde{p}) , \qquad (9.34)$$

subject to

$$\int_0^{R_g} F_g(t)\mathrm{d}t\ \tilde{p} - \int_{R_g}^T F_g(t)\mathrm{d}t\ x_g \geq B_g , \qquad (9.35)$$

$$\widetilde{W}_b(B_b) \geq V_b^*(x_g, R_g, \tilde{p}) \,, \tag{9.36}$$

$$\mu B_g + (1 - \mu)B_b \geq 0 \,, \tag{9.37}$$

and

$$B_b \leq 0 \,. \tag{9.38}$$

Here (9.35) and (9.37) represent the feasibility and (9.36) the incentive-compatibility constraint. Further, (9.38) ensures that (9.16) is met. This transformation of the optimization problem is very convenient, since (9.35)–(9.37) can always be shown to be binding in the optimum. Thus, it only remains to be shown whether (9.38) is binding. If it is, type-g consumers' expected lifetime utility could only be increased by extracting positive transfers from type-b consumers — hence, violating (9.16). Using the now familiar short-hand notation, the first-order conditions can be derived as

$$\frac{\partial V_{gg}^*}{\partial x} - \Lambda^I \int_{R_g^I}^T F_g(t)\,dt - \Phi^I \frac{\partial V_{bg}^*}{\partial x} = 0 \tag{9.39}$$

$$\frac{\partial V_{gg}^*}{\partial R} + \Lambda^I F_g(R_g^I)[\tilde{p} + x_g^I] - \Phi^I \frac{\partial V_{bg}^*}{\partial R} = 0 \tag{9.40}$$

$$\Phi^I \frac{\partial \widetilde{W}_b(B_b^I)}{\partial B_b} + \Gamma^I(1 - \mu) + \Psi_B^I = 0 \tag{9.41}$$

$$-\Lambda^I + \Gamma^I \mu = 0 \tag{9.42}$$

In these equations Λ, Φ, Γ — all non-negative — represent the multipliers associated with constraints (9.35) — (9.37). Further, $\Psi_B \leq 0$ is associated with constraint (9.38). Rearranging (9.39) and (9.40) can be seen to restate (9.23) from above. Since transfers do not alter type-b's optimal pension, (9.14) can be utilized in (9.41) above. Then inserting from (9.41) and (9.42) it follows that:

$$\frac{(1 - \mu)}{\mu} \left[1 - \frac{MRT_{gg}^{x,R} - MRS_{gg}^{x,R}}{MRT_{gg}^{x,R} - MRS_{bg}^{x,R}} \right]$$

$$- \frac{MRT_{gg}^{x,R} - MRS_{gg}^{x,R}}{MRT_{gg}^{x,R} - MRS_{bg}^{x,R}} \frac{G \int_{R_g^I}^T F_g(t)\,dt}{\int_{R_g^I}^T U'(z_b(t; \tilde{p}, x_g^I, R_g^I))F_b(t)\,dt} \geq 0 \tag{9.43}$$

Now, the condition stated in the proposition can be verified to be sufficient by noting that, if the expression in (9.43) is smaller than zero for $x_g^I = x_g^0$ and $R_g^I = R_g^0$, $B_g^I > 0$ must be optimal. The remaining statements in the Proposition are easily shown to hold, since — starting from the no-transfer situation — type-g consumers'

welfare can only be improved by increasing the replacement ratio. Nevertheless, type-g consumers still retire inefficiently early.
$Q.E.D.$

Figure 9.4 depicts a situation in which transfers from type-g to type-b consumers are optimal. As stated in Proposition 17, (x_g^0, R_g^0) is associated with the highest attainable welfare level for type-g individuals, if no transfers were made. By construction, there exists a combination (x_g^I, R_g^I)—involving $B_g^I = -((1 - \mu)/\mu)B_b^I > 0$—such that this solution is dominated. Obviously, $\{(x_g^I, R_g^I), (\tilde{x}, \tilde{R}_b(B_b^I))\}$ also satisfies feasibility and incentive-compatibility.

Proposition 17 basically identifies two properties which make optimal transfers more likely. First, note that the term in the first line of the condition is positive and smaller than unity. It approaches unity as the difference between the marginal rates of substitution for the two consumer-types vanishes—hence, if the two individual-types accumulation behavior becomes 'more similar'. In this case the $\tilde{i}_g$-curve is not too steep compared to the i_b^0 indifference curve at point (x_g^0, R_g^0) in Figure 9.4. Thus, it becomes more likely that there exists some per-capita transfer B_g^I, shifting ξ_g^M to the right and type-b consumers' indifference curves to the left,

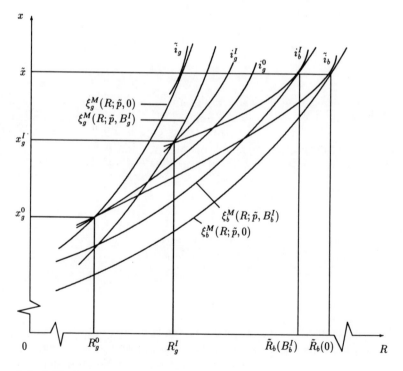

Figure 9.4   Self-selection with optimal transfers

which can yield a new point of intersection within the area between $\xi_g^M(R; \tilde{p}, 0)$
and $\tilde{i}_b$. Similarly, the term $G \int_{R_g^0}^T F_g(t) \mathrm{d}t / \int_{R_g^0}^T U'(z_b(t; \tilde{p}, x_g^0, R_g^0)) F_b(t) \mathrm{d}t$ becomes
large, if (a) g-types' remaining life-expectancy as of age R_g^0 is large relative to
b-types', and/or (b) the difference $\tilde{x} - x_g^0$ is rather small. Both conditions imply
that the slope of the indifference curve $\tilde{i}_b$ is very flat compared to the slope of the
benefit schedule $\xi_g^M(R; \tilde{p}, 0)$.

Whereas these arguments impose qualifications on the risk-taking behavior of
the individuals and the differences in the survival probabilities, relative frequencies
of consumer-types in the population determine whether transfers will be optimal
as well. In particular, if there are relatively many type-g consumers, the cost for
each type-g individual associated with subsidizing type-b consumers in order to
increase this type's preference for the undistorted offer is comparably small. In
this case, rather small per-capita transfer payments B_g^I, inducing small rightward
shifts of the ξ_g^M-curve, generate large per-capita transfers B_b^I to be received by each
type-b individual — reflected by large leftward shifts in the respective indifference
curve. Hence, by accepting relatively small decreases in the actuarial value of their
pension flow, g-types can attain rather significant increases in the replacement
ratio — implying improved risk-shifting.

Note that the presence of transfers does not affect most of the conclusions
obtained before. Benefits still increase with the retirement age chosen. Further,
despite type-g consumers subsidizing type-b individuals, early benefits appear
to be better than fair, utilizing average survival probabilities for reference. Any
group including 'bad' risk consumers would induce losses, if choosing the option
(x_g^I, R_g^I). Nevertheless, the possibility of an efficient transfer system gives rise
to deviations from individual fairness. In particular, accounting for the fact that
x_g^I is chosen by g-types exclusively, early retirement benefits may involve larger
than fair deductions — taking $\tilde{x}$ as a reference. Moreover, 'good' risks retire inefficiently early by Definition 4. However, transfers increase (decrease) the lifetime
labor supply of 'good' ('bad') risks compared with the no-transfer separating offers.
Due to the fact that relative frequencies of consumer-types in the population, properties of the instantaneous preference structure, and differences in the survival risk
co-determine the size of the transfers paid/received, it is not possible to derive
clearcut conclusions concerning the aggregate effect on the lifetime labor supply
of the cohort. In fact, examples can be constructed in which the retirement age of
type-g consumers exceeds their best age $\tilde{R}_g(0)$.

Yet, so far the analysis has maintained that the contribution is exogenously fixed
at $\tilde{p}$. On first sight, deviating from this welfare-maximizing contribution appears
to bear potential benefits for type-g consumers. Since 'good' risk individuals do
not attain an undistorted allocation, it is obviously possible to construct alternative
offers with contributions $p \neq \tilde{p}$, so as to keep this individual-type indifferent.
It could then be assumed that the risk-taking behavior and the differences in the
survival risk again govern whether or not the incentive-compatibility constraint

can be relaxed by such deviations. As pointed out by Cooper (1984), the analysis of self-selection models turns out to be rather problematic, when more than two variables can be chosen in order to achieve separations. Restricting the attention to insurance schemes in which all participants must pay an identical contribution, the following can be obtained, however:

Proposition 18.   *The optimal common contribution (rate) is $\tilde{p}$.*

Proof.   Consider the optimization problem (9.15)–(9.17), and (9.10) again. In addition to the first-order conditions (9.18)–(9.21), maximization with respect to p yields

$$\frac{\partial V_{gg}^*}{\partial p} + \Lambda^I \left(\mu \int_0^{R_g^I} F_g(t)\mathrm{d}t + (1 - \mu) \int_0^{R_b^I} F_b(t)\mathrm{d}t \right)$$

$$-\Phi^I \frac{\partial V_{bg}^*}{\partial p} = -[\Psi^I + \Phi^I]\frac{\partial V_{bb}^*}{\partial p}. \qquad (9.44)$$

Conditions (9.19) and (9.21) immediately show that type-b consumers always attain an efficient lifetime labor supply contingent on the optimal contribution p^I. Hence,

$$x_b^I = x^*(p^I, B_b^I); \quad R_b^I = R^*(p, B_b^I) . \qquad (9.45)$$

Inserting from (9.18)–(9.21) into (9.44) with some rearrangements reveals

$$\frac{MRT_{gg}^{x,p} - MRS_{gg}^{x,p}}{MRT_{gg}^{x,R} - MRS_{gg}^{x,R}} \; \begin{array}{c} \geq \\ \leq \end{array} \; \frac{MRT_{gg}^{x,p} - MRS_{bg}^{x,p}}{MRT_{gg}^{x,R} - MRS_{bg}^{x,R}} \; , \qquad (9.46)$$

depending on whether

$$[\Psi^I + \Phi^I]\frac{\partial V_{bb}^*}{\partial p} \left(MRT_{bb}^{x,p} - MRS_{bb}^{x,p} \right) \; \begin{array}{c} \leq \\ \geq \end{array} \; 0. \qquad (9.47)$$

As shown before, $\Psi^I + \Phi^I > 0$. Consider the following arbitrage arguments now: define an adjustment rule for the pension flow according to

$$\mathrm{d}x_g^I = MRT_{gg}^{x,p}\mathrm{d}p^I + MRT_{gg}^{x,R}\mathrm{d}R_g^I . \qquad (9.48)$$

It can easily be seen that B_g^I remains constant for all changes in the contribution and retirement age, as long as benefits are adjusted according to (9.48). Totally differentiating V_{kg}^*, $k = g, b$, and utilizing this rule implies

$$\mathrm{d}V_{kg}^* \cdot \frac{\partial V_{kg}^*}{\partial x} = \left(MRT_{gg}^{x,p} - MRS_{kg}^{x,p} \right) \mathrm{d}p^I + \left(MRT_{gg}^{x,R} - MRS_{kg}^{x,R} \right) \mathrm{d}R_g^I . \qquad (9.49)$$

If the LHS of (9.46) is unequal to the respective RHS, it is always possible to simultaneously alter (p, R), so as to keep type-b consumers' welfare constant, while increasing the expected lifetime utility of g-type individuals. Hence, in the optimum (9.46) must hold with equality. Thus, the third term in (9.47) must be equal to zero. Yet, (9.45) states that type-b consumers always attain an efficient lifetime labor supply. By virtue of Proposition 2, the only case in which this also generates a replacement rate equal to unity occurs when $p = \tilde{p}$. Q.E.D.

Interpreting this result, the following should be noted: since (9.16) must be satisfied, any deviation from the welfare-maximizing contribution — applied to type-b consumers as well — is associated with a necessity to compensate accordingly. Every self-selection policy incorporating a different contribution thus also generates transfers. Holding these transfers constant, it is also possible to calculate the corresponding expected utilities — given the contributions were $\tilde{p}$. Then, it must only be checked whether the implied transfers are optimal in this context as well. Otherwise, there always exists a dominating solution with contribution $\tilde{p}$. In other words, the transfer system generated under a deviating contribution must duplicate the optimal system derived for $p = \tilde{p}$. Now, recall that any deviation from this contribution requires additional compensating per-capita transfers to be received by b-types. This contradicts that transfers can be identically equal. Only given this contribution, b-types attain an undistorted allocation. Hence, the model confirms a finding by Wilson (1977): Whereas in best situations all consumers attain an undistorted allocation, this must remain to be true for 'bad' risk consumers in second-best problems. If this were not so — as in the case where the consumer-types share an offer discussed above, for instance — it is always possible to achieve Pareto-improvements.

9.4   THE VALUE OF ADDITIONAL INFORMATION

9.4.1   IMPERFECT RISK-CATEGORIZATION

So far, the analysis has only considered cases in which the individuals' information regarding their risk-classification is perfectly private. In many circumstances, however, it is plausible to assume that both the insurance agency and the consumers share some information. In the context of old-age insurances the health status of an individual — as proved in medical examinations — can provide informative signals concerning the survival risk. Contingent on these signals it is then possible to distinguish consumer groups characterized by differences in the respective average survival risk. The question remains, whether an optimal policy — as defined above — will establish health-contingent retirement schemes. This issue will be addressed in the following.

In order to keep the analysis simple again, assume that at date 0 the health status of the consumers is known to the insurance agency and the individual. Again, this date does not necessarily mark the individual's entrance to the labor force in the current framework. Moreover, there exist only two possible states: an individual can either be 'healthy' or show 'poor health' by some standard utilized by the old-age insurance agency. The probability that type-g (type-b) individuals exhibit health deficits is Q_g (Q_b). It appears natural to assume $Q_g > Q_b$. Thus, 'good' risk individuals from the point of view of old-age insurance prove to be of 'poor health' more frequently than 'bad' risk consumers. Yet, this analysis abstracts from additional implicit health insurance provisions. Rather, the instantaneous preferences and the survival risk of the consumers are taken to be unaffected by the health status of the individual. Here only the fact that a consumer's health condition constitutes an informative signal with regard to the respective survival risk matters. Further, $Q_k \in (0, 1)$, for $k = b, g$. Thus, the health status of the consumers only allows for an imperfect risk-categorization. It is generally known that the group of healthy individuals (on average) exhibits a higher survival risk than the group of individuals with documented health deficits. Nevertheless, both groups comprise both consumer-types defined before. Again, the risk-type constitutes private information of the consumers. This is intended to capture the notion that results from health examinations do not reveal all the information known to the individual concerning the survival risk.

Since the information about a consumer's health status is revealed *ex-ante* as well, there actually exist four individual-types, now. Hence, let subscripts 'kn' refer to an individual of type-k, $k = g, b$, associated with health tests providing signals $n = p, h$ — according to whether or not 'poor health' is documented, respectively. Applying the concept of voluntary participation again, an optimal policy must now solve two optimization problems. For consumers who exhibit 'poor health' the policy must choose a contribution p_p and two offers (x_{kp}, R_{kp}), $k = g, b$, such as to maximize (9.15), subject to (9.16), (9.17), and feasibility. The latter now implies

$$\mu Q_g \int_0^{R_{gp}} F_g(t)\mathrm{d}t\, p_p + (1 - \mu)Q_b \int_0^{R_{bp}} F_b(t)\mathrm{d}t\, p_p$$

$$-\mu Q_g \int_{R_{gp}}^T F_g(t)\mathrm{d}t\, x_{gp} - (1 - \mu)Q_b \int_{R_{bp}}^T F_b(t)\mathrm{d}t\, x_{bp} \geq 0. \qquad (9.50)$$

Similarly, for the group of 'healthy' individuals feasibility can be written as

$$\mu(1 - Q_g) \int_0^{R_{gh}} F_g(t)\mathrm{d}t\, p_h + (1 - \mu)(1 - Q_b) \int_0^{R_{bh}} F_b(t)\mathrm{d}t\, p_h$$

$$-\mu(1 - Q_g) \int_{R_{gh}}^T F_g(t)\mathrm{d}t\, x_{gh} - (1 - \mu)(1 - Q_b) \int_{R_{bh}}^T F_b(t)\mathrm{d}t\, x_{bh} \geq 0. \qquad (9.51)$$

It should be clear that the two optimization problems jointly characterizing an optimal policy exhibit the same basic characteristics intensively discussed in the previous sections. Hence, it is not necessary to derive additional formal descriptions. In particular, the contribution will uniformly be set equal to $\tilde{p}$ — regardless of whether the health contingent benefit rules differ. Further, type-b consumers always attain an undistorted lifetime allocation:

$$x_{bn}^I = \tilde{x} \; ; \; R_{bn}^I = \tilde{R}(B_{bn}^I), \; n = p, h. \tag{9.52}$$

Then the offer claimed by type-g individuals satisfies

$$x_{gn}^I < \tilde{x}; \; R_{gn}^I < \tilde{R}(B_{bn}^I), \; n = p, h \, . \tag{9.53}$$

A more interesting question concerns the existence of transfers between the consumers-types within the two retirement schemes. A condition for $B_{gp}^I = -(((1 - \mu)Q_b)/\mu Q_g)B_{bp}^I > 0$ can rather easily be obtained as:

$$\left[\frac{MRT_{g0}^{x,R} - MRS_{g0}^{x,R}}{MRT_{g0}^{x,R} - MRS_{b0}^{x,R}} \right] \left(1 + \frac{\mu Q_g}{(1 - \mu)Q_b} \frac{G \int_{R_g^0}^T F_g(t)dt}{\int_{R_g^0}^T U'(z_b(t; \tilde{p}, x_g^0, R_g^0))F_b(t)dt} \right) > 1. \tag{9.54}$$

Here the index '0' again refers to marginal rates of substitution and transformation evaluated at the offer (x_g^0, R_g^0) associated with the highest attainable lifetime utility for type-g individuals, if transfers were restricted to equal zero.

Similarly, $B_{gh}^I = -((1 - \mu)(1 - Q_b)/\mu(1 - Q_g))B_{bh}^I > 0$, if

$$\left[\frac{MRT_{g0}^{x,R} - MRS_{g0}^{x,R}}{MRT_{g0}^{x,R} - MRS_{b0}^{x,R}} \right]$$

$$\times \left(1 + \frac{\mu(1 - Q_g)}{(1 - \mu)(1 - Q_b)} \frac{G \int_{R_g^0}^T F_g(t)dt}{\int_{R_g^0}^T U'(z_b(t; \tilde{p}, x_g^0, R_g^0))F_b(t)dt} \right) > 1. \tag{9.55}$$

Conditional on whether (9.54) and (9.55) are satisfied, three cases can now be distinguished.

(I)   Given that the expressions in (9.54) and (9.55) are both smaller than unity, $B_{gp}^I = B_{gh}^I = 0$. Consequently, the retirement schemes are identical, implying

$$x_{gp}^I = x_{gh}^I = x_g^0 \, ,$$

$$R_{gp}^I = R_{gh}^I = R_g^0 \, ,$$

and

$$\tilde{R}_b(B_{bp}^I) = \tilde{R}_b(B_{bh}^I) = \tilde{R}_b(0) .$$

Here the signals received by the agency — despite being informative — will not be utilized to establish separate health-contingent retirement schemes. Obviously, this case also requires that transfers from type-g to type-b individuals are not optimal in the no-signal model analyzed before.

(II)   If condition (9.54) is satisfied, but (9.55) is not, only type-b consumers who document 'poor health' will be subsidized. Two health-contingent retirement schemes will be established, and

$$x_{gh}^I = x_g^0 < x_{gp}^I < \tilde{x} ,$$

$$R_{gh}^I = R_g^0 < R_{gp}^I < \tilde{R}_b(B_{bp}^I) < \tilde{R}_b(0) .$$

Due to

$$\frac{Q_g}{Q_b} \frac{\mu}{(1-\mu)} > \frac{\mu}{(1-\mu)} > \frac{(1-Q_g)}{(1-Q_b)} \frac{\mu}{(1-\mu)} ,$$

this case can arise, either if the no-signal model generates an optimal transfer system, or if transfers between consumer-types equal zero here.

(III) If both (9.54) and (9.55) are met, two health-contingent retirement schemes will be established. The benefit rules in both schemes entail type-g consumers subsidizing type-b individuals. Further, it must be true that

$$x_{g0}^I < x_{gh}^I < x_{gp}^I < \tilde{x} .$$

As far as the respective retirement ages are concerned, similar clearcut conclusions cannot be obtained, however. The respective first-order conditions only reveal

$$R_{gh}^I < \tilde{R}_b(B_{bh}^I) < \tilde{R}_b(0) ,$$

and

$$R_{gp}^I < \tilde{R}_b(B_{bp}^I) < \tilde{R}_b(0)$$

here. This case necessarily requires that the no-signal model entails a non-trivial optimal transfer system as well.

Graphical illustrations of the first two cases have implicitly been provided before already. Note that Case I can be depicted as shown in Figure 9.2. Since both optimization problems generate the no-transfer solution, the realized offers for type-g individuals must be identical and located on the marginally fair benefit schedule $\xi_g^M(R, \tilde{p}, 0)$. Since the availability of the signal does not change the insurance offers chosen by the consumers, the expected lifetime utilities are unaffected as well. Similarly, the qualitative aspects of the optimal policy arising under the conditions of Case II are captured by Figure 9.4. Here only the notation must be altered somewhat. In particular, the offer (x_g^I, R_g^I) depicted in the figure now corresponds to (x_{gp}^I, R_{gp}^I), and $\tilde{R}_b(B_{bp}^I)$ can be identified with $\tilde{R}_b(B_b^I)$. The respective offers in the scheme for 'healthy' consumers are $\{(x_g^0, R_g^0), (\tilde{x}, \tilde{R}_b(0))\}$. In contrast to Case I, the availability of signals obviously bears welfare impacts — the direction of which depends on the reference situation without signaling.

Clearly, if the no-signal model generates per-capita transfers equal to zero, but non-trivial transfers turn out to be beneficial, given that signals allow for imperfect risk-categorization, all 'poor health' consumers' welfare is increased, while 'healthy' individuals maintain their welfare level. Thus, the availability of an informative signal is Pareto-improving. On the other hand, given that the no-signal model entails an optimal transfer system, only the welfare of type-g individuals who document 'poor health' can always be shown to increase. Type-b consumers who also prove to be of 'poor health' are better off than those documenting to be 'healthy'. Nevertheless, only if transfers in the 'poor health' scheme exceed the transfers received in the no-signal model does their lifetime utility increase as well. This cannot be guaranteed, however. On the one hand, subsidizing type-b consumers becomes 'cheaper' for each type-g individual. Turning to Figure 9.4 — relatively small increases in B_g^I (associated with rightward shifts of the $\xi_g^M(R, \tilde{p}, B_g^I)$-curve) yield rather large leftward shifts of the i_b^I-indifference curve of type-b consumers. This tends to encourage increases in the transfers received by b-types, compared with the original no-signal model. At the same time, relatively large decreases in B_g^I (associated with leftward shifts of the $\xi_g^M(R, \tilde{p}, B_g^I)$-curve) yield rather small changes in the per-capita transfer received by type-b consumers. Thus, the i_b^I-curve shifts to the right — but this effect is relatively weak and, therefore, tends to encourage a decrease in B_b^I. As far as 'healthy' consumers are concerned, both types unambiguously suffer welfare losses compared to the no-signal framework.

Moreover, the positive implications of Case II appear questionable: although two separate health-contingent retirement schemes are established, the implied choices of the retirement ages do not seem to comply with the stylized facts, when maintaining the interpretation of the signal as referring to the health status of an individual. 'Healthy' type-g consumers can be verified to retire earlier than all individuals with documented health deficits. However, health-contingent retirement schemes are naturally associated with overall earlier retirement. While this view may be misleading, accounting for the rather complex structure of retirement schemes incorporating employment-related allowances as well, it is interesting to note that Case III may in fact reverse this order of retirement.

The respective arguments are illustrated in Figure 9.5. Here the reference situation, when additional signals are not available, entails transfers $B_g^I = -((1 - \mu)/\mu)B_b^I > 0$ from type-g to type-b individuals. The corresponding optimal policy is characterized by the two offers $\{(x_g^I, R_g^I), (\tilde{x}, \tilde{R}_b(B_b^I))\}$. Exploiting the

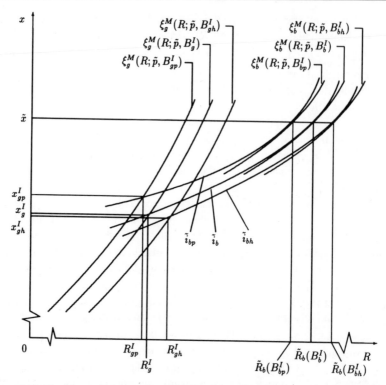

Figure 9.5 Health-contingent retirement schemes — Case III

additional information, 'healthy' g-types now experience a comparative disadvantage in subsidizing type-b individuals — if compared to 'poor health' g-types. It is therefore plausible to assume that this change induces per-capita transfers paid by 'healthy' ('poor health') type-g consumers to increase (decrease). At the same time, per-capita transfers received by 'healthy' ('poor health') type-b consumers decrease (may still increase). In Figure 9.5 this has been indicated by the locations of the respective marginally fair benefit schedules $\xi_k^M(R, \tilde{p}, B_{kn}^I)$, with $k = g, b$ and $n = p, h$, as compared to the schedules $\xi_k^M(R, \tilde{p}, B_k^I)$ capturing the transfer system which arises in absence of the additional information. The self-selection offers are again characterized by the intersections of type-b consumers' indifference curves with the corresponding ξ_g^M-schedules. As exemplified in the figure it is now possible to obtain $R_{gp}^I < R_{gh}^I$ and $\tilde{R}_b(B_{bp}^I) < \tilde{R}_b(B_{bh}^I)$. Given the situation illustrated, the two sets of benefit rules applied in fact 'overlap': There exist (type-b) 'poor health' individuals who retire later than (type-g) 'healthy' consumers. However, examples can also be constructed in which $R_{gh}^I > \tilde{R}_b(B_{bp}^I)$. Given such situations, 'very early' retirement options would be exclusively confined to consumers with documented health deficits.

Although Figure 9.5 does not show the respective indifference curves for type-g individuals, it can rather easily be seen that 'poor health' g-types always benefit from the availability of the additional information. At the same time, 'healthy' consumers, regardless of type, experience welfare losses compared to the no-signal case. Despite the example discussed above, it cannot be guaranteed that per-capita transfers to 'poor health' type-b consumers actually increase if risk-categorization becomes possible. Hence, no clearcut welfare conclusions can be derived for this individual-type. Summarizing, it can thus be stated that symmetric, but imperfect, *ex-ante* information only generates Pareto-improvements, if two conditions are met: first, without the additional signal, the optimal policy does not incorporate transfers. Second, with available health information, the retirement scheme offered to 'poor health' individuals entails subsidizing b-types.

9.4.2   A NOTE ON RANDOM SIGNALING

The welfare implications derived above seem to comply with Hoy (1988, 1989). This previous research also shows that additional symmetric information need not be welfare enhancing. However, the analysis presented here differs in several respects. First, Hoy considers a framework, in which both the insurance agency and the consumers are *ex-ante* perfectly uninformed with regard to the risk-classification of a particular individual. Signals allowing for imperfect categorization are only received after the insurance scheme is specified. Risk-aversion on the side of the agency then yields signal-contingent insurance. Since the consumers would prefer uncontingent offers *ex-ante*, in order to obtain insurance against the uncertainty of being classified as 'bad' risks, the additional information yields deteriorations in the consumers' *ex-ante* expected utility. In contrast, the present study assumes that the individuals are always perfectly informed about their risk-type. Thus, given the objective function specified an optimal *ex-ante* insurance separates consumer-types. Nevertheless, it is worth questioning whether *ex-ante* signaling will always result in the establishment of health-contingent retirement schemes. In order to highlight the basic arguments and following Hoy (1988) rather closely, suppose that the health examinations take place after the retirement schemes are specified, but before the actual economic life commences. Thus, the individuals always choose an optimal consumption plan under certainty with respect to the pension/retirement age offers applicable. Further, the health information becomes publicly available, irrespective of whether a consumer wishes so. Also, the probabilities Q_k, $k = g, b$, are publicly known *ex-ante*.

The objective of the insurance agency is now defined so as to maximize[9]

$$Q_g V_g^*(\tilde{p}, x_{gp}, R_{gp}) + (1 - Q_g)V_g^*(\tilde{p}, x_{gh}, R_{gh}) , \tag{9.56}$$

---

[9]For simplicity, the contribution is held constant at $\tilde{p}$ again.

subject to

$$\int_0^{R_{gn}} F_g(t)\mathrm{d}t\ \tilde p - \int_{R_{gn}}^{T} F_g(t)\mathrm{d}t\, x_{gn} \geq B_{gn} , \tag{9.57}$$

defining surpluses B_{gn} in the retirement schemes indexed $n = p, h$. Further, incentive compatibility in both programs requires

$$\widetilde W_b(B_{bn}) \geq V_b^*(\tilde p, x_{gn}, R_{gn}) . \tag{9.58}$$

Feasibility is ensured by

$$\mu[Q_g B_{gp} + (1 - Q_g)B_{gh}] + (1 - \mu)[Q_b B_{bp} + (1 - Q_b)B_{bh}] \geq 0 . \tag{9.59}$$

Since the *ex-ante* expected utility of type-b consumers is linear in B_{bn}, it suffices to add

$$Q_b B_{bp} + (1 - Q_b)B_{bh} \leq 0 , \tag{9.60}$$

in order to ensure that it is greater than or equal to $\widetilde W_b(0)$.

It should be obvious that the qualitative results concerning the structure of the separating offers in the two schemes, if established, remain unaffected. Hence, it is more interesting to note that rearranging the first-order conditions also yields

$$\frac{Q_g}{Q_b}\left[\frac{\partial V_{ggp}^*}{\partial x} - \Gamma' \mu \int_{R_{gp}^I}^{T} F_g(t)\mathrm{d}t\right] = \left[\frac{\Gamma'(1 - \mu) + \Psi'}{G}\right]\frac{\partial V_{gbp}^*}{\partial x}, \tag{9.61}$$

$$\frac{(1 - Q_g)}{(1 - Q_b)}\left[\frac{\partial V_{ggh}^*}{\partial x} - \Gamma' \mu \int_{R_{gh}^I}^{T} F_g(t)\mathrm{d}t\right] = \left[\frac{\Gamma'(1 - \mu) + \Psi'}{G}\right]\frac{\partial V_{gbh}^*}{\partial x}, \tag{9.62}$$

$$\frac{Q_g}{Q_b}\left[\frac{\partial V_{ggp}^*}{\partial R} + \Gamma' \mu F_g(R_{gp}^I)[\tilde p + x_{gp}^I]\right] = \left[\frac{\Gamma'(1 - \mu) + \Psi'}{G}\right]\frac{\partial V_{gbp}^*}{\partial R}, \tag{9.63}$$

$$\frac{(1 - Q_g)}{(1 - Q_b)}\left[\frac{\partial V_{ggh}^*}{\partial R} + \Gamma' \mu F_g(R_{gh}^I)[\tilde p + x_{gh}^I]\right] = \left[\frac{\Gamma'(1 - \mu) + \Psi'}{G}\right]\frac{\partial V_{gbh}^*}{\partial R}. \tag{9.64}$$

Here, subscripts 'kln' refer to respective derivative of type-k consumers' expected lifetime utility, evaluated at the offer (x_{ln}, R_{ln}), with $l = g, b$ and $n = p, h$. Further, $\Gamma' \geq 0$ and $\Psi' \leq 0$ denote the optimal values of the multipliers associated with constraints (9.59) and (9.60), respectively. For $\Psi' = 0$—i.e. if (9.60) is not binding in the optimum—it is immediately clear that an optimal policy will never choose to set $(x_{gp}, R_{gp}) = (x_{gh}, R_{gh})$—unless $Q_g = Q_b$. This result is rather obvious: when transfers are mutually welfare-enhancing in either one of two separate health-contingent schemes, then it is also possible to strictly improve type-g consumers' *ex-ante* expected utility by establishing such programs. It must only be noted that the respective alternative would be to have all g-types receiving

(x_g^0, R_g^0) — as defined before. More interestingly, however, inspecting (9.61)–(9.64) also verifies that the policy always establishes two separate health-contingent retirement schemes, if the signal derived from the health-examination is informative. The only possibility to find identical offers in the two schemes — which is equivalent to not establishing health-contingent offers — occurs, when $\Gamma^I(1 - \mu) = -\Psi^I$. Then rearranging the first-order conditions again reveals that g-types receive an undistorted offer with pension $\tilde{x}$ as well — indicated by point A in Figure 9.3 again. However, as argued above, type-g consumers can receive a strictly dominating, certain[10] *ex-ante* expected lifetime utility by implementing the separating policy $\{(x_g^I, R_g^I), (\tilde{x}, \tilde{R}_b(B_b^I))\}$ discussed in the previous sections.

The reason for this result is rather obvious and can be clarified by recalling the illustration in Figure 9.2, for instance. Here the initial situation is characterized by no transfers paid by g-types in order to subsidize type-b consumers. Note, however, that simple redistributions between 'healthy' and 'poor health' type-g individuals — holding B_{bn}^I constant and equal to zero — bears welfare effects. Increasing (decreasing) B_{gp}^I (B_{gh}^I) — starting from $B_{gn}^I = 0$ in both schemes — will produce shifts of the ξ_{gp}^M-curve (ξ_{gh}^M-curve) to the left (right) of the ξ_g^M-benefit schedule depicted in the figure, for instance. The respective separating offers will be found moving along the $\tilde{i}_b$-curve. Hence, in this example of redistribution among g-types only, the welfare of type-g consumers is increased (decreased) in the 'poor health' ('healthy') individuals' retirement scheme. Similarly, holding B_{gn}^I constant and equal to zero, type-g consumers' welfare in the two schemes can be influenced by redistributing B_b^I without violating (9.60). For instance, decreasing (increasing) B_{bp}^I (B_{bh}^I) will shift the respective $\tilde{i}_b$-curve to the left (right). The separating offers can then be found moving along the $\xi_g^I(R, \tilde{p}, 0)$-curve until the new points of intersection with b-types indifference curves are reached. Given the example formulated, this will again raise 'poor health' type-g consumers' welfare, and induce respective losses for 'healthy' g-types.

It is immediately clear that an optimal *ex-ante* policy must balance these possible welfare losses/gains for g-types by choosing the transfer system $(B_{gp}^I, B_{gh}^I, B_{bp}^I, B_{bh}^I)$ appropriately. Some rather simple arbitrage arguments reveal transfers between retirement schemes to be always welfare enhancing, unless the relative frequencies of consumer-types in the two schemes are identical. However, due to the complex structure of the model, the exact directions of these transfers remain ambiguous. In particular, it cannot be ruled out that 'poor health' consumers subsidize 'healthy' ones. This may seem to be counter-intuitive — given a common-sense notion of health-contingent retirement. However, it should be emphasized that in each of the schemes established the basic feature of seemingly better than fair early retirement pensions is always maintained.

---

[10]This obviously only refers to the fact that there exists no uncertainty with respect to the offers available for g-types.

9.5   CRITICAL COMMENTS

The analysis pursued in this chapter underlines that, while seemingly unfair benefit rules may only reflect the fact that early retirements exhibit lower than average survival risks, pensions which increase with retirement ages chosen require an additional adverse selection argument. Transfers between consumer-types have then to be demonstrated to be mutually welfare-enhancing under certain circumstances. Although the direction of these transfers is always described as shifting resources from 'good' risks to 'bad' risks, early retirement benefits remain to be better than actuarially fair — utilizing the average survival risk as a point of reference. Finally, given that the insurance agency possesses some, though imperfect, information with respect to a consumer's risk-classification, separate signal-contingent retirement schemes (may) evolve. If subsidizing 'bad' risks turns out to be beneficial for 'good' risks in both schemes, the resulting benefit rules can reproduce the stylized facts of co-existing health-contingent variable retirement programs. Nevertheless, the model utilizes a set of assumptions which can be viewed as questionable.

- Assuming more general survival probability functions, for instance, can render the current analysis suspect. If marginally fair benefit schedules intersect, best solutions, even without *a priori* transfers, may by chance turn out to be implementable under private information as well. This arises when the best retirement ages happen to be identical. On the other hand, if best retirement induces one consumer-type to claim the respective other type's offer, only two possibilities arise: either marginal rates of transformation and substitution for the individual-types can be ordered such as to allow one to pursue the analysis above, or pooling the different types under one offer will be the only alternative[11].

- Further, under the assumptions of Section 9.2.1, but focusing on exogenously specified contributions $p \neq \tilde{p}$, it is immediately clear that the qualitative results obtained carry over to cases with $p > \tilde{p}$. Under best conditions and without *a priori* transfers, $x_g^*(p, 0) = x_h^*(p, 0)$ and $R_g^*(p, 0) < R_h^*(p, 0)$ in this regime. However, it is possible that separation can be achieved setting $x_g^I < x_g^*(p, 0)$, but maintaining $(1 - p) \leq x_g^I$ in the second-best. Hence, adverse selection does not necessarily induce private accumulation of g-types here. On the other hand, $p < \tilde{p}$ generally implies private accumulation of both consumer groups under best and second-best conditions. Yet, for these cases it cannot be precluded that private information is compatible with implementing the best. This follows, since $x_g^*(p, 0)$ can be greater than, equal to, or smaller than $x_h^*(p, 0)$ here. Again, however, if adverse selection is present, the qualitative aspects of the model presented above can be maintained.

---

[11] Compare Cooper (1984) and Nalebuff and Zeckhauser (1985).

- The model can rather easily be extended to incorporate more than just two consumer-types. The second-best retirement age/benefit combinations for the different types can be characterized as follows: The 'highest' risk class always attains an undistorted offer. All other groups' pensions and retirement ages are then determined as points of intersections of the respective marginally fair benefit schedules with the indifference curve derived for the 'highest' risk class individuals. Thus, the slope of this indifference curve, rather than actuarial calculations, determines the adjustment of pensions to alternative choices of retirement ages. Recall that this slope is always smaller than the slope of a corresponding marginally fair benefit schedule designed for the 'highest' risk group. Thus, early benefits appear to be better than fair — using average survival risks to calculate actuarial deductions. It should be noted that, if one of the 'lower' risk groups can benefit from subsidizing the 'highest' risk class, all other risk groups incur welfare gains as well. This is so, since transfers received by the 'highest' risk consumers shift the respective indifference-curve to the left, as intensively discussed before . Hence, all other 'low' risk-types can attain more favorable separating offers as well. Yet, such transfers may reverse the order of retirement again — depending on the particular structure of the survival risk and the risk-taking behavior of the individuals. Thus, they may also give rise to additional moral hazard problems. Consequently, the present analysis should once more be emphasized to provide exemplifications of some basic arguments, rather than a complete description of all possible cases.

It must further be conceived that the concept of 'optimality' utilized above is subject to more fundamental criticism. Referring to social security arrangements Kuhn and Davies (1992), for instance, note: 'Since the government can force everyone to purchase its "annuities", unlike private insurers it is not subject to adverse selection'. As pointed out above already, this view need not necessarily be shared, however. Although the current approach has been based on a concept of 'voluntary participation' — restricting the role of government to enforcing the insurance scheme, rather than forcing consumer groups under a particular arrangement — it remains to be shown that socially optimal policies always induce transfers between consumer-types, such that the different groups are in effect pooled under a single benefit/retirement age offer. This obviously requires particular assumptions concerning the social welfare function to be maximized, in addition to merely stating the government's capability to force individuals to participate[12]. Generally, it should be clear that any other policy incorporating a priori transfers between consumer-groups can only fall within one of two possible categories: either these transfers are such that the best solution remains to be non-implementable under private information of the consumers, due to 'bad' risks preferring 'good' risk individuals' allocation. Then the analysis shown above applies with only slight

---

[12]Compare Townley and Boadway (1988) again.

modifications. On the other hand, if *a priori* transfers from g-types to b-types are large enough to induce $\tilde{R}_b(B_b^I) \leq \tilde{R}_g(B_g^I)$, the only possible solution arising under second-best conditions must set pensions uniformly equal to $\tilde{x}$. The common retirement age is then determined so as to ensure feasibility. Again, either adverse selection is present, or it is *a priori* ruled out by the particular objective of the insurance agency. Obviously, the more interesting case — from the point of view of theory — has been discussed in this chapter.

Moreover, as pointed out in the introduction, there exists some empirical support for the hypothesis that self-selection of consumers, characterized by different mortality expectations, actually occurs in old-age insurances. Also, these expectations correspond to respective realizations of remaining lifetimes. In this respect, it is rather irrelevant whether policy-makers intend to induce the separation of consumer-types. Uhlenberg (1988), for instance, agrees that differentiating risk-classes in principle reflects greater 'equity' in the old-age insurance. On the other hand, due to the variety of factors influencing longevity, 'refusing to discriminate on the basis of individual characteristics appears to be the only reasonable way to avoid splintering the population into numerous competing factions'. Yet, variable retirement options obviously constitute a common feature of old-age insurance schemes. Hence, if these systems in fact induce a self-selection of risk-classes, efficiency considerations as exposed in this chapter can also be assumed to influence the design of benefit rules, irrespective of the reasons for introducing early retirement allowances.

In general, opinions concerning the applicability of approaches based on private information of the consumers to problems of old-age insurances vary greatly. Whereas Nalebuff and Zeckhauser (1985) state that '[i]ndividuals have quite adequate incentives, apart from pensions they receive, to increase their survival', Davies and Kuhn (1992), dismissing the relevance of adverse selection problems for public old-age insurances, turn to the analysis of a 'hidden action' model. In particular, the survival risk is seen to depend on the consumption of a health-related commodity. Increasing longevity induces costs by raising the actuarial premium. At the same time, there is some direct welfare effect associated with the consumption of the health commodity, as well as an indirect benefit derived from the increased longevity. The level of health-related consumption cannot be observed by insurers. The study then considers premium/benefit rules designed so as to induce a particular consumption behavior of the individuals ensuring the feasibility of the insurance. Following Cooper (1984), however, 'hidden action' and 'adverse selection' problems share the same basic features[13]. This can also be illustrated utilizing the present model again. Thus, suppose that individuals are in fact identical, but the survival risk associated with b-types in the preceding sections can only be attained by some investment in health-related activities. Then, the separating policies derived above

---

[13]Correspondingly, the distinction between 'moral hazard', referring only to 'hidden action' models, and 'adverse selection' often found in the relevant literature is rather misleading.

can also be interpreted as providing incentives to increase longevity. The interpretation of the offers would change rather drastically, however: Since all consumers are *ex-ante* indifferent between the offers (x_g^I, R_g^I) and $(\tilde{x}, \tilde{R}_b(0))$, they can be assumed to invest in order to increase longevity. Consequently, one would only observe one consumer-type (b-types) and no early retirement occurs. Individually different retirement behavior could only be re-introduced if consumer-types were distinguished according to the 'safety'-technology available to them. Moreover, this technology must constitute *ex-ante* private information of the consumers[14].

---

[14]Compare Hoy (1989) again.

CHAPTER 10

Summary and conclusions

The present study has attempted to provide both an overview of the existing literature on pension economics, with particular reference to retirement issues, and to formulate an approach towards an institutional theory of variable retirement schemes. The stylized facts of the development and current structure of old-age insurance systems in developed countries, and economic theories concerned with the role of public pensions, identify two basic explanatory approaches. Insurance-theoretic arguments point at the welfare-enhancing properties of public transfer systems, when, due to myopia, asymmetric information structures, or the existence of non-insurable risks, private insurance arrangements fail to provide for efficient risk-shifting. In contrast, a second line of arguments stresses the inter-generational redistribution of pay-as-you-go financed social security. Since, under plausible assumptions, this financing method must be associated with long-run welfare losses, both this choice of financing and significant extensions in the pension provisions are often seen to reflect the political power of the elderly.

This view is not undisputed, however. First, it cannot be distinguished whether the systems reflect political majorities or altruism on the part of the young. Second, arguments based on political power do not guarantee the future stability of the schemes. Finally, the inter-generational transfers implemented can be counteracted, and thus remain neutral, if the consumers possess an effective bequest motive. Since the empirical evidence is split, it is impossible to rule out particular points of view. Within this debate the problem of determining the retirement age enters in two ways: On the one hand, the extensions of the benefits, in particular, as expressed by the introduction of flexible retirement age allowances, are claimed to have induced a decrease in the average retirement age. Moreover, this development is seen to contribute strongly to the financial problems of social security systems. In contrast, recent work suggests that the removal of lifetime labor supply inefficiencies, resulting from the particular ways of tying benefit claims to withdrawal decisions, may reinstate the possibility of Pareto-efficient transitions from pay-as-you-go to capital-funded systems.

Efficient lifetime labor supply decisions are noted to require actuarially fair adjustments of benefits to choices of the retirement age, irrespective of the financing method employed. Hence, the call for a realignment of flexible retirement age schemes so as to meet this rule can be found throughout the literature on social security reform. While deviations from actuarial fairness within public schemes are thus frequently associated with the general extension of the benefit provisions, the governments' attempts to regulate private pension plans have introduced an increased necessity to calculate pensions utilizing actuarial methods. On first sight, this should also yield benefit rules which entail actuarially fair adjustments to retirement ages chosen. Otherwise, the schemes must incorporate some redistribution among cohort members, given that in the end the actuarial values of contributions and benefits within the plans must coincide. These observations define the task performed in the remaining chapters. If deviations from actuarial fairness can be shown to characterize efficient private pension arrangements, this argument may also apply to social security benefit formulas. Consequently, the standard view that such deviations constitute part of the inter-generational transfer package need not be shared.

Focusing on theories of retirement behavior, the 'induced retirement' approach, relating lifetime labor supply decisions to income flows received, constitutes a natural starting point. Moreover, since benefit/retirement rules are the center of interest, a model, based on missing private annuity insurance and liquidity-constrained consumers under uncertain lifetimes, is identified to generate the necessary sensitivity of retirement decisions with respect to the income structure. It follows that the framework introduced utilizes insurance-theoretic arguments. Most importantly, the formal analysis of this model shows that the choice of the contribution rate alone determines whether or not the individuals turn out to be underinsured, and therefore accumulate privately as well, or overinsured. The result hinges on the complementarity between self-protection, via variations of the retirement age, and the insurance coverage obtained. This effect also governs the respective comparative statics of the model. In particular, whenever the consumers save privately, the retirement effects of income changes are shown to be ambiguous.

Whereas this analysis *assumed* actuarially fair adjustments, the study also identifies two efficiency conditions which are suited to allow a classification of the reactions of individuals to more general benefit rules. For every given contribution rate, efficient lifetime labor supply decisions require actuarially fair adjustments. This restates earlier findings noting that inter-generational transfers should be implemented lump-sum, rather than manipulating benefit schedules. However, within the present framework efficient lifetime allocations also require that the retirement scheme must provide for perfect income insurance. Given the complementarity between self-protection and insurance, this can be verified to demand a particular contribution rate. Hence, for every rate chosen a retirement scheme may induce inefficient early, efficient, or inefficient late retirement. Nevertheless, even efficient lifetime labor supply decisions, relative to a contribution rate specified, do not rule out that further improvements in the induced lifetime allocation remain possible. This is solely due to the fact that optimal retirement decisions of individuals do not entail efficient risk-shifting, unless a particular welfare-maximizing contribution is levied.

The following chapters then turn to analyzing variable retirement age policies applied to heterogeneous populations. In a first step, comparative static results with respect to marginal changes in the labor income, the disutility of labor, and the survival risk are generated. Thus, it is assumed that all individuals face a single, differentiable benefit schedule. Again, due to counteracting income and substitution effects, the impacts of changes in the labor supply and the survival risk are ambiguous, while decreases in the disutility of labor always yield delayed retirement age choices. However, variable retirement schemes are observed not only to involve deviations from actuarial fairness. In addition, the adjustment rules seem to entail 'kinks'. This suggests that the simple comparative static analysis may be misleading. Consequently, the analysis turns to a more detailed investigation of efficient benefit/retirement age rules designed for heterogeneous populations. The first case assumes that two individual-types, characterized by different disutilities of labor, must be covered in an insurance system levying a common contribution rate. Since the welfare-maximizing contribution is contingent on the disutility of labor, it is immediately clear that this institutional constraint precludes efficient lifetime allocations to be attained by all consumers. In fact, intra-generational efficient policies are verified to entail allocational distortions for both consumer-types. Moreover, individuals with low disutility of labor turn out to be overinsured, while the respective other consumer-type is underinsured. In general, the efficient policy entails non-trivial transfers between individual-types. These transfers translate into deviations from actuarial fairness in observed retirement rules. In particular, early benefits appear to be better than fair, when the consumer-type characterized by a high disutility of labor receives a positive transfer.

Focusing on the issue of determining the direction of the transfers, the analysis highlights the relevance of reference policies. Specifically, if the initial situation is characterized by an exogenous contribution and a single marginally fair benefit schedule, the directions of the transfers solely depend on the contribution rate specified. On the other hand, the analysis also derives efficient policies from maximizing a weighted average of the type-specific expected lifetime utilities — either restricting the initial choice to policies incorporating a single fair benefit schedule, or ensuring 'voluntary participation' of all consumer-groups. It is interesting to note that, if the weights equal the relative frequencies of consumer-types in the cohort under consideration, the optimal policy entails a transfer to be received by consumers exhibiting a high disutility of labor. Finally, as a consequence of the transfer system established, the implementation of the second-best policies may be subject to moral hazard. If self-selection constraints are binding, the subsidized individuals' retirement decision is shown to be inefficient. Given that transfers flow from consumers with low (high) disutility of labor to individuals exhibiting a high (low) disutility, the latter retire inefficiently early (late).

A second approach picks up the problem of adverse selection which arises when consumers characterized by different survival risks are distinguished according to the retirement age chosen. Optimal policies then design benefit rules such as to induce a self-selection of consumer-types over a menu of benefit/retirement age offers. It is assumed that, with unobservable consumer-types, 'bad' risk consumers exhibiting high survival risks impose a threat of claiming the offer designed for 'good' risk individuals. This would render the flexible retirement age allowance infeasible. Second-best policies are then shown to induce inefficient early retirement of 'good' risks and an increasing benefit schedule. Since early benefits are always claimed by individuals with low survival risks, they still appear to be better than fair, however. This result can be maintained for situations in which it is mutually beneficial to subsidize 'bad' risks. As efficient best policies are seen to require no differentiation with respect to the contribution rate, the optimal common rate under second-best conditions remains unaltered as well. This reflects the fact that it is always optimal to let the potential 'shirking' individual-type attain an undistorted lifetime allocation.

Finally, given that the insurance agency and the consumers share some information concerning the risk-classification of individuals, separate signal-contingent retirement schemes may evolve. Thus, the study confirms the possibility of welfare-enhancing, coexisting health-contingent variable retirement age programs, for instance. Each scheme is characterized by increasing benefit profiles, with early benefits seemingly calculated better than fair. Moreover, the differences in the benefit rules between the schemes solely depend on the additional information revealed by observing a particular health-status. Hence, the current framework suggests an alternative interpretation of health-contingent early retirement. Even with overall improvements in the physical health condition of a cohort, an increased use of disability programs for early retirement can merely reflect an improved signaling of survival risks by documenting 'poor health' as defined in the standards of the insurance agency. Similarly, increased 'generosity' of disability benefits can be associated with differences in the intra-generational transfer systems between retirement schemes, rather than additional inter-generational transfers.

The problem remains to characterize efficient benefit rules, when individuals exhibit differences in the instantaneous preference structure and survival risks at the same time. 'Adverse correlation' — as defined by Nalebuff and Zeckhauser (1985) — occurs when individuals exhibiting a high disutility of labor are also characterized by lower survival risks, for instance. Obviously, a number of different scenarios can emerge under such conditions. However, clearcut results are not to be expected from analyzing the general case. The virtue of the present analysis can thus be seen in untangling the impacts of institutional and informational constraints in designing intra-generational efficient flexible retirement programs. This has been demonstrated to be particularly important for the identification of lifetime labor supply decisions as inefficient. Additional insights and alternative interpretations of observed benefit rules are obtained by distinguishing between intra-generational transfers and differences in survival risks in explaining deviations from actuarial fairness.

References

Aaron, H. J. (1966) The Social Insurance Paradox. *Canadian Journal of Economics and Political Science* **32**: 371–374.

Abel, A. B. (1985) Precautionary Saving and Accidental Bequests. *American Economic Review* **75**: 777–791.

Abel, A. B. (1986) Capital Accumulation and Uncertain Lifetimes with Adverse Selection. *Econometrica* **54**: 1079–1097.

Adden, H. (1991) Perspektiven eines künftigen gesamtdeutschen Alterssicherungssystems. *Acta Demographica* 1991: 101–133.

Akerlof, G. A. (1970) The Market for 'Lemons': Qualitative Uncertainty and the Market Mechanism. *Quarterly Journal of Economics* **84**: 488–500.

Ando, A. and Modigliani, F. (1957) The 'Life-cycle' Hypothesis of Saving: Aggregate Implications and Tests. *American Economic Review* **53**: 55–84.

Aschauer, D. A. (1985) Fiscal Policy and Aggregate Demand. *American Economic Review* **75**: 117–127.

Atkinson, A. B. (1991) The Development of State Pensions in the United Kingdom. In Schmähl, W. (ed.) *The Future of Basic and Supplementary Pension Schemes in the European Community: 1992 and Beyond*: 71–89. Nomos, Baden-Baden.

Auerbach, A. J. and Kotlikoff, L. J. (1984) Social Security and the Economics of Demographic Transition. In Aaron, H. J. and Burtless, G. (eds) *Retirement and Economic Behavior*: 255–278. The Brookings Institution, Washington, D. C.

Auerbach, A. J., Kotlikoff, L. J., Hagemann, R. P. and Nicoletti, G. (1989) The Economic Dynamics of an Aging Population: The Case of Four OECD Countries. In *OECD Economic Studies* No. **12**: 97–130. OECD Head of Publication Services, Paris.

Balasko, Y. and Shell, K. (1980) The Overlapping Generations Model, I: The Case of Pure Exchange Without Money. *Journal of Economic Theory* **23**: 281–306.

Balasko, Y. and Shell, K. (1981) The Overlapping Generations Model, II: The Case of Pure Exchange With Money. *Journal of Economic Theory* **24**: 112–142.

Barro, R. J. (1974) Are Government Bonds Net Wealth? *Journal of Political Economy* **82**: 1095–1117.

Barro, R. J. (1976) Reply to Feldstein and Buchanan. *Journal of Political Economy* **84**: 343–349.

Barro, R. J. and Friedman, J. W. (1977) On Uncertain Lifetimes. *Journal of Political Economy* **85**: 843–849.

Becker, G. S. (1962) Investment in Human Capital. *Journal of Political Economy* **70**: 9–49.

Bellmann, L. (1989) Seniority-Based Wage System and Postponed Retirement. In Schmähl, W. (ed.) *Redefining the Process of Retirement—An International Perspective*: 151–162. Springer, Berlin, etc.

Benjamin, B., Haberman, S., Helowicz, G., Kaye, G. and Wilke, D. (1987) *Pensions*. Allen & Unwin, London.

Bental, B. (1989a) Capital Accumulation and Population Growth in Two Sector Closed and Open Economies. In Wenig, A. and Zimmermann, K. F. (eds) *Demographic Change and Economic Development*: 94–109. Springer (Studies in Contemporary Economics), Berlin, etc.

Bental, B. (1989b) The Old-Age Security Hypothesis and Optimal Population Growth. *Journal of Population Economics* **1**: 285–301.

Ben-Zion, U. and Gradstein, M. (1988) Equilibrium and Efficiency in Intergenerational Transfers. In Wenig, A. and Zimmermann, K. F. (eds) *Demographic Change and Economic Development*: 152–165. Springer (Studies in Contemporary Economics), Berlin, etc.

Bernheim, B. D. (1987a) The Economic Effects of Social Security: Towards a Reconciliation of Theory and Measurement. *Journal of Public Economics* **33**: 273–304.

Bernheim, B. D. (1987b) Dissaving after Retirement: Testing the Pure Life-cycle Hypothesis. In Bodie, Z., Shoven, J. B. and Wise, D. A. (eds) *Issues in Pension Economics*: 237–274. University of Chicago Press, Chicago and London.

Bernheim, B. D. (1988) Social Security Benefits: An Empirical Study of Expectations and Realizations. In Ricardo-Campbell, R. and Lazear, E. P. (eds) *Issues in Contemporary Retirement*: 312–352. The Hoover Institution, Stanford, Ca.

Bernheim, B. D. (1989) The Timing of Retirement: A Comparison of Expectations and Realizations. In Wise, D. A. (ed.) *The Economics of Aging*: 335–358. University of Chicago Press, Chicago and London.

Bernheim, B. D. (1991) How Strong Are Bequest Motives? Evidence based on Estimates of the Demand for Life Insurance and Annuities. *Journal of Political Economy* **99**: 899–927.

Bernheim, B. D., Shleifer, A. and Summers, L. H. (1985) — The Strategic Bequest Motive. *Journal of Political Economy* **93**: 1045–1076.

Bernholz, P. and Breyer, F. (1984) *Grundlagen der politischen Ökonomie*. J. C. B. Mohr (Paul Siebeck), Tübingen.

Berthold, N. (1991) Ansätze einer ökonomischen Theorie der Sozialpolitik. *Jahrbuch für Sozialwissenschaft* **42**: 145–178.

Blinder, A. S., Gordon, R. H. and Wise, D. A. (1980) Reconsidering the Work-disincentive Effects of Social Security. *National Tax Journal* **33**: 431–442.

Boadway, R. and Wildasin, D. E. (1989) A Median Voter Model of Social Security. *International Economic Review* **30**: 307–328.

Bodie, Z. (1990) Inflation Insurance. *Journal of Risk and Insurance* **57**: 634–645.

Börsch, M. (1987) *Umverteilung, Effizienz und demographische Abhängigkeit von Rentenversicherungssystemen.* Springer (Studies in Contemporary Economics), Berlin, etc.

Börsch-Supan, A. (1991) Aging Population. *Economic Policy* **6**: 103–139.

Börsch-Supan, A. and Stahl, K. (1991) Life-cycle Savings and Consumption Constraints: Theory, Empirical Evidence, and Fiscal Implications. *Journal of Population Economics* **4**: 233–255.

Boskin, M. J. (1977) Social Security and Retirement Decisions. *Economic Inquiry* **15**: 1–25.

Brandts, J. and De Bartolome, C. A. M. (1992) Population Uncertainty, Social Insurance and Actuarial Bias. *Journal of Public Economics* **47**: 361–380.

Breton, A. (1974) *The Economic Theory of Representative Government.* Aldine (Aldine Treatise in Modern Economics), Chicago.

Breyer, F. (1989) On the Intergenerational Pareto-efficiency of Pay-as-you-go Financed Pension Systems. *Zeitschrift für die gesamte Staatswissenschaft — Journal of Institutional and Theoretical Economics* **145**: 643–658.

Breyer, F. (1990) *Ökonomische Theorie der Alterssicherung.* Franz Vahlen, Munich.

Breyer, F. (1991) *Voting on Social Security when Labor Supply is Endogenous.* Discussion Paper No. 175, Dept. of Economics, Fern Universität, Hagen.

Breyer, F. and von der Schulenburg, J.-M. Graf (1987) Voting on Social Security: The Family as Decision-making Unit. *Kyklos* **40**: 529–547.

Breyer, F. and Straub, M. (1993) Welfare Effects of Unfunded Pension Systems when Labor Supply is Endogenous. *Journal of Public Economics* **50**: 77–93.

Brown, D. J. (1977) Philosophical Basis of the National Insurance Program. In McGill, D. M. (ed.) *Social Security and Private Pensions — Competitive or Complementary*: 1–13. Richard D. Irwin, Homewood, Il.

Browning, E. K. (1975) Why the Social Security Budget is Too Large in a Democracy. *Economic Inquiry* **16**: 373–388.

Browning, E. K. (1979) The Politics of Social Security Reform. In Campbell, C. D. (ed.) *Financing Social Security*: 187–207. American Enterprise Institute, Washington, D. C.

Brugiavini, A. (1993) Uncertainty Resolution and the Timing of Annuity Purchases. *Journal of Public Economics* **50**: 31–62.

Brunner, J. K. (1990) *Optimum Social Security and Intragenerational Transfers.* Discussion Paper No. 9028, Institute for Economics, Johann-Keppler-University, Linz.

Buchanan, J. M. (1976) Barro on the Ricardian Equivalence Theorem. *Journal of Political Economy* **84**: 337–342.

Burkhauser, R. V. and Quinn, J. F. (1983) Is Mandatory Retirement Overrated? — Evidence from the 1970's. *Journal of Human Resources* **18**: 337–358.

Burkhauser, R. V. and Quinn, J. F. (1989) American Patterns of Work and Retirement. In Schmähl, W. (ed.) *Redefining the Process of Retirement — An International Perspective*: 91–113. Springer, Berlin, etc.

Burkhauser, R. V. and Turner, J. A. (1982) Social Security, Preretirement Labor Supply and Saving: A Confirmation and a Critique. *Journal of Political Economy* **90**: 643–646.

Burtless, G. and Moffitt, R. A. (1984) The Effect of Social Security on the Labor Supply of the Aged. In Aaron, H. J. and Burtless, G. (eds) *Retirement and Economic Behavior*: 135–174. The Brookings Institution, Washington, D. C.

Burtless, G. and Moffitt, R. A. (1985) The Joint Choice of Retirement Age and Postretirement Hours of Work. *Journal of Labor Economics* **3**: 209–236.

Cagan, P. (1965) *The Effect of Pension Plans on Aggregate Savings: Evidence from a Sample Survey*. NBER Occasional Paper No. 95, Columbia University Press, New York.

Casey, B. (1989) Early Retirement: The Problems of 'Instrument Substitution' and 'Cost-Shifting' and Their Impact for Restructuring the Process of Retirement. In Schmähl, W. (ed.) *Redefining the Process of Retirement—An International Perspective*: 133–150. Springer, Berlin.

Casmir, B. (1989) *Staatliche Rentenversicherungssyteme im internationalen Vergleich*. Peter Lang, Frankfurt a. M.

Chang, F.-R. (1991) Uncertain Lifetimes, Retirement and Economic Welfare. *Economica* **58**: 215–232.

Clark, R. L., Kreps, J. L. and Spengler, J. J. (1978) The Economics of Aging: A Survey. *Journal of Economic Literature* **16**: 919–962.

Cook, F. L. (1990) Congress and the Public: Convergent and Divergent Opinions on Social Security. In Aaron, H. J. (ed.) *Social Security and the Budget*: 79–107. University Press of America (National Academy of Social Insurance), Lanham, Ma. and London.

Cooper, R. (1984) On Allocative Distortions in Problems of Self-Selection. *Rand Journal of Economics* **15**: 568–577.

Crane, R. (1992) Voluntary Income Redistribution with Migration. *Journal of Urban Economics* **31**: 84–98.

Crawford, V. P. and Lilien, D. M. (1981) Social Security and the Retirement Decision. *Quarterly Journal of Economics* **95**: 505–529.

Crimmins, E. M. and Pramaggiore, M. T. (1988) Changing Health of the Older Working-age Population and Retirement Patterns over Time. In Ricardo-Campbell, R. and Lazear, E. P. (eds): *Issues in Contemporary Retirement*: 132–161. The Hoover Institution, Stanford, Ca.

Danziger, S., van der Gaag, J., Smolensky, E. and Taussig, M. (1982) The Life-cycle Hypothesis and the Consumption Behaviour of the Elderly. *Journal of Post-Keynesian Economics* **5**: 208–227.

David, M. and Menchik, P. L. (1985) The Effect of Social Security on Lifetime Wealth Accumulation and Bequests. *Economica* **52**: 421–434.

Davies, J. B. (1981) Uncertain Lifetimes, Consumption, and Dissaving in Retirement. *Journal of Political Economy* **89**: 561–577.

Davies, J. B. and Kuhn, P. (1992) Social Security, Longevity, and Moral Hazard. *Journal of Public Economics* **49**: 91-106.

D'Herbais, P.-G. (1991) A Comparison of Private and Public Sector Supplementary Pension Systems in the Countries of the European Community. In Schmähl, W. (ed.) *The Future of Basic and Supplementary Pension Schemes in the European Community: 1992 and Beyond*: 71-89. Nomos, Baden-Baden.

Diamond, P. A. (1965) National Debt in a Neoclassical Growth Model. *American Economic Review* **55**: 1126-1150.

Diamond, P. A. (1977) A Framework for Social Security Analysis. *Journal of Public Economics* **8**: 275-298.

Diamond, P. A. and Hausman, J. A. (1984a) Individual Retirement and Savings Behavior. *Journal of Public Economics* **23**: 81-114.

Diamond, P. A. and Hausman, J. A. (1984b) The Retirement Behavior of Older Workers. In Aaron, H. J. and Burtless, G. (eds) *Retirement and Economic Behavior*: 97-134. The Brookings Institution, Washington, D. C.

Diamond, P. A., Helms, L. J. and Mirrlees, J. A. (1980) Optimal Taxation in a Stochastic Economy: A Cobb-Douglas Example. *Journal of Public Economics* **14**: 1-29.

Diamond, P. A. and Mirrlees, J. A. (1978) A Model of Social Insurance with Variable Retirement. *Journal of Public Economics* **10**: 295-336.

Diamond, P. A. and Mirrlees, J. A. (1985) Insurance Aspects of Pensions. In Wise, D. A. (ed.) *Pensions, Labor, and Individual Choice*: 317-356. Chicago University Press, Chicago and London.

Diamond, P. A. and Mirrlees, J. A. (1986) Payroll-tax Financed Social Insurance with Variable Retirement. *Scandinavian Journal of Economics* **88**: 25-50.

Dicks-Mireaux, L.-D. L. and King, M. A. (1984) Pension Wealth and Private Savings: Tests of Robustness. *Journal of Public Economics* **23**: 115-139.

Dinkel, R. H. (1988) Ökonomische Einflußfaktoren für die individuelle Entscheidung des Übertritts in den Ruhestand. In Schmähl, W. (ed.) *Verkürzung oder Verlängerung der Erwerbsphase*: 128-150. J. C. B. Mohr (Paul Siebeck), Tübingen.

Dinkel, R. H. (1990) Der Einfluß von Wanderungsbewegungen auf die langfristige Bevölkerungsdynamik. *Acta Demographica* 1990: 47-62.

Doherty, N. A. and Garven, J. R. (1986) Price Regulation in Property Liability Insurance: A Contingent-Claims Approach. *Journal of Finance* **41**: 1031-1050.

Doherty, N. A. and Schlesinger, H. (1990) Rational Insurance Purchasing: Considerations of Contract Non-performance. *Quarterly Journal of Economics* **105**: 243-253.

Donaldson, D. and Eaton, B. C. (1976) Firm-specific Human Capital: A Shared Investment or Optimal Entrapment. *Canadian Journal of Economics* **9**: 462-472.

Dowell, R. S. and McLaren, K. R. (1986) An Intertemporal Analysis of the

Interdependence between Risk Preference, Retirement, and Work Rate Decisions. *Journal of Political Economy* **94**: 667–682.

Drissen, E. and van Winden, F. (1991) Social Security in a General Equilibrium Model with Endogenous Government Behavior. *Journal of Population Economics* **4**: 89–110.

Dye, R. F. (1985) Influencing Retirement Behavior: Untangling the Effects of Taxation of Social Security Benefits. *Journal of Policy Analysis and Management* **5**: 150–154.

Dyer, J. K. (1977) Coordination of Private and Public Pension Plans: An International Summary. In McGill, D. M. (ed.): *Social Security and Private Pensions — Competitive or Complementary*: 29–40. Richard D. Irwin, Homewood, Il.

Eckstein, Z., Eichenbaum, M. and Peled, D. (1985a) Uncertain Lifetimes and the Welfare Enhancing Properties of Annuity Markets and Social Security. *Journal of Public Economics* **26**: 303–326.

Eckstein, Z., Eichenbaum, M. and Peled, D. (1985b) The Distribution of Wealth and Welfare in the Presence of Incomplete Annuity Markets. *Quarterly Journal of Economics* **100**: 789–806.

Ehrlich, I. and Becker, G. S. (1972) Market Insurance, Self-Insurance and Self-Protection. *Journal of Political Economy* **80**: 623–648.

Eichenbaum, M. and Peled, D. (1987) Capital Accumulation in an Adverse Selection Economy. *Journal of Political Economy* **95**: 334–354.

Elbers, L. and Weddepohl, H. N. (1986) Steady-State Equilibria with Saving for Retirement in a Continuous Time Overlapping Generations Model. *Zeitschrift für Nationalökonomie — Journal of Economics* **46**: 253–288.

Ermish, J. (1989) Intergenerational Transfers in Industrialized Countries: Effects of Age Distribution and Economic Institutions. *Journal of Population Economics* **3**: 269–284.

Fabel, O. (1992) Social Security, Optimal Retirement, and Savings. Discussion Paper No. 236, University of Bielefeld. Forthcoming in the *European Journal of Political Economy*.

Famula, R. and Spreemann, K. (1980) Generationsverträge und Rentenversicherung als Ponzi GmbH. *Zeitschrift für öffentliche und gemeinwirtschaftliche Unternehmen* **3**: 379–403.

Feinstein, J. S. and McFadden, D. (1989) The Dynamics of Housing Demand by the Elderly: Wealth, Cash-flow and Demographic Effects. In Wise, D. A. (ed.) *The Economics of Aging*: 55–88. University of Chicago Press, Chicago and London.

Felder, S. (1992) *The Welfare Effects of Tax Reforms in a Life-cycle Model: An Analytical Approach*. Discussion Paper, University of Western Ontario.

Feldstein, M. S. (1974) Social Security, Induced Retirement, and Aggregate Capital Accumulation. *Journal of Political Economy* **82**: 905–926.

Feldstein, M. S. (1976a) Perceived Wealth in Bonds and Social Security: A Comment. *Journal of Political Economy* **84**: 331–336.

Feldstein, M. S. (1976b) Social Security and the Distribution of Wealth. *Journal of the American Statistical Association* **71**: 800–807.

Feldstein, M. S. (1978) Do Private Pensions Increase National Savings? *Journal of Public Economics* **10**: 277–293.

Feldstein, M. S. (1980) International Differences in Social Security and Savings. *Journal of Public Economics* **14**: 225–244.

Feldstein, M. S. (1982a) Social Security and Private Savings: Reply. *Journal of Political Economy* **90**: 630–642.

Feldstein, M. S. (1982b) Government Deficits and Aggregate Demand. *Journal of Monetary Economics* **9**: 1–20.

Feldstein, M. S. (1983) Should Private Pensions Be Indexed? In Bodie, Z. and Shoven, J. B. (eds) *Financial Aspects of the United States Pension System*: 211–232. University of Chicago Press, Chicago and London.

Feldstein, M. S. (1985) The Optimal Level of Social Security Benefits. *Quarterly Journal of Economics* **100**: 303–320.

Fields, G. S. and Mitchell, O. S. (1984) *Retirement, Pensions, and Social Security.* MIT Press, Cambridge, Ma. and London.

Fischer, S. (1973) A Life Cycle Model of Life Insurance Purchases. *International Economic Review* **14**: 132–152.

Fitzgerald, J. (1987) The Effects of Social Security on Life Insurance Demand by Married Couples. *Journal of Risk and Insurance* **54**: 86–99.

Flaig, G. (1987) Staatsausgaben, Staatsverschuldung und die makroökonomische Konsumfunktion. *Zeitschrift für Wirtschafts- und Sozialwissenschaften* **107**: 337–359.

Franz, W. (1976) Die Lebenszyklushypothese der Konsumfunktion: Eine empirische Überprüfung für die Bundesrepublik Deutschland. *Jahrbücher für Nationalökonomie und Statistik* **191**: 97–116.

Friedman, B. M. and Warshawsky, M. (1988) Annuity Prices and Savings Behavior in the United States. In Bodie, Z., Shoven, J. B. and Wise, D. A. (eds) *Pensions in the US Economy*: 53–85. University of Chicago Press, Chicago and London.

Friedman, B. M. and Warshawsky, M. (1990) The Cost of Annuities: Implications for Saving Behavior and Bequests. *Quarterly Journal of Economics* **104**: 135–154.

Gale, D. G. (1973) Pure Exchange Equilibrium of Dynamic Economic Models. *Journal of Economic Theory* **6**: 12–36.

Gale, D. G. (1992) A Walrasian Theory of Markets with Adverse Selection. *Review of Economic Studies* **59**: 229–255.

Gehrels, F. (1991) Risk-Averse, Time Optimizing Behaviour of Households: Comparisons with German Microcensus Data. *Zeitschrift für Wirtschafts- und Sozialwissenschaften* **111**: 169–185.

Genosko, J. (1983) Erwerbsbeteiligung und gesetzliche Rentenversicherung: Der Fall der 60- bis 65jährigen Männer. *Zeitschrift für die gesamte*

Staatswissenschaft—Journal of Institutional and Theoretical Economics **139**: 625–642.

Genosko, J. (1985) *Arbeitsangebot und Alterssicherung.* Transfer Verlag, Regensburg.

Gordon, R. H. and Blinder, A. S. (1980) Market Wages, Reservation Wages, and Retirement Decisions. *Journal of Public Economics* **14**: 277–308.

Gordon, R. H. and Varian, H. R. (1988) Intergenerational Risk Sharing. *Journal of Public Economics* **37**: 185–202.

Green, J. R. (1977) *Mitigating Demographic Risk through Social Insurance.* NBER Working Paper No. 215.

Green, J. R. (1988) Demographics, Market Failure, and Social Security. In Wachter, M. S. (ed.) *Social Security and Private Pensions*: 3–16. Lexington, Ma.

Gustman, A. L. and Steinmeier, T. L. (1986) A Structural Retirement Model. *Econometrica* **54**: 555–584.

Hakansson, N. H. (1969) Optimal Investment and Consumption Strategies under Risk, an Uncertain Lifetime, and Insurance. *International Economic Review* **10**: 443–466.

Hakansson, N. H. (1970) Optimal Investment and Consumption Strategies under Risk for a Class of Utility Functions. *Econometrica* **38**: 587–607.

Hall, R. E. and Mishkin, F. (1982) The Sensitivity of Consumption to Transitory Income: Estimates from Panel Data on Households. *Econometrica* **50**: 461–481.

Hammermesh, D. S. (1984) Life-cycle Effects on Consumption and Retirement. *Journal of Labor Economics* **2**: 353–370.

Hammermesh, D. S. (1985) Expectations, Life Expectancy, and Economic Behavior. *Quarterly Journal of Economics* **100**: 389–408.

Hammond, P. (1975) Charity: Altruism or Cooperative Egoism? In Phelps, E. S. (ed.) *Altruism, Morality, and Economic Theory*: 115–131. The Russel Sage Foundation, New York.

Hanoch, G. and Honig, M. (1983) Retirement, Wages, and the Labor Supply of the Elderly. *Journal of Labor Economics* **1**: 131–151.

Haveman, R. H. and Wolfe, B. L. (1984) Disability Transfers and Early Retirement: A Causal Relationship? *Journal of Public Economics* **24**: 47–66.

Hellwig, M. F. (1987) Some Recent Developments in the Theory of Competition in Markets with Adverse Selection. *European Economic Review* **31**: 319–325.

Hellwig, M. F. (1988) A Note on the Specification of Intra-Firm Communication in Insurance Markets with Adverse Selection. *Journal of Economic Theory* **46**: 154–163.

Hemming, R. C. L. (1977) The Effect of Private Pensions on Retirement Behavior and Personal Capital Accumulation. *Review of Economic Studies* **44**: 169–172.

Holler, M. (1986) Intergenerational Solutions to the Social Security Dilemma. In Graf von der Schulenburg, J.-M. (ed.) *Essays in Social Security Economics*: 54–74. Springer (Microeconomic Studies), Berlin, etc.

Homburg, S. (1988) *Theorie der Alterssicherung.* Springer (Studies in Contemporary Economics), Berlin, etc.

Homburg, S. (1990) The Efficiency of Unfunded Pension Schemes. *Zeitschrift für die gesamte Staatswissenschaft—Journal of Institutional and Theoretical Economics* **146**: 640–647.

Homburg, S. and W. Richter (1991) *Harmonizing Public Debt and Public Pension Schemes in the European Community.* Discussion Paper, Dept. of Economics, University of Dortmund.

Hornung-Draus, R. (1989) Das Vermögen der privaten Haushalte in Deutschland: Bestand, Entwicklung und Verteilung. *Jahrbücher für Nationalökonomie und Statistik* **206**: 18–47.

Hoy, M. (1988) Risk Management and the Value of Symmetric Information in Insurance Markets. *Economica* **55**: 355–364.

Hoy, M. (1989) The Value of Screening Mechanisms under Alternative Insurance Possibilities. *Journal of Public Economics* **39**: 177–206.

Hu, S. C. (1978) On the Dynamic Behaviour of the Consumer and the Optimal Provision of Social Security. *Review of Economic Studies* **45**: 437–445.

Hu, S. C. (1979) Social Security, the Supply of Labor, and Capital Accumulation. *American Economic Review* **69**: 274–283.

Hu, S. C. (1986) Uncertain Life Span, Risk-Aversion, and the Demand for Pension Annuities. *Southern Economic Journal* **52**: 933–947.

Hubbard, R. G. (1985) Social Security, Liquidity Constraints, and Pre-Retirement Consumption. *Southern Economic Journal* **52**: 471–483.

Hubbard, R. G. (1987) Uncertain Lifetimes, Pensions, and Individual Saving. In Bodie, Z., Shoven, J. B. and Wise, D. A. (eds) *Issues in Pension Economics*: 175–210. University of Chicago Press, Chicago and London.

Hubbard, R. G. and Judd, K. L. (1987) Social Security and Individual Welfare: Precautionary Saving, Borrowing Constraints, and the Payroll Tax. *American Economic Review* **77**: 630–646.

Hurd, M. D. (1987) Savings of the Elderly and Desired Bequests. *American Economic Review* **77**: 298–312.

Hurd, M. D. (1989) Mortality Risk and Bequests. *Econometrica* **57**: 779–813.

Hurd, M. D. (1990) Issues and Results from Research on the Elderly: Economic Status, Retirement, and Savings. *Journal of Economic Literature* **28**: 565–637.

Hurd, M. D. and Boskin, M. J. (1984) The Effect of Social Security on Retirement in the Early 1970s. *Quarterly Journal of Economics* **99**: 767–790.

Jackson, P. A. (1977) Philosophical Basis of the Private Pension Movement. In McGill, D. M. (ed.) *Social Security and Private Pensions—Competitive or Complementary*: 14–28. Richard D. Irwin, Homewood, Il.

Jacobs, K. and Schmähl, W. (1989) The Process of Retirement in Germany. In Schmähl, W. (ed.) *Redefining the Process of Retirement—An International Perspective*: 13–37. Springer, Berlin, etc.

Jäger, N. (1990) *Die Umstellung der Gesetzlichen Rentenversicherung auf ein partiell kapitalgedecktes Finanzierungsverfahren — Eine Simulationsanalyse.* Peter Lang, Frankfurt a. M.

Jaynes, G. D. (1978) Equilibria in Monopolistically Competitive Insurance Markets. *Journal of Economic Theory* **19**: 394-422.

Kahn, J. A. (1988) Social Security, Liquidity and Early Retirement. *Journal of Public Economics* **35**: 97-117.

Katona, G. (1964) *Private Pensions and Individual Savings.* University of Michigan — Survey Research Center, Ann-Arbor, Mi.

King, M. A. and Dicks-Mireaux, L.-D. L. (1982) Asset Holdings and the Life-cycle. *Economic Journal* **92**: 706-732.

Kochin, L. A. (1974) Are Future Taxes Anticipated by Consumers? *Journal of Money, Credit and Banking* **6**: 385-394.

Kohli, M. (1988) Die gesellschaftliche und individuelle Bedeutung der Altersgrenze. In Schmähl, W. (ed.) *Verkürzung oder Verlängerung der Erwerbsphase*: 36-53. J. C. B. Mohr (Paul Siebeck), Tübingen.

Kormedi, R. C. (1983) Government Debt, Government Spending and Private Sector Behavior. *American Economic Review* **73**: 994-1010.

Kotlikoff, L. J. (1979a) Social Security and Equilibrium Capital Intensity. *Quarterly Journal of Economics* **93**: 233-253.

Kotlikoff, L. J. (1979b) Testing the Theory of Social Security and Lifetime Accumulation. *American Economic Review* **69**: 396-410.

Kotlikoff, L. J. (1988a) The Relationship of Productivity to Age. In Ricardo-Campbell, R. and Lazear, E. P. (eds) *Issues in Contemporary Retirement*: 100-125. Hoover Institution Press, Stanford, Ca.

Kotlikoff, L. J. (1988b) Intergenerational Transfers and Savings. *Journal of Economic Perspectives* **2**: 41-58.

Kotlikoff, L. J., Shoven, J. B. and Spivak, A. (1987) Annuity Markets, Savings, and the Capital Stock. In Bodie, Z., Shoven, J. B. and Wise, D. A. (eds) *Issues in Pension Economics*: 211-236. University of Chicago Press, Chicago and London.

Kotlikoff, L. J. and Spivak, A. (1981) The Family as an Incomplete Annuity Market. *Journal of Political Economy* **89**: 372-391.

Kotlikoff, L. J., Spivak, A. and Summers, L. H. (1982) The Adequacy of Savings. *American Economic Review* **72**: 1056-1069.

Kotlikoff, L.J and Summers, L. H. (1981) The Role of Intergenerational Transfers in Aggregate Capital Accumulation. *Journal of Political Economy* **89**: 706-732.

Kotlikoff, L. J. and Wise, D. A. (1987) Incentive Effects of Private Pension Plans. In Bodie, Z., Shoven, J. B. and Wise, D. A. (eds) *Issues in Pension Economics*: 283-336. University of Chicago Press, Chicago and London.

Kuné, J. B. (1983) Studies on the Relationship Between Social Security and Savings: A Tabular Survey. *Kredit und Kapital* **16**: 371-380.

Kruse, A. and Söderström, L. (1989) Early Retirement in Sweden. In Schmähl, W.

(ed.) *Redefining the Process of Retirement—An International Perspective*: 46–61. Springer, Berlin.

Laitner, J. (1979a) Household Bequests, Perfect Expectations, and the National Distribution of Wealth. *Econometrica* **47**: 1175–1193.

Laitner, J. (1979b) Bequests, Golden-age Capital Accumulation and Government Debt. *Economica* **46**: 403–414.

Laitner, J. (1979c) Household Bequest Behaviour and the National Distribution of Wealth. *Review of Economic Studies* **46**: 467–483.

Laitner, J. (1988) Bequests, Gifts, and Social Security. *Review of Economic Studies* **55**: 275–299.

Lam, D. (1989) Population Growth, Age Structure, and Age-specific Productivity: Does a Uniform Age Structure Minimize Lifetime Wages? *Journal of Population Economics* **2**: 189–210.

Lapp, J. J. (1985) Mandatory Retirement as a Clause in Employment Insurance Contracts. *Economic Inquiry* **23**: 69–92.

Lazear, E. P. (1979) Why Is There Mandatory Retirement? *Journal of Political Economy* **87**: 1261–1284.

Lazear, E. P. (1983) Pensions as Severance Pay. In Bodie, Z. and Shoven, J. B. (eds) *Financial Aspects of the United States Pension System*: 57–89. University of Chicago Press, Chicago and London.

Lazear, E. P. (1985) Incentive Effects of Pensions. In Wise, D. A. (ed.) *Pensions, Labor, and Individual Choice*: 253–282. University of Chicago Press, Chicago and London.

Leimer, D. R. and Lesnoy, S. D. (1982) Social Security and Private Savings: New Time Series Evidence. *Journal of Political Economy* **90**: 606–629.

Leimer, D. R. and Richardson, D. H. (1992) Social Security, Uncertainty Adjustments and the Consumption Decision. *Economica* **59**: 311–335.

Leland, H. E. (1978) Optimal Risk-sharing and the Leasing of Natural Resources, with Applications to Oil and Gas Leasing on the OCS. *Quarterly Journal of Economics* **92**: 413–437.

Levhari, D. and Srinivasan, T. N. (1969) Optimal Savings under Uncertainty. *Review of Economic Studies* **36**: 153–164.

Lindbeck, A. (1985) Redistributive Policy and the Expansion of the Public Sector. *Journal of Public Economics* **28**: 309–328.

Longman, P. L. (1990) Costs of Aging Population: Financing the Future. In Aaron, H. J. (ed.) *Social Security and the Budget*: 63–74. University Press of America (National Academy of Social Insurance), Lanham, Ma. and London.

Lundholm, M. (1991a) *Compulsory Social Insurance: A Critical Review*. Economic Studies (1991:1), Dept. of Economics, Uppsala University.

Lundholm, M. (1991b) *Compulsory Social Insurance: The Case of Paternalism Revisited*. Working Paper (1991:8), Dept. of Economics, Uppsala University.

Lupu, W. A. (1984) Influencing Retirement Behavior: A Further Analysis. *Journal of Policy Analysis and Management* **3**: 439–459.

Mackenroth, G. (1952) Die Reform der Sozialpolitik durch einen deutschen Sozialplan. In Albrecht, G. (ed.) *Die Berliner Wirtschaft zwischen Ost und West—Die Reform der Sozialpolitik durch einen deutschen Sozialplan*: 39–76. Duncker & Humblot (Schriften des Vereins für Sozialpolitik, Neue Folge, No. 4), Berlin.

Mayers, D. and Smith, C. W., Jr. (1983) The Interdependence of Individual Portfolio Decisions and the Demand for Insurance. *Journal of Political Economy* **91**: 304–311.

Menchik, P. A. and David, M. (1983) Income Distribution, Lifetime Savings, and Bequests. *American Economic Review* **73**: 672–690.

Merton, R. C. (1969) Lifetime Portfolio Selection under Uncertainty: The Continuous-time Case. *Review of Economics and Statistics* **51**: 247–257.

Merton, R. C. (1983a) On Consumption-indexed Public Pension Plans. In Bodie, Z. and Shoven, J. B. (eds) *Financial Aspects of the United States Pension System*: 259–289. University of Chicago Press, Chicago and London.

Merton, R. C. (1983b) On the Role of Social Security as a Means for Efficient Risk-sharing in an Economy where Human Capital is Not Tradeable. In Bodie, Z. and Shoven, J. B. (eds):*Financial Aspects of the United States Pension System*: 325–358. University of Chicago Press, Chicago and London.

Merton, R. C., Bodie, Z. and Marcus, A. J. (1987) Pension Plan Integration as Insurance against Social Risk. In Bodie, Z., Shoven, J. B. and Wise, D. A. (eds) *Issues in Pension Economics*: 147–174. University of Chicago Press, Chicago and London.

Mirer, T. (1979) The Wealth–age Relationship Among the Aged. *American Economic Review* **69**: 435–443.

Mirer, T. (1980) The Dissaving Behavior of the Aged. *Southern Economic Journal* **46**: 1197–1205.

Mitchell, O. S. and Fields, G. S. (1984) The Economics of Retirement Behavior. *Journal of Labor Economics* **2**: 84–105.

Modigliani, F. (1988) The Role of Intergenerational Transfers and Life Cycle Saving in the Accumulation of Wealth. *Journal of Economic Perspectives* **2**: 15–40.

Modigliani, F. and Brumberg, R. (1954) Utility Analysis and the Consumption Function: An Interpretation of Cross-section Data. In Kurihana, K. K. (ed.) *Post-Keynesian Economics*: 388–436. Rutgers University Press, New Brunswick, N. J.

Morrison, M. H. (1988) Changes in the Legal Mandatory Retirement Age: Labor Force Participation Implications. In Ricardo-Campbell, R. and Lazear, E. P. (eds) *Issues in Contemporary Retirement*: 378–411. The Hoover Institution, Stanford, Ca.

Mossin, J. (1968a) Aspects of Rational Insurance Purchasing. *Journal of Political Economy* **76**: 553–568.

Mossin, J. (1968b) Optimal Multiperiod Portfolio Decisions. *Journal of Business* **41**: 215–225.

Müller, H.-N. and Roppel, U. (1990) Lösung der demographisch bedingten Probleme durch Kapitaldeckung? Zur Abschätzung der Anwartschaften in der GRV der Bundesrepublik Deutschland. *Acta Demographica* 1990: 107–130.

Mumy, G. M. (1985) The Role of Taxes and Social Security in Determining the Structure of Wages and Pensions. *Journal of Political Economy* 93: 574–585.

Munnel, A. H. (1974) The Impact of Social Security on Personal Saving. *National Tax Journal* 27: 553–567.

Munnel, A. H. (1982) *The Economics of Private Pensions.* The Brookings Institution, Washington, D. C.

Nalebuff, B. and Zeckhauser, R. J. (1985) Pensions and the Retirement Decision. In Wise, D. A. (ed.) *Pensions, Labor, and Individual Choice:* 283–316. University of Chicago Press, Chicago and London.

Naquib, F. M. (1985) Some Redistributive Aspects of Social Security and Their Impact on the Supply of Labor. *Public Finance* 40: 230–246.

Neher, P. A. (1971) Peasants, Procreation, and Pensions. *American Economic Review* 61: 380–389.

Neumann, M. (1986) *Möglichkeiten zur Entlastung der gesetzlichen Rentenversicherung durch kapitalbildende Vorsorgemaßnahmen.* J. C. B. Mohr (Paul Siebeck), Tübingen.

Neumann, M. (1987) Gesamtwirtschaftliche Aspekte der privaten Altersvorsorge. In von Wartenberg, L. (ed.) *Die wirtschafts- und sozialpolitische Bedeutung der privaten Altersvorsorge:* 15–22. Kohlhammer, Stuttgart, etc.

Newberry, D. M. and Stiglitz, J. E. (1987) Wage Rigidity, Implicit Contracts, Unemployment and Efficiency. *Economic Journal* 97: 416–430.

Ng, Y.-K. (1992) The Older the More Valuable: Divergence Between Utility and Dollar Values of Life as One Ages. *Zeitschrift für Nationalökonomie — Journal of Economics* 55: 1–16.

Niskanen, W. A. (1971) *Bureaucracy and Representative Government,* Chicago, Aldine-Atherton.

OECD (1988a) *Ageing Populations: The Social Policy Implications.* OECD Publication Services, Paris.

OECD (1988b) *Reforming Public Pensions.* OECD Social Policy Studies — No. 5. OECD Publications Services, Paris.

OECD (1992) *Employment Outlook.* OECD Publication Services, Paris

Packard, M. D. and Reno, V. P. (1988) A Look at Very Early Retirees. In Ricardo-Campbell, R. and Lazear, E. P. (eds) *Issues in Contemporary Retirement:* 243–272. The Hoover Institution, Stanford, Ca.

Palgrave's Dictionary of Political Economy (1910). Macmillan, London.

Pauly, M. V. (1974) Overinsurance and the Public Provision of Insurance: The Role of Moral Hazard and Adverse Selection. *Quarterly Journal of Economics* 88: 44–54.

Peracchi, F. and Welch, F. (1991) *Labor Force Participation of Older Workers: Evidence from CPS Data.* C. V. Starr Center of Applied Economics at New

York University, and Texas A & M and Unicon Research Group, respectively, mimeo.

Peters, W. (1988) A Pension Insurance Model in an Overlapping Generations Model. *Zeitschrift für die gesamte Staatswissenschaft—Journal of Institutional and Theoretical Economics* **144**: 813–830.

Peters, W. (1989) *Theorie der Renten- und Invaliditätsversicherung.* Springer (Studies in Contemporary Economics), Berlin.

Peters, W. (1992) *Public Pensions, Family Allowances and Endogenous Growth.* Discussion Paper, SFB 303, University of Bonn.

Petersen, J. H. (1989) The Process of Retirement in Denmark: Trends, Public Discussion and Framework. In Schmähl, W. (ed.) *Redefining the Process of Retirement—An International Perspective*: 63–81. Springer, Berlin, etc.

Pfaff, M., Hurler, P. and Dennerlein, R. (1979) Old Age Security and Saving in the Federal Republic of Germany. In von Furstenberg, G.M (ed.) *Social Security versus Private Savings*: 277–312. Ballinger, Cambridge, Ma.

Pfeiffer, D. (1989) *Verteilungswirkungen der Alterssicherung.* Transfer Verlag, Regensburg.

Phelps, E. S. (1961) The Golden Rule of Accumulation: A Fable for Growthmen. *American Economic Review* **51**: 638–643.

Plosser, C. J. (1982) Government Financing Decisions and Asset Returns. *Journal of Monetary Economics* **9**: 325–352.

Pogue, T. F. and Sgontz, L. G. (1977) Social Security and Investment in Human Capital. *National Tax Journal* **30**: 157–169.

Quinn, J. F. and Burkhauser, R. V. (1983) Influencing Retirement Behavior: A Key Issue for Social Security. *Journal of Policy Analysis and Management* **3**: 1–13.

Reimers, C. and Honig, M. (1989) The Retirement Process in the United States. In Schmähl, W. (ed.) *Redefining the Process of Retirement—An International Perspective*: 115–131. Springer, Berlin.

Richter, W. (1991) *Public Debt in a Two-country OLG-model with Endogenous Migration.* Discussion Paper, Dept. of Economics, University of Dortmund.

Romer, T. and Rosenthal, H. (1982) Median Voters or Budget Maximizers: Evidence from Social Expenditure Referenda. *Economic Inquiry* **20**: 556–578.

Rosa, J. J. (1982) *The World Crisis in Social Security*: A Joint Project of the Fondation Nationale D'Économie Politique, Based in Paris, and the Institute of Contemporary Studies, Based in San Francisco, Calif.. Transaction Books, New Brunswick, N. J.

Rothschild, M. and Stiglitz, J. E. (1976) Equilibrium in Competitive Insurance Markets: An Essay on the Economics of Imperfect Information. *Quarterly Journal of Economics* **90**: 629–649.

Rust, J. (1989) A Dynamic Programming Model of Retirement. In Wise, D. A. (ed.) *The Economics of Aging*: 359–403. University of Chicago Press, Chicago and London.

Samuelson, P. A. (1958) An Exact Consumption–Loan Model of Interest With or Without the Social Contrivance of Money. *Journal of Political Economy* **66**: 467–482.

Samuelson, P. A. (1969) Lifetime Portfolio Selection by Dynamic Stochastic Programming. *Review of Economics and Statistics* **51**: 239–246.

Samuelson, P. A. (1975) Optimum Social Security in a Life-cycle Growth Model. *International Economic Review* **16**: 531–538.

Sanmartino, F. J. and Kasten, R. A. (1985) The Distributional Consequences of Taxing Social Security Benefits: Current Law and Alternative Schemes. *Journal of Post-Keynesian Economics* **8**: 28–46.

Schlesinger, H. and Graf von der Schulenburg, J.-M. (1987) Risk-Aversion and the Purchase of Risky Insurance. *Zeitschrift für Nationalökonomie—Journal of Economics* **47**: 309–314.

Schmähl, W. (1974) *Systemveränderung in der Altersvorsorge*. Westdeutscher Verlag, Opladen.

Schmähl, W. (1986) Lohnentwicklung im Lebensverlauf: Zur Gestalt der Alters-Lohn-Profile von Arbeitern in Deutschland. *Allgemeines Statistisches Archiv* **70**: 180–203.

Schmähl, W. (1988) Verkürzung oder Verlängerung der Erwerbsphase? Fragen, Ziele, Wirkungen — ein Überblick. In Schmähl, W (ed.) *Verkürzung oder Verlängerung der Erwerbsphase*: 1–35. J. C. B. Mohr (Paul Siebeck), Tübingen.

Schmähl, W. (1989) Retirement at Cross-Roads — Tasks and Problems under Changing Economic and Demographic Conditions. Some Introductory Remarks. In Schmähl, W. (ed.) *Redefining the Process of Retirement—An International Perspective*: 1–12. Springer, Berlin.

Schmähl, W. (1990) Demographic Change and Social Security: Some Elements of a Complex Relationship. *Journal of Population Economics* **3**: 159–177.

Schmähl, W. (1991) On the Future Development of Retirement in Europe, Especially of Supplementary Pension Schemes — An Introductory Overview. In Schmähl, W. (ed.) *The Future of Basic and Supplementary Pension Schemes in the European Community: 1992 and Beyond*: 31–70. Nomos, Baden-Baden.

Schultze, C. L. (1990) Setting Long-Run Deficit Reduction Targets: The Economics and Politics of Budget Design. In Aaron, H. J. (ed.) *Social Security and the Budget*: 15–42. University Press of America (National Academy of Social Insurance), Lanham, Ma. and London.

Schwarz, K. (1991) Drei 'Mythen' in der deutschen Demographie. *Acta Demographica* 1991: 1–14.

Schwarz-Schilling, C. (1987) *Die Rentenreform: Anpassungsrahmen und strukturelle Neuansätze*. Mittelstands-Verlag, Bonn.

Schwödiauer, G. and Wenig, A. (1989) Accidental Bequests, Social Security, and the Distribution of Wealth. In Felderer, B. (ed.) *Einkommensverteilung und Bevölkerungsentwicklung*: 133–154. Duncker & Humblot (Schriften des Vereins für Sozialpolitik, Neue Folge, No. 187), Berlin.

Schwödiauer, G. and Wenig, A. (1990) The Impact of Taxation on the Distribution of Wealth in an Economy with Changing Population. *Journal of Population Economics* **3**: 53–71.

Sheshinski, E. (1978) A Model of Social Security and Retirement Decisions. *Journal of Public Economics* **10**: 337–360.

Sheshinski, E. and Weiss, Y. (1981) Uncertainty and Optimal Social Security Systems. *Quarterly Journal of Economics* **96**: 189–206.

Shorrocks, A. F. (1975) The Age–Wealth Relationship: A Cross-section and Cohort Analysis. *Review of Economics and Statistics* **42**: 155–163.

Sjoblom, K. (1985) Voting for Social Security. *Public Choice* **45**: 225–240.

Smith, A. (1982) Intergenerational Transfers as Social Insurance. *Journal of Public Economics* **19**: 97–106.

Solow, R. M. (1956) A Contribution to the Theory of Economic Growth. *Quarterly Journal of Economics* **70**: 65–94.

Spreemann, K. (1984) Intergenerational Contracts and their Decomposition. *Zeitschrift für Nationalökonomie — Journal of Economics* **44**: 237–253.

Summers, L. (1983) Observations on the Indexation of Old-age Pensions. In Bodie, Z. and Shoven, J. B. (eds) *Financial Aspects of the United States Pension System*: 231–258. University of Chicago Press, Chicago and London.

Tanner, E. J. (1979) An Empirical Investigation of Tax Discounting. *Journal of Money, Credit and Banking* **11**: 214–218.

Testafion, L. (1984) Welfare Implications of Net Social Security Wealth. *Journal of Public Economics* **24**: 1–27.

Thompson, L. G. (1983) The Social Security Reform Debate. *Journal of Economic Literature* **21**: 1425–1467.

Thornborrow, N. (1985) Social Security's Effect on Retirement Assets. *Quarterly Journal of Business and Economics* **24**: 51–72.

Todo-Rivera, A. and Pérez-Amaral, T. (1988) Social Security and Private Savings: A Reconsideration of the Assumptions. *Applied Economics* **20**: 1057–1069.

Townley, P. G. C. (1981) Public Choice and the Social Insurance Paradox: A Note. *Canadian Journal of Economics* **14**: 712–717.

Townley, P. G. C. and Boadway, R. W. (1988) Social Security and the Failure of Annuity Markets. *Journal of Public Economics* **35**: 75–96.

Turnbull, S. M. (1983) Additional Aspects of Rational Insurance Purchasing. *Journal of Business* **56**: 217–229.

Turner, J. A. (1984) Population Age Structure and the Size of Social Security. *Southern Economic Journal* **50**: 1131–1146.

Uhle, C. (1987) *Betriebliche Sozialleistungen*. Müller-Botermann, Cologne.

Uhlenberg, P. (1988) Population Aging and the Timing of Old-age Benefits. In Ricardo-Campbell, R. and Lazear, E. P. (eds) *Issues in Contemporary Retirement*: 353–377. Hoover Institution, Stanford, Ca.

Van Immhoff, E. (1987) On the Independence of Financing Methods and Redistributive Aspects of Public Pensions: A Comment. *Public Finance* **42**: 448–453.

Van Praag, B. and Poeth, G. (1975) The Introduction of an Old-age Pension in a Growing Economy. *Journal of Public Economics* **4**: 87-100.

VDR — Verband Deutscher Rentenversicherungsträger (1988) *Rentenversicherungen im internationalen Vergleich*. A. Metzner, Frankfurt/Neuwied.

Veall, M. R. (1986) Public Pensions as Optimal Social Contracts. *Journal of Public Economics* **31**: 237-251.

Venti, S. F. and Wise, D. A. (1989) Aging, Moving and Housing Wealth. In Wise, D. A. (Ed.) *The Economics of Aging*: 9-48. University of Chicago Press, Chicago and London.

Verbon, H. A. A. (1985) On the Independence of Financing Methods and Redistributive Aspects of Public Pensions. *Public Finance* **40**: 280-289.

Verbon, H. A. A. (1986) Altruism, Political Power and Public Pensions. *Kyklos* **39**: 343-358.

Verbon, H. A. A. (1987a) The Rise and Evolution of Public Pension Systems. *Public Choice* **52**: 75-100.

Verbon, H. A. A. (1987b) On the Independence of Financing Methods and Redistributive Aspects of Public Pensions: Reply. *Public Finance* **42**: 454-456.

Verbon, H. A. A. (1988a) *The Evolution of Public Pension Schemes*. Springer (Microeconomic Studies), Berlin.

Verbon, H. A. A. (1988b) Explaining Pay-as-you-go Financed Public Pensions. *Economics Letters* **28**: 181-187.

Verbon, H. A. A. (1990) Transfers to the Old, Government Debt and Demographic Change. *Journal of Population Economics* **3**: 89-104.

Verbon, H. A. A. and van Winden, F. A. A. M. (1986) Public Pensions and Political Decision Making. In Graf von der Schulenburg, J.-M. (ed.) *Essays in Social Security Economics*: 32-53. Springer (Microeconomic Studies), Berlin, etc.

Viscusi, W. K. (1980) Self-Selection, Learning-induced Quits, and the Optimal Wage-structure. *International Economic Review* **21**: 529-546.

Viscusi, W. K. (1985) The Structure of Uncertainty and the Use of Non-transferable Pensions as a Mobility-reducing Incentive Device. In Wise, D. A. (ed.) *Pensions, Labor, and Individual Choice*: 223-251. University of Chicago Press, Chicago and London.

Von Furstenberg, G. M. and Malkiel, B. G. (1977) The Government and Capital Formation: Recent Issues. *Journal of Economic Literature* **15**: 835-878.

Von Wartenberg, L. (1987) Ergänzung der gesetzlichen Rentenversicherung durch private Altersvorsorge. In von Wartenberg, L. (ed.) *Die wirtschafts- und sozialpolitische Bedeutung der privaten Altersvorsorge*: 7-14. Kohlhammer, Stuttgart, etc.

Wagner, G. (1986) *Umverteilung in der gesetzlichen Rentenversicherung*. Campus, Frankfurt a. M. and New York.

Wagner, M. and Huinink, J. (1991) Neuere Trends beim Auszug aus dem Elternhaus. *Acta Demographica — 1991*: 39-62.

Watson, H. (1982) Saving, Social Security and Uncertainty. *Southern Economic Journal* **49**: 330–341.

Weaver, C. L. (1982) *The Crisis in Social Security*. Duke University Press (Duke Press Policy Studies), Durham, N. C.

Weiss, Y. (1972) On the Optimal Lifetime Pattern of Labor Supply. *Economic Journal* **82**: 1293–1315.

Whinston, M. D. (1983) Moral Hazard, Adverse Selection, and the Optimal Provision of Social Insurance. *Journal of Public Economics* **22**: 49–71.

Wildasin, D. E. (1991) The Marginal Cost of Public Funds with an Aging Population. *Journal of Population Economics* **4**: 111–135.

Wilson, C. (1977) A Model of Insurance Markets with Incomplete Information. *Journal of Economic Theory* **16**: 167–207.

Wolfe, J. R. (1983) Perceived Longevity and Early Retirement. *Review of Economics and Statistics* **65**: 544–551.

Yaari, M. E. (1964) On the Consumer's Lifetime Allocation Process. *International Economic Review* **5**: 304–317.

Yaari, M. E. (1965) Uncertain Lifetime, Life Insurance, and the Theory of the Consumer. *Review of Economic Studies* **32**: 137–150.

Zabalza, A., Pissarides, C. and Barton, M. (1980) Social Security and the Choice between Full-time Work, Part-time Work, and Retirement. *Journal of Public Economics* **14**: 145–276.

Index

Index compiled by Michael J. Heary